Islamic Life and Thought

Islamic Life and Thought

by
SEYYED HOSSEIN NASR

STATE UNIVERSITY OF NEW YORK PRESS
ALBANY

First published in USA by State University of New York Press, Albany, 1981

Printed in the United States of America

For information, address State University of New York Press, State University Plaza, Albany, N.Y., 12246

Library of Congress Cataloging in Publication Data

Nasr, Seyyed Hossein.
Islamic life and thought.

Includes index.
1. Islam—Addresses, essays, lectures. I. Title.
BP25.N27 909'.097671 81-4723
ISBN 0-87395-490-4 AACR2
ISBN 0-87395-491-2 (pbk.)

Contents

In the Name of God – Most Merciful, Most Compassionate

بسم الله الرحمن الرحيم

Introduction

Islam is at once a religion and a civilisation and social order based upon the revealed principles of the religion. It is an archetypal reality, residing eternally in the Divine Intellect, and an unfolding of this reality in history and in the lives of numerous generations of men from different races and ethnic groups and different localities spreading over most of the surface of the earth. Islam cannot be reduced to a historical phenomenon because its immutable principles and sacred forms are of a non-temporal nature; yet it is also a historical reality of dazzling dimensions. Nor can Islam be considered solely in its cultic sense, although the cult and the practices related to it lie at the heart of the Islamic tradition.

Moreover, the Islamic tradition cannot be confined solely to the message which was received in the form of the Holy Quran by the Blessed Prophet – upon whom be blessings and peace – fourteen centuries ago, although of course this message has been and will always remain the heart of all that is Islamic. Islam includes, in addition to this heart, its unfolding in time and space and all that it absorbed according to its own genius and made its own through its power of transformation and synthesis. Thus not only are the Holy Quran and *Ḥadīth* Islamic, but also the sacred forms of Islamic art, schools of Islamic philosophy and the sciences, and Islamic social and political institutions are Islamic whatever may have been the historical origin of the 'matter' which the Islamic tradition absorbed and imbued with the form of Islam. The Holy Quran and *Ḥadīth*, as well as the oral instructions and the grace or *barakah* issuing from the revelation of the Holy Quran and its recipient, the Blessed Prophet, are like the roots and the trunk of the tree of the Islamic tradition. The arts and sciences, social institutions and the like are the branches of the tree, some located closer to the trunk and others farther away but all a part of its organism and nourished ultimately by the roots. Some of the 'branches' like Islamic art reflect directly the inner aspects of the Islamic revelation and are indispensable to the tradition. Others like certain schools of thought reflect these principles less directly and are more incidental to the tradition. Yet they too have fulfilled and continue to fulfil a necessary function for certain types of mentalities. Otherwise they would not have come into being nor gained the right of entrance into the 'city' (*madīnah*) of Islam.

In modern times, as a result of the loss of the universal perspective of tradition or *dīn* among the vast majority of Western orientalists as well as among modernised Muslims, men have lost sight of the unity of the Islamic tradition and the unifying principles which over the ages have bound together the diverse elements of the Islamic tradition. Studies limited to historical and analytical methods have tended through their method of dissection to neglect the living character of the subject of their treatment. They have tended to forget that one can only dissect a living entity after divesting it of its life. People have laboured hard to show that this stone of the courtyard of a particular mosque comes from Roman or Byzantine ruins near by or that that particular word or idea entered into Arabic from Assyrian or Greek, forgetting the function of this stone in the totality of the sacred space of the mosque or that word or idea in the poem or intellectual edifice into which it has become integrated. In too many cases, the loss of vision of principles has turned portents (*āyāt*) into brute facts and a living organism into a cadaver.

It is not that careful historical or analytical studies are illegitimate. On the contrary, they have even existed in traditional Islamic scholarship and have their rightful place in Islamic studies. What is illegitimate from the Islamic point of view is the secular perspective itself to which the analytical method is usually wed and the historicism which opposes metaphysics and the transcendent, and wishes to reduce reality itself to its reflection upon the surface of the flowing river of time. Otherwise, analytical and historical methods can legitimately be used in traditional scholarship and in conformity with the dictates of logic and common sense. They can be integrated into a higher point of view so that their positive features remain but their limitation does not damage the total and universal understanding of things.

Today in the West, as well as in the Islamic world itself, there is an ever greater need to study both the principles and manifestations of Islam from its own authentic point of view and in a manner comprehensible to contemporary man, or at least to one who possesses sufficient intelligence and good intentions. Moreover, this needs to be achieved by using methods of analysis and description which are at once logical and in conformity with the Islamic perspective; for this latter places the highest value upon intelligence (*al-'aql*) and logic, which is inseparable from it, although of course the transcendent realities cannot be reduced to logical categories. This type of writing which can 'translate' Islamic teachings into a contemporary idiom without betraying it is very important not only for non-Muslims who wish to learn about Islam but most of all for young Muslims, who are now mainly products of modern educational systems.

Fortunately works of this type in European languages are becoming more numerous, with the publication of the diverse books and articles of such authors as F. Schuon, T. Burckhardt, M. Lings and others. It is only to be hoped that such works will increase and gain wider recognition and also become better known in the Islamic world itself, where there is such a profound need for a re-presentation of the Islamic tradition, especially in its intellectual and spiritual aspects. The result would provide the necessary means with which to combat the follies and inanities of the modern world – the fashions of the day – and to unmask that systematic 'learned ignorance' which passes today for wisdom.

The essays which comprise this volume are a humble effort to revive and re-present various facets of the Islamic tradition from the Islamic point of view, in a contemporary medium and with full awareness of modern scholarship in both East and West. Written over the years, they have appeared for the most part in an earlier form in various reviews and collections all over the world. But they are all concerned with a single subject, namely the integral Islamic tradition, and have been written from a single point of view, which is that of the Islamic tradition. Moreover, they have been thoroughly revised and rewritten so that the components, although of diverse origin, have been integrated into a single work on Islamic studies.

In our other works we have had occasion to deal with various facets of things Islamic, including the religion itself, Sufism, philosophy and science. Usually each work has been devoted to one subject or to several interrelated themes within one broad domain of the Islamic tradition. In the present work, however, we have devoted separate studies to many different aspects of Islam, ranging from social and political thought to philosophy and Sufism. We have therefore chosen to call it *Islamic Life and Thought*. Although no one aspect of Islamic life or thought is studied in an all-inclusive and exhaustive manner, many facets have been investigated and described in a way which might be compared to so many sketches of both the thought and life of the Islamic tradition. Some of the sketches are metaphysical and philosophical studies and interpretations, and others works of scholarship and the result of the scholarly research of the author himself, based upon the work carried out so far in the field in question.

The first section concerns Islamic Law and society, including the confrontation of traditional Islamic doctrines on spiritual and temporal authority, freedom, the sacred nature of law and traditional Islamic education with those modern ideas which challenge and oppose the very foundations of these traditional doctrines. In the second section, two extensive studies deal, on the one hand, with the typology of Islamic culture and the different zones and areas of this culture and, on the other, with an extensive survey of Islamic intellectual life. In a sense, these two chapters complement each other in that one deals with the extension and diversity of the Islamic tradition 'horizontally' and among different ethnic groups, and the other with the manifestation of this tradition in the world of the mind and the spirit.

We have dealt exclusively with the Islamic sciences in two of our works, *Science and Civilization in Islam* and *Islamic Science – An Illustrated Study*, and with cosmology in our *An Introduction to Islamic Cosmological Doctrines*. Yet the domain of Islamic cosmology and the sciences is so vast that we have been forced to devote several separate studies over the years to the subject. These essays on cosmology, alchemy and natural history are collected in the next section dealing with the sciences.

The same is true of the section on philosophy, which deals on the one hand with modern challenges to Islamic philosophy and on the other with Mullā Ṣadrā and his school. These studies again complement our works devoted to philosophy, especially the recent *Ṣadr al-Dīn Shīrāzī and His Transcendent Theosophy*. Two studies concerning Sufism bring the main body of these sketches to their conclusion.

In the postscript four short studies written as the result of recent acute problems and debates within the Islamic world have been brought together. They are answers to concrete debates but at the same time address themselves more generally to all those concerned with things Islamic since those same issues are still very much alive and continue to be discussed and debated between traditionalists and modernists in various Islamic countries and climes.

In these studies we have of necessity repeated certain themes and arguments found in our other writings. But this is inevitable since the exposition of a certain aspect of the Truth requires the return to certain principles and elements related to other aspects of the Truth. This lies in the nature of tradition itself, which is a whole and a totality, a unity within diversity, a circle with a centre which itself is found everywhere and on every point of the circumference.

In conclusion, we wish to thank Dr H. Sharifi for his valuable aid in this undertaking and Mrs I. Hakemi, Miss K. Grant and Mrs Montagu for their aid in typing and preparing the manuscript for publication.

wa mā tawfiqī illā bi'Llāh

Tehran – Rajab 1398 (AH) June 1978 (AD)

Seyyed Hossein Nasr

Law and Society

1

Religion and Secularism, Their Meaning and Manifestation in Islamic History

I

Those whose minds have been nurtured on Western thought turn inevitably to the concepts of religion and secularism when they wish to study the Islamic world. But words do not always have the same meaning within differing contexts. This is especially true in the perspective of different civilisations. Therefore, it is necessary to define what is meant by religion and secularism in relation to Islam before discussing their significance in Islamic history. To anyone familiar with Islam, it is only too obvious that these terms do not have the same meaning in languages connected with Muslim civilisation as they have in various European languages. In fact there exists no term in classical Arabic or Persian which is exactly synonymous with the word 'secularism'.[1] Nor is there in Islam the distinction between the religious and secular, or the sacred and the profane, as there is in Christianity.

In the unitary perspective of Islam, all aspects of life, as well as all degrees of cosmic manifestation, are governed by a single principle and are unified by a common centre. There is nothing outside the power of God and in a more esoteric sense nothing 'outside' His Being, for there cannot be two orders of reality. *Lā ilāha illa'Llāh* means ultimately that there is no being or reality other than the Absolute Being or the Absolute Reality. In essence, therefore, everything is sacred and nothing profane because everything bears within itself the fragrance of the Divine.

In such a perspective, the meaning of religion and secularism appears in a new light. Religion becomes the revelation sent by God to man to guide him towards Unity and to help him become what he always 'was' but has forgotten; that is, to make him remember and regain the celestial beatitude which he once enjoyed before falling into the prison of the senses. Religion may be considered ultimately as the Divine guide by the help of which man can overcome the ontological barrier separating him from his Divine Origin, although in essence he has never been separated from it. Moreover, religion becomes not a single instance of Divine guidance but all the revelations sent through the 124,000 prophets mentioned in traditional Islamic sources to the peoples of all ages and nations, of which the last in the present cycle of humanity is Muḥammad – upon whom be blessings and peace.[2] So it is that the Prophet claimed not to have brought anything new but to have re-stated the Truth claimed by all the previous prophets and to have re-established the primordial tradition (*al-dīn al-ḥanīf*) which is the Truth lying within the nature of things.

The mystery of creation lies in the fact that God, despite His perfection and His plenitude, brings into being a world which, although nothing but Himself, does not share His perfection. In fact, manifestation means imperfection, because it means separation from the source of all goodness. It is this separation which, although an illusion with respect to the Divine, is nevertheless quite real with respect to cosmic existence, and which is the source of all secularism, or of all that is, from the human point of view, non-sacred or non-divine.

Secularism, therefore, may be considered as everything whose origin is merely human and therefore non-divine, and whose metaphysical basis lies in this ontological hiatus between man and God. Of course in reality even this void is a symbol of the Divine, just as Satan is the ape of God, but, from the point of view of man in his earthly imperfection or what in Christianity is called the state of 'fallen man', this separation is real with a reality matching that of the Divine order itself. Thus in man's social and historic existence secularism has come to acquire a reality as great as religion itself. Or, in today's world, in which to most modern men God seems to be nowhere and in which He has become eclipsed by the shadows of forgetfulness, it has even come to occupy the centre of the stage and to claim all rights for itself.

Considered from this point of view, religion in Islam means first of all the Islamic revelation and all the truths, both exoteric and esoteric, revealed in the Holy Quran and interpreted by the Prophet in his sayings and traditions. In the case of the Shiʿah the sayings of the Imams are included along with those of the Holy Prophet. Secondly, religion means all the teachings and institutions of Divine origin revealed through other prophets before Islam, many of which Islam, through the universality and synthetic power which is its *raison d'être*, integrated into its own perspective.

Similarly, secularism implies ideas and institutions of purely human origin, not derived from an inspired source. Therefore, we should not consider anything that does not lie specifically within the teachings of Islam as secular, nor everything practised by those who profess Islam as necessarily religious. The Pythagorean-Platonic wisdom derived from the Orphic mysteries and inherited later by the Muslims cannot be called secular, and some of the apologetic writings of the Muslim modernists cannot be considered as religious, although they may be dressed in Islamic terms.

II

Islamic history presents several instances in which foreign ideas have intruded into the world view of Muslim civilisation, ideas which have in more than one instance been secular in the sense defined above. As mentioned earlier, the first set of historical circumstances in the career of Islam concerned the Arab environment in which Islam was revealed. There were many 'pagan' Arabic practices and traditions such as blood-feuds, absolute allegiance to the tribe, and cults of idol worship which were banned in the unitarian and universal perspective of Islam. Islam waged a battle against many such elements, not only during its early life in Arabia, but also in another form during the Umayyad caliphate. During the first struggle of its terrestrial existence, Islam succeeded in freeing itself from becoming a local Arabic religion, but nevertheless it acquired a certain Arabic character, since all revelation is coloured by the world in which it is first revealed and it is also spoken in the language of the people to whom it is revealed. Furthermore, despite the victory of Islam over 'pagan' ideas, the aftermath of the battle of Ṣiffīn and the later establishment of the Umayyad caliphate by Mu'āwiyah mark the first intrusion of secularism into the political life of Islam in the sense that politics, or at least a part of it, became divorced from divinely revealed principles and fell into the arena of power politics in which human ambition was the dominant factor.[3]

In spreading northward into what was previously the domain of the Persian and the Byzantine empires, Islam encountered another set of political, administrative, and fiscal institutions and laws which presented a challenge to the unified structure of the earlier Medinan community. By the power of integration inherent within Islam, many of these institutions were Muslimised and absorbed into the structure of Muslim society so that they lost their foreign attributes. Yet other adaptations of Byzantine and Persian customs and procedures, especially in the fields of taxation, introduced a certain heterogeneity into Islamic law which later played an important part when much of the law in the Muslim world was secularised during the thirteenth/nineteenth and fourteenth/twentieth centuries. There were also cultural movements of a national character in this encounter between Islam and the Persian and Byzantine civilisations in the second and third centuries AH, especially among the Persians. The latter were finally absorbed into the bosom of Islam and at this point no major secular ideas were able to penetrate the Islamic world view.

During the succeeding period, the intrusion of an ancient political institution became a reality as the Abbasid caliphate weakened in the fourth/tenth and fifth/eleventh centuries. At the very moment when al-Māwardī was defining the function of the caliph, the power of the caliphate was for all practical purposes being replaced by that of local princes. However, it was not until the establishment of the Seljuks that the existence of a third authority, the *sulṭān*, became recognised alongside that of the Sacred Law and the caliph. In this new adjustment, which is reflected in the writings of such theologians as al-Ghazzālī and especially in the *Siyāsat-nāmah* of Khwājah Niẓām al-Mulk, the sultanate, an institution based on Sassanid models and alien to the early political organisation of Islam, became recognised as the necessary factor for the preservation of religion in society.[4] This view was accepted to such an extent that many of the Sufis, philosophers and scientists of the Mongol period, such as Najm al-Dīn Rāzī and Khwājah Naṣīr al-Dīn Ṭūsī, wrote in its support.[5]

Turning from social and political matters to cultural and intellectual questions, once again we meet with the introduction of foreign elements into the Muslim world – this time, the vast heritage of the ancient Mediterranean civilisations, Persia and to some extent India. But here also a close study reveals that the Muslims accepted only those elements of this heritage which were ultimately of an inspired origin and not the secular and naturalistic aspects of the Graeco-Roman heritage which ultimately led to the death of classical civilisation. So we see the Muslim sages turning eagerly to the teachings of the Pythagorean-Platonic school and the writings of the Aristotelians viewed through the commentaries of the neo-Platonists. The Muslims, much like the Jewish philosopher Philo, considered these sages the heirs to the wisdom of the prophets, and in their wisdom they saw the reflection of the doctrine of Divine Unity taught by the sacred scriptures.

Similarly, Muslims made the scientific heritage of Alexandria their own, because these forms of knowledge, like other ancient and medieval cosmological sciences, sought to show the unicity of Nature and the interrelatedness of all that exists.[6] Therefore, far from being secular modes of knowledge, they were closely related to the central theme of Islamic wisdom, unity, and throughout Islamic history, the sciences and religious and metaphysical doctrines were knit together, as in the Jābirian corpus or the *Rasā'il* of the Ikhwān al-Ṣafā'. For example, the mathematics of the Greeks and the Hindus were united in the writings of the Muslim mathematicians, thereby creating or giving further development to several new branches of this science including algebra. But here, too, mathematics was considered not a secular technique but more as the ladder of Jacob extending from the sensible to the intelligible world and as the science which the Pythagoreans considered to be the key to the treasury of Divine mysteries.

There were, of course, also aspects of the classical culture which scarcely interested the Muslims, among them the secularist philosophies of the Epicureans and of some of the Cynics or the naturalism of the atomists. The one element of potential secular nature, however, which did penetrate into the Islamic world view was the rationalism inherent in Peripatetic philosophy. Rationalism, basing itself on the exclusive validity of judgement of the human reason which is but a reflection of the Intellect, tends towards the secular by nature, because human reason, although real on its own level, is but a limitation and dispersion of the Intellect and to that extent rooted in that illusory void which separates our existence from Ultimate Reality. This rationalism, based neither upon Islamic revelation nor on other inspired doctrines which are largely gnostic and illuminationist rather than rationalistic, was for several centuries the main source of potential secularism in the cultural life of Islam. It manifested itself primarily in the form of various philosophical and theological movements. The most famous of these was that of the Mu'tazilites and it was not weakened until the fifth/eleventh and sixth/twelfth centuries. At that time, under the pressure of both theology and Sufism, the danger of the suffocation of spiritual life under rationalism was curtailed, and the scene prepared for the expansion of the sapiental doctrines of sages like Shaykh al-Ishrāq Shihāb al-Dīn Suhrawardī and Ibn 'Arabī. In this challenge, the spiritual principles of Islam met secularism in its most basic form, and in restricting its influence enabled the Islamic world to continue its life upon the foundations established by the Quranic revelation.

III

The most devastating attack of secularism upon Islam did not begin until the thirteenth/nineteenth century, and then by a civilisation which, unlike that of the defunct Greeks, was materially more powerful than the Islamic world and politically and economically interested in overcoming it. This attack, facilitated by internal weakness within much of the territory of Islam which had set in during the latter part of the twelfth/eighteenth century, and the partial destruction of some of the Sufi brotherhoods by new forms of puritanical rationalism like Wahhabism in Arabia and the *Ahl-i ḥadīth* in India, began to affect nearly every realm of Muslim life, including law, government and administration, education, and even religion itself.[7]

In the field of law, through a series of changes or *tanẓīmāt* carried out in the Ottoman Empire, that part of the law which from the beginning had remained outside Quranic legislation was converted to various European codes. These codes did not originate from theocratic societies like Byzantium and Persia but from the modern West, which ever since the Renaissance has moved with ever-increasing speed towards the complete secularisation of all life and the divorce of things from their spiritual principles. The acceptance of European codes for commercial and civil matters has been followed in the fourteenth/twentieth century by the demand for the 'modernisation', which always means secularisation, of even personal law which is clearly outlined in the Holy Quran. And so we find such well-known modernists as al-Zahāwī, Ṭāhir al-Ḥaddād and many others pleading for the legal 'equality' of women in the European sense within a secular law and apologists like Sayyid Amīr 'Alī feeling ashamed of the Islamic conception of the status of women because it does not agree with the modern European view.[8]

In the field of government, there has been no uniformity of action. Each Muslim land has a political form peculiar to itself. It may be said in general that throughout the Islamic world, many ideas concerning government and administration have been spread which are not only of non-Islamic origin but which are, moreover, fruits of the various revolutions of the past two centuries in Europe. Each of these has aimed at a greater degree of secularisation of the society. Among these ideologies, not the least of them is Western-style nationalism, which in most areas of the Muslim world has become a powerful force in the secularising of Islamic society.

Nowhere is the intrusion of secularism into the Islamic world more evident than in the field of education. Here, from the thirteenth/nineteenth century onward, schools on a European model and teaching European subjects have often been built by Muslim authorities. The original hope was to enable Muslims to overcome their European invaders. However, the consequence of such schools has been the growth of a segment of Muslim society into a class with views differing radically from the majority of Muslims and the creation of serious rifts in the Muslim social order.[9] To see this difference of approach, it is enough to speak with a student of a modern university in the Muslim world and compare his ideas with those of a student from a religious school or *madrasah*.

The new education represents an important factor in the introduction of secularism. This is especially true not so much because of the subject-matter taught but because of the point of view from which the subjects are taught. The medieval Muslim schools also taught mathematics, the natural sciences, languages, and letters, besides theology, jurisprudence, and philosophy. However, the modern subjects bearing the same name are not simply the continuation of the Islamic sciences, as is claimed by many Muslim apologists.

It is true that the modern sciences have borrowed many techniques and ideas from the ancient and medieval sciences, but the point of view in the two cases is completely different. The Islamic sciences breathed in a Universe in which God was everywhere. They were based upon certainty and searched after the principle of Unity in things which is reached through synthesis and integration. The modern sciences, on the contrary, live in a world in which God is nowhere or, even if there, is irrelevant to the sciences. They are based on doubt. Having once and for all turned their back on the unifying principle of things, they seek to analyse and divide the contents of Nature to an ever greater degree, moving towards multiplicity and away from Unity. That is why, for the majority of Muslim students studying them, they tend to cause a dislocation with regard to the Islamic tradition. Unfortunately, not everyone is able to see the heavens as both the Pedestal of God's Throne and incandescent matter whirling through space.[10] Therefore, by teaching the various modern European arts and sciences which are for the most part alien to the Islamic perspective, the curriculum of the schools and universities in the Muslim countries has injected an element of secularism into the mind of a fairly sizeable segment of Islamic society.

Finally, in the field of religion itself, secularism has made a certain encroachment in the form of rationalism or of various apologetic tendencies.[11] The movement begun by Jamāl al-Dīn Astarābādī, known usually as al-Afghānī, and Shaykh Muḥammad 'Abduh to consider once again the basis of Islamic Law and theology was marked often by a tendency to belittle or even deny elements that were not in conformity with modern thought. This finally led to the neo-Wahhābī Salafiyyah movement in Egypt and spread to other lands, including Persia, where a few of the religious leaders like Sharī'at-i Sangilajī became its advocates. Even more in India, where modernism has spread more in the philosophical and educational fields than in the Middle East, nearly all of the modernist leaders from Sir Aḥmad Khān and Sayyid Amīr 'Alī to contemporary figures have been influenced to some extent by secularism. Although most of the above mentioned authors still thought within the unified view of Islam, some, like the Egyptians 'Alī Abdal-Rāziq, Shaykh Khālid, and Ṭaha Ḥusayn (at least in his early period), moved a step further and preached openly the separation of religion from temporal life, recognising secularism as a legitimate pole of life alongside religion. In Persia and other areas of the Muslim world, the Bahā'ī movement has introduced Western and secular ideas in a religious dress and has played some role in spreading secularism among certain classes of the countries involved.

We see, therefore, that in nearly every domain of life the unitary principles of Islam are challenged by secular ideas and the Islamic world is faced with the mortal danger of 'polytheism' or *shirk*, that is the setting up of various modern European ideas as gods alongside Allah. As to what will be the outcome of this struggle between a weakened defender and a materially powerful enemy it is difficult to predict. Certainly the Islamic world cannot hope to return to a homogeneous and integrated life while the ever increasing disorder in the Western world continues. Moreover, Islam is not exclusively a way of love like Christianity and therefore cannot remain oblivious to any form of knowledge. The way of Islam is essentially gnostic. Therefore it must have a response to other systems which claim to expound a science of things and must be able to place all orders of existence within its universal perspective.

Whatever the immediate outcome of this struggle, there is no doubt that ultimately the clouds of illusion and unreality will fade away. No matter how much secularist thought may appear dominant, it has no more substance than the fragile and changing human nature from which it derives its being. When the illusion of the separation between the soul and the Divine Self is removed, we realise that there is but one Principle dominant in every mode of manifestation, and that the reality we saw in secularism as a competing principle with religion has been no more than the reality of the fantasies of a soul not yet awakened from the dream of negligence and forgetfulness.

Notes

1 However there is the word '*urfi* which refers essentially to law, *dunyawī*, which means this-worldly in contrast to other-worldly, and *zamānī* which means temporal as opposed to eternal, but none of these has exactly the same meaning as secular.

2 Actually Islam, in the most universal sense, means reassertion of the Truth which always was and always will be and of which all orders of existence partake including Nature.

3 See Gibb, H. A. R., 'An Interpretation of Islamic History. I', *Muslim World*.

4 See Lambton, A. K. S., 'Quis custodiet custodes? Some Reflections on the Persian Theory of Government', *Studia Islamica*, vol. V, 1965, pp. 130 ff.; and Binder, L., 'Al-Ghazali and Islamic Government', *Muslim World*, XLV, No. 2, July 1955.

5 See *Mirṣād al-'ibād* of Najm al-Dīn Rāzī and the *Nasirean Ethics* of Ṭūsī.

6 See Burckhardt, T., 'Nature de la perspective cosmologique', *Études traditionelles*, vol. 49, 1948, pp. 216–19.

7 For a detailed study of Western influence on these and other aspects of life in the Ottoman Empire, see Gibb, H. A. R., and Bowen, H., *Islamic Society and the West*, Oxford University Press, 1957 on. Needless to say, modernism, which is for the most part synonymous with secularism, has also affected the daily life of the Muslims, their dress, architecture, city planning, interior decoration, diet, and other aspects of similar nature which have a profound influence on the whole of man's outlook. Although we cannot delve into this question at the present moment, we wish to emphasise the importance of these factors in preparing the way for the spread of secularism.

8 For a thorough study of modernism in Islam see Gibb, H. A. R., *Modern Trends in Islam*, Chicago, 1947.

9 'It is important for us to appreciate the breadth of this rift between religious and secular education in Egypt and its far reaching consequences. Not only has it ranged school against school and university against university, but it has contributed more than any other factor to the division in Muslim society . . . ranging orthodox against 'Westernizer' in almost every department of social and intellectual activity, in manner of dress, living, social habits, entertainment, literature, and even speech'. Gibb, H. A. R., *Modern Trends . . .*, p. 42. The same could be said of Persia, Pakistan, and most other Muslim countries.

10 For a profound discussion of this question, see F. Schuon, *L'Œil du cœur*, Paris, 1974, pp. 95–7.

11 See L. Gardet, *La Cité musulmane*, Paris, 1954, pp. 350–62.

2

The Concept and Reality of Freedom in Islam and Islamic Civilisation

In the modern world one concept which is most affected by the dominance of secularism is that of freedom. The discussion of the concept of freedom in the West today is so deeply influenced by the Renaissance and post-Renaissance notion of man as a being in revolt against Heaven and master of the earth that it is difficult to envisage the very meaning of freedom in the context of a traditional civilisation such as that of Islam. It is necessary, therefore, to resuscitate the concept of man as understood in Islam in order to be able to discuss in a serious way the meaning of freedom in the Islamic context. It is meaningless to try to study the notion of freedom in Islam from the point of view of the meaning which has been attached to this term in the West since the rise of humanism.

It might be said that most of the discussion in the West concerning freedom involves in one way or another the freedom to do or to act, whereas in the context of traditional man the most important form of freedom is the freedom to *be*, to experience pure existence itself. This is the most profound form of freedom but it is nearly completely forgotten today because modern man who is so fond of collecting experiences has ceased to remember what the experience of pure existence, which is a reflection of Being Itself and which is at once beauty, consciousness and bliss, means and therefore how precious is the freedom which makes this experience possible and, from another point of view, issues from this experience.

Humans are, according to the Islamic perspective, created in the 'image of God' and are also God's vicegerents (*khalīfah*) on earth. But they are both, by virtue of their servitude to God which makes it possible for them to receive from Heaven and to administer on earth. By virtue of their centrality in the cosmic scheme, proven in reverse if proof is necessary for the sceptic by the nearly complete destruction they have brought upon the environment, they participate in the

Divine freedom, and by virtue of being earthly creatures they are beset by all the limitations which a lower degree of existence implies. God is both pure freedom and pure necessity. Man as the theophany of the Divine Names and Qualities, or as the 'image of God', participates in both this freedom and this necessity. Personal freedom lies in fact in surrender to the Divine Will and in purifying oneself inwardly to an ever greater degree so as to become liberated from all external conditions, including those of the carnal soul (*nafs*), which press upon and limit one's freedom.

Pure freedom belongs to God alone; therefore the more we *are*, the more are we free. And this intensity in the mode of existence cannot be reached save through submission and conformity to the Will of God who alone *is* in the absolute sense. There is no freedom possible through flight from and rebellion against the Principle which is the ontological source of human existence and which determines ourselves from on high. To rebel against our own ontological Principle in the name of freedom is to become enslaved to an ever greater degree in the world of multiplicity and limitation. It is to forfeit the illimitable expanses of the world of the Spirit for the indefinitely extended labyrinth of the psycho-physical world, where the only freedom is to pursue an ever more accelerated life of action devoid of meaning and end.

Infinity resides in the centre of our being, a centre which is hidden from the vast majority of those who live on the periphery of the wheel of existence. Yet only at the centre are we free in an absolute and infinite sense. Otherwise each of us is limited in both our powers and rights *vis-à-vis* God, nature, and other human beings. To seek infinity in the finite is the most dangerous of illusions, a chimera which cannot but result in the destruction of the finite itself. 'Infinite freedom' exists only in the proximity of the Infinite. At all lower levels of existence freedom is conditioned by the limitations of cosmic existence itself and is meaningful only with respect to the limitations and obligations which the very structure of Reality imposes upon us.

The principles outlined briefly thus far form the background of all Islamic thought on freedom, but the degree to which they are explicitly formulated depends upon the perspective within Islamic civilisation in question. The Islamic intellectual world is a hierarchic one in which the same truths are reflected in differing forms on various levels and modes of understanding ranging from the exoteric law to pure esotericism. Here it is sufficient to discuss the concept of freedom as understood by the jurisprudents (*fuqahā'*), the theologians (*mutakallimūn*), the philosophers and Sufis to grasp its basic meaning within the Islamic world view.

The jurisprudents are concerned with the codification of Islamic

Law (*Sharī'ah*) and their discussion of freedom is naturally from a juridical point of view rather than a metaphysical one. Nevertheless the metaphysical background is present even in their juridical discussions for they are dealing with the same *homo islamicus* to whom the whole of the Islamic revelation is addressed. The jurisprudents envisage human freedom as a result of personal surrender to the Divine Will, rather than as an innate personal right. For them, since we are created by God and have no power to create anything by ourselves (in the sense of creation *ex nihilo*), we are ontologically dependent on God and therefore can only receive what is given to us by the source of our own being.

Human rights are, according to the *Sharī'ah*, a consequence of human obligations and not their antecedent. We possess certain obligations towards God, nature, and other humans, all of which are delineated by the *Sharī'ah*. As a result of fulfilling these obligations we gain certain rights and freedoms which are again outlined by the Divine Law. Those who do not fulfil these obligations have no legitimate rights, and any claims of freedom that they make upon the environment or society is illegitimate and a usurpation of what does not belong to them, in the same way that those persons who refuse to recognise their theomorphic nature and act accordingly are only 'accidentally' human and are usurping the human state which by definition implies centrality and Divine vicegerency. Islam holds this conception not only for its own followers but also for the followers of all other religions who, therefore, as religious minorities, are given rights under their own religious codes.

The technical discussion of freedom (*ḥurriyyah* in Arabic and *āzādigī* in Persian) as far as jurisprudence is concerned usually involves the question of slavery, the means whereby slaves are freed, the duties free men have towards them, etc. But in a more general sense, not necessarily bound to the technical term *ḥurriyyah* itself, jurisprudence defines human freedom in the context of a Divine Law which concerns not only our relation to God but also our relation to nature, to other men and even to ourselves since we are not free to do anything we wish with our own lives, which we have not created. For example, suicide is considered as a great sin because it is the usurpation of the right of God. Man is not free to take his life because he did not bring it into being in the first place. On this question Islam stands at the very antipodes of the agnostic existentialism which envisages complete freedom for human existence without considering the source, and also the end, of this existence. The *Sharī'ah* also imposes limitations upon human freedom, but in return bestows a sacred character upon human life which in turn makes possible a greater inner freedom. Ultimately the limitations imposed by the *Sharī'ah* are in the direction of removing from human life certain negative possibilities and freedoms to do evil. They aim to establish the maximum amount of equilibrium in the human collectivity which then serves as outward basis for the inner life which in turn leads to freedom in its most universal sense.

As far as the theologians are concerned, the most famous school among them, namely the Ash'arite, negates human freedom (*ikhtiyār*) completely in favour of a determinism (*jabr*) which is all-embracing. Other theological schools such as the Mu'tazilite and most of the Shi'ite schools do believe in human freedom in its theological sense and reject the total determinism of the Ash'arites. Altogether the debate concerning free will and determinism is a central one to *kalām* and nearly every theologian has participated in it. The debates are in many ways the reverse of what is seen today among philosophers some of whom seek to safeguard the free will of the individual in one form or another before materialistic determinism, whether it be biological, behavioural, or of any other sort, while others try to defend these forms of determinism. Among Muslim theologians there has been, of course, no question of an outward 'material' factor determining human freedom. The problem has always been the relationship of human will to the Divine Will and the extent to which the latter determines the former.

Muslim theology, especially in its prevalent Ash'arite form, tends toward a totalitarian voluntarism not seen usually in Christian theology, but there are many other views among Muslims. It is also important to remember that, despite all the debates among theologians, men did and do continue to live with a consciousness of their free will and hence responsibility before God. As the remarkable dynamism of Islamic history proves, the Muslims are not at all the fatalists they are made out to be in Western sources. But their reliance upon the Divine Will and awareness of the operation of that Will, as shown in their incessant use of the term *inshā'Allāh* (if God wills) in daily discourse, is more noticeable than in most other cultures. The debates of the theologians reflect this general religious concern for submission to the Divine Will and conformity to Its injunctions. Nevertheless no rational theology could overcome certain dichotomies and polarisations, which the theological debate of the subject created, so certain hardened positions were then pushed to extremes. Theologians went so far as to deny human freedom against both the immediate experience of man and the religious injunctions concerning men being held responsible before God for their actions.

The philosophers in general reacted severely against the theologians on this question and asserted fully the reality of human freedom. The early Muslim Peripatetics such as al-Fārābī, Abu'l-Ḥasan al-'Āmirī, Ibn Sīnā (Avicenna) as well as the Andalusian philosophers such as Ibn

Bājjah (Avempace) and Ibn Rushd (Averroes) were greatly interested in political philosophy and well acquainted with Plato and Aristotle and even with some of the Stoics. On the question of freedom, however, they regarded the problem from the point of view of the Islamicised political philosophy of al-Fārābī rather than in purely Greek terms. For all of them, the *Sharī'ah* (which al-Fārābī equated with the Pythagorean-Platonic *nomos*) was a reality, as was the Islamic community (*ummah*) and the legitimacy of political rule derived from the source of revelation, whether this was seen in terms of its Sunni or Shi'ite interpretations. The reality of human freedom was asserted by them, but in the context of the nomocratic society of Islam and not from the point of view of a secularist humanism. Later Islamic philosophers such as Mullā Ṣadrā reverted mostly to a more theological and religious debate about free will and determinism and shied away from the discussions on political philosophy of the kind seen in an al-Fārābī or Averroes. But they too were adamant in asserting the reality of human freedom and also the necessity to conform to the Divine Will which rules over both the cosmos and human society and which alone can prevent men from becoming imprisoned in the narrow confines of their own passions.

Finally something must be said about the Sufis who more than any other group in Islam have spoken about freedom. The verses of such Sufi poets as Rūmī and Ḥāfiẓ are replete with the word *āzādigī* and similar terms denoting freedom. In one of his most famous verses Ḥāfiẓ says:

غلام همّت آنم که زیر چرخ کبود   زهرچه رنگ تعلّق پذیرد آزاداست

I am the slave of the spiritual will of him who
under the azure wheel
Is free (*āzād*) from whatever possesses the colour
of dependence.

The goal of Sufism is union with the One Who is both Absolute and Infinite, Who alone is beyond all limitation, the One Who is absolutely free. The Sufis therefore consider freedom (*ḥurriyyah* or *āzādigī*) as being almost synonymous with the goal of Sufism itself. However, for them freedom does not mean individualism, for their whole aim is to integrate the individual into the universal. Rather, for them freedom means to gain inner detachment through the help of the revealed forms, whether they be cultic or artistic, forms which are outwardly limited but open inwardly towards the Infinite. Sufis, therefore, have always been the most rigorous in the observation of forms, in regard for the *Sharī'ah* and its meticulous practice; yet they have 'broken' these forms from within and attained complete freedom. They have, moreover, done so not in spite of the revealed forms but because of them. No one can transcend what he does not possess. The Sufis transcended forms not by rebelling individualistically against them but by penetrating their inner dimension which because of the sacred character of these forms opens unto the Infinite. Sufis also practised detachment and were often indifferent towards worldly authority. But there were also those among them who were outwardly rich or who even wielded political power. But in both cases there existed an inner detachment and spiritual poverty (*faqr*) which alone make inner freedom possible, for men lose their freedom to the extent that they become enslaved not only by external factors but also by passionate attachments and by their needs, whether these be artificial or real. Freedom in Sufism means ultimately deliverance (*najāt*) from all bondage and an experience of the world of the Spirit where alone freedom in its real sense is to be found.

The realisation of freedom in Islamic civilisation must be studied also on several levels, especially those of action and thought as well as the actual possibility of attaining inner freedom and deliverance. On the level of external action, the immediate question which arises is that of political freedom *vis-à-vis* forms of a government following the period of the first four 'rightly guided' caliphs. Much has been written about 'Oriental despotism' and the lack of freedom of men in various Islamic states in the face of political and military authority. But it must be remembered that for ages the Divine Law remained as a protective code whose bounds even the most ruthless ruler could not transgress. There remained within Islamic society a continuous tension between the political authority of the caliph, sultan, or *amīr* and the religious scholars (*'ulamā*), who played a major role in protecting the *Sharī'ah* and, therefore, those freedoms of the individual guaranteed by the *Sharī'ah*.

Also it is important to mention that the '*ulamā*' do not play the same role in Islam as the clergy do in Christianity. As mentioned earlier, there is no sacerdotal hierarchy in Islam; instead there is an element of 'sacred democracy' in this tradition which enters directly into daily religious life and has much to do with the guarantee of considerable religious freedom in the life of individuals and the community. The role of the *Sharī'ah* and its institutions as protection for the community against arbitrary military and political oppression needs to be emphasised especially since most modern studies on the subject only view the external political institutions and not the personal relationships, family structure, individual rights, etc., all embraced within the comprehensive fold of the *Sharī'ah*.

The lack of an organised religious structure is combined in Islam with the lack of a strictly defined creed in the Christian sense and therefore a much less rigorously defined notion of what is doctrinally acceptable. In Islam, orthodoxy is defined by the testimonial of Islam or *Shahādah, Lā ilāha illa' Llāh* (There is no divinity but the Divine), which is the most universal formulation possible of Divine Unity and not a closely defined theological formulation. There has also been no institution in Islam to define the meaning of the *Shahādah* and its legitimate interpretations. Of course, there *is* orthodoxy in Islam without which, in fact, no truth and no tradition is possible. But this orthodoxy has not been defined in any limited sense nor has there been a particular religious institution to decide who is orthodox and who is not. The community (*ummah*) has been the ultimate judge in the long run. Those in Islamic history who were persecuted or even put to death for their words or writings, such as Ibn Ḥanbal the jurist, al-Ḥallāj the Sufi, or Suhrawardī the Sufi and philosopher, were all involved in political situations with religious implication, the problem of al-Ḥallāj being, however, of a rather special nature. But even cases of persecution such as those cited are few in comparison with what is found elsewhere. By and large, the Islamic tradition has provided a vast umbrella under which views as different as those of a Rhazes and an Ibn 'Arabī have been expressed and taught. If there has been tension, it has usually been between the exoteric and the esoteric dimensions of the tradition but this is a tension which is of a creative nature and lies within the structure of the Islamic tradition itself.

The most crucial test for the actual realisation of means to attain freedom in Islam has been the degree to which it has been able to keep alive within its bosom ways of spiritual realisation leading to inner freedom. And in this matter of central concern, as far as man's entelechy is concerned, Islam has been eminently successful. Over the ages and despite all the obstacles which the gradual darkening of man's outward nature has placed before authentic spiritual paths, Islam has been able to preserve intact to this very day ways of attaining freedom in its absolute and unconditional sense, that is in the sense of complete detachment from everything except God, which is in fact exactly how Sufis have defined freedom or *ḥurriyyah*. Its spiritual techniques and methods, contained mostly within Sufism, are doors which open inwardly to the only freedom which is real and abiding but which is imperceptible to the outward eye. Any discussion of the concept and reality of freedom in Islam must take into account, besides outward manifestations of freedom on the plane of action, the inner freedom which is related to the experience of being itself, and which transforms us in such a way that outward forms of freedom gain a completely different meaning for us. In modern times, men may have gained many outward forms of freedom but they have also lost that most fundamental freedom which is the freedom to be oneself, not the coagulated cloud of the ego with which we usually identify ourselves, but the immortal soul which resides in the proximity of the Self and which enjoys immortality and freedom because of its very nature.

3*

The Sharī'ah and Changing Historical Conditions

I

In the tension between tradition and modernism, one of the most acute problems faced by the contemporary Muslim is the relationship between the *Sharī'ah*, and especially the parts belonging to the domain of personal law, and modern theories and legal practices. However, being neither a jurisprudent or *faqīh* in the traditional sense, nor an advocate in the modern one, but rather a student of Islam and Islamic civilisation in its intellectual and spiritual aspects, we feel it our duty to confine ourselves to the analysis and clarification of the general principles which underlie the very issue implied by the subject of this essay. The discussion of their detailed application we leave to those more competent in matters of jurisprudence.

It must be made clear that in discussing Muslim personal law, we are dealing with the *Sharī'ah* and not simply man-made laws. Thus, the emphasis is more on religion than on law, as these two terms are used in European languages today. Every discussion of Islamic Law involves the most basic religious beliefs and attitudes of Muslims. This is because in Islam the Divine Will manifests itself concretely as specific law, and not abstractly as more or less general moral injunctions. Christianity teaches that God asks man to be charitable or humble as the teachings of Christ clearly indicate. However, one is not told how in a concrete sense one should apply these virtues, so that the general

* This essay is the development of a paper which was delivered originally in India some years ago on the occasion of a colloquium on Muslim personal law. It is, therefore, concerned as much with a particular 'climate' and situation as with general principles. Also certain arguments have been repeated as a result of the particular circumstances in which this paper was delivered and the conditions which resulted from the cogency of the subject matter for the millions of Muslims of India whose personal lives depended upon the conclusions reached in the colloquium.

religious teaching remains on an abstract level unaffected by changes in the concrete laws which govern human society. That is why Europeans, as well as modernised Muslims who are more at home in Western culture than in their own, cannot understand the insistence of traditional Muslims on preserving the letter of the Divine Law.

It could be said quite justifiably that the modern West is not the product of Christianity. Yet even those who oppose Christianity in the modern world cannot eradicate *ad hoc* two thousand years of a heritage which they carry in their souls in spite of themselves. This heritage manifests itself clearly when such a question as Muslim personal law is approached. Here, the attitude of secularists and Christians, and also many modernised Muslims, is the same. All is based on the general attitude taken towards law in Western civilisation derived mostly from the particular nature of Christianity as a 'way of love' without a Divine Law.

What must be taken into account is the profound difference between the Semitic and more particularly Islamic conception of law on the one hand and the modern one on the other. The Semitic conception, shared by Judaism and Islam, sees law as the embodiment of the Divine Will, as a transcendent reality which is eternal and immutable, as a model by which the perfections and shortcomings of human society and the conduct of the individual are judged, as the guide through which man gains salvation and, by rejecting it, courts damnation and destruction. It is like the Law of Manu of Hinduism and the *dharma* which each human being must follow in order to gain felicity. To discuss law in Islam is therefore as essential to the Islamic religion as the discussion of theology is to Christianity. To discuss, much less change, Islamic Law cannot be done by anyone except those competent in the *Sharīʻah*, no more than Christian theology could be discussed and doctrines of the Christian church altered by any other than those vested with authority in such matters. It would be as unthinkable from the Islamic point of view to change Muslim personal law through any simply elected legislative body as it would be to change doctrines of the Christian church through a similar body of laymen. It is only because the similarity of the role of theology in Christianity to the Divine Law in Islam is not understood that the validity of such an analogy is not accepted by so many people today.

Let us now examine how the *Sharīʻah* is related to the world in which we live. To many people, reality is exhausted by the physico-psychological world which surrounds us and what does not conform to this world is considered to be unreal. Islamic doctrine, like all other traditional metaphysics, is based on the belief that reality is comprised of multiple states of existence (*marātib al-wujūd*) of which the physical world is the lowest and furthest removed from the Divine Origin of all reality. Therefore the *Sharī'ah*, being an eternal truth belonging to a higher order of existence, is by no means abrogated if it does not conform to the particular conditions of a certain point in space or moment in time. Rather, it is the world which must conform to the Divine Law. The Law loses nothing if it is not followed by men. Conversely man and his world lose everything by not conforming to the Divine Will of which the *Sharī'ah* is the concrete embodiment.

These days we are often told that we must keep up with the times. Rarely does one ask what have the 'times' to keep up with. For men who have lost the vision of a reality which transcends time, who are caught completely in the mesh of time and space and who have been affected by the historicism prevalent in modern European philosophy, it is difficult to imagine the validity of a truth that does not conform to their immediate external environment. Islam, however, is based on the principle that truth transcends history and time. Divine Law is an objective transcendent reality, by which man and his actions are judged, not vice versa. What are called the 'times' today are to a large extent a set of problems and difficulties created by man's ignorance of his own real nature and his stubborn determination to 'live by bread alone'. To attempt to shape the Divine Law to the 'times' is therefore no less than spiritual suicide because it removes the very criteria by which the real value of human life and action can be objectively judged and thus surrenders man to the most infernal impulses of his lower nature. To say the least, the very manner of approaching the problem of Islamic Law and religion in general by trying to make them conform to the 'times' is to misunderstand the whole perspective and spirit of Islam.

Islam has always considered the positive aspect of the intellect (*'aql*) and man's ability to reach the cardinal doctrine of Islam, that is to say the doctrine of Unity (*tawḥīd*), through his *'aql*. In fact, the Quran often describes those who have gone astray from religion as those who cannot 'intellect' (*lā ya'qilūn*). But this is no licence for rationalism and an *ad hoc* treatment of the *Sharī'ah* as judged by human reason, because man can reach *tawḥīd* through his own *'aql* only under the condition that this *'aql* is in a wholesome state (*salīm*). And it is precisely the *Sharī'ah* whose practice removes the obstacles in the soul which prevent the correct functioning of the intellect and obscure its vision. It is the *Sharī'ah* that guarantees the wholesomeness of the intellect so that to change the *Sharī'ah* through the judgement of human reason with the excuse that the Quran has ordered man to use his intellectual faculties, is no more than sheer sophistry and a chimerical manner of leading simple souls astray.

II

We may ask why the question of changing Muslim personal law has been posed at all in so many parts of the Islamic world. Having briefly outlined the nature of Islamic law, we must now turn to two elements which deserve to be analysed: one the question of change and the other personal law. In traditional Muslim sources, there is no term to denote personal law, because theoretically the *Sharī'ah* covers all human life, both personal and social. If such a term has come into recent usage and has even found its way into contemporary Islamic law (the adjective *shakhṣiyyah* being usually used for personal), it is because even during the Umayyad period the *Sharī'ah* was in practice not applied fully in certain realms such as that of general taxation. Also, many political dealings of Muslim rulers remained outside its injunctions. That is why the so-called reforms carried out by many Muslim states in their attempt to introduce certain European codes, such as the *Tanẓīmāt* of the Ottomans, did not profoundly affect the structure of Islamic society. What has remained intact through the ages has been that aspect of the *Sharī'ah* which concerns directly the human person, such as marriage, divorce and inheritance. These are thus labelled as personal law. This domain has been the refuge and stronghold that has enabled Islamic society to remain Islamic in spite of the various forms of political institution that have ruled over it in past centuries. Therefore what is under discussion is the last refuge of the legal aspect of the *Sharī'ah* in Islamic society as a whole.

As for the question of change involved in the subject matter of this essay, it lies in that complex set of factors which characterise modernism in general, in the West as well as in the East. First of all, through the spread of belief in that false idol of eighteenth- and nineteenth-century European philosophy, namely progress, many in the East unconsciously equate change with progress. And, since they have surrendered their intelligence to the dictum of historicism, they evaluate all things in the light of change and becoming rather than with regard to their immutable aspect. They thus equate the immutability of the Truth with solidification and petrifaction. Secondly, the structure of Western civilisation, even before modern times, was such as to view law only in its mutable aspect. This trait has been inherited by modernism, which is naturally a product of Western civilisation. Christianity was by nature an esotericism (*ṭarīqah*) externalised. It was devoid of a *Sharī'ah* so that it had to integrate Roman law into its structure in order to become the religion of a whole civilisation. Therefore, even if Roman law had a Divine aspect from the point of view of Roman religion, it was not an integral part of the Christian revelation, so that the Christians never regarded their law in the same manner as did the

Jews and Muslims, or the Hindus for that matter. That is the basic reason why Westerners cannot usually understand the meaning of the *Sharī'ah* and Westernised Muslims approach the problems of Islamic Law in the modern world from the point of view so prevalent today.

To this misunderstanding must be added the psychological factors which are the result of centuries of pressure imposed by the West on all Oriental civilisations. In the minds of many Muslims, there is a sense of inferiority *vis-à-vis* the West, which forces them to be its blind followers and to regard their own tradition either with disdain or at best with an attitude of apologetic acceptance. In that state of mind, they usually try to change those aspects of their religion and law which do not conform to today's fashions and which, to cover one's intellectual and spiritual weakness, is called 'keeping up with the times'.

For example, let us take the question of polygamy, which is far from limited to Islam (we remember that Charlemagne had many wives). Many modernised Muslims feel embarrassed by this feature of the *Sharī'ah* for no other reason than that Christianity eventually banned it and that in the West today it is forbidden. The arguments against it are not so much logical as sentimental and carry mainly the weight and prestige of the modern West with them. All the arguments given, based on the fact that polygamy is the only way of preventing many social ills of today, have no effect on those for whom the fashion of the day has replaced the *Sunnah* of the Holy Prophet. One can speculate that, if modernism had originated in the Himalayan states rather than in Europe, the modern Muslim apologists would not have tried to interpret the teachings of the *Sharī'ah* as permitting polyandry, as today they interpret its teaching only in the monogamous sense which is current Western practice.

Of course we do not propose that Muslims should remain oblivious of the world around them. This is neither desirable nor possible. No Islamic state can avoid owning trains and planes, but Muslims can avoid hanging surrealistic paintings on their walls. By this is meant that there are certain conditions in twentieth-century life which the Muslim world cannot alter and with which it must live while others can be avoided. The whole difference lies in the attitude towards the modern world. One can regard a situation as one in which it is difficult to practise the *Sharī'ah* fully, not because the *Sharī'ah* itself is imperfect, but because the conditions in which we live have fallen short of those immutable principles which of necessity ultimately govern all things. One can still follow and practise Islamic Law in such conditions by following the teachings of Islam itself, for the Prophet even allowed prayers to be said on horseback in time of war.

Or one can, as is so common today, take the world as the sole reality and judge the validity of the *Sharī'ah* according to its degree of conformity to this world. This attitude is totally un-Islamic and is like putting the cart before the horse. Such an attitude makes the world and man's imperfect judgements informing it take the place of God. Such an attitude commits the sin which theologically is the gravest of all in Islam, namely *shirk* or 'polytheism'.

Islam is a way of peace based on the establishment of equilibrium between all human tendencies and needs, which must of necessity serve as a basis for all man's spiritual strivings. The *Sharī'ah* is the maker and preserver of this equilibrium and the personal laws play a particularly significant role in keeping this human order and equilibrium. Were this equilibrium to be destroyed, both inner and outward peace, which everyone seeks today but rarely finds, would disappear. All 'reforms' and changes–especially in matters of personal law–proposed today should aim to preserve and build rather than destroy this equilibrium whose chief symbol in Islam is the square Ka'bah. The question of changing Islamic personal law should be approached with the spirit of belief in the *Sharī'ah*, thereby attempting to apply and preserve it to the extent possible in the modern world, and to build the life of Muslim society according to it. It should not be approached with a firm belief in all 'values' and norms prevalent in the West today according to which one should seek to change Islamic Law. These practices and 'values' which seem permanent today are as impermanent as the most impermanent aspect of human nature upon which they are based.

If the question of changes in Islamic Law is approached by the Muslim intelligentsia in the spirit thus proposed, it will be seen in a completely different light. The rift between the Western-educated classes and the rest of the Muslim community will pass and everyone will realise the real significance of the *Sharī'ah* as the basis of stability in human life. They will also learn that, although to concern oneself with matters pertaining to Islam is the duty of every Muslim, applying the *Sharī'ah* in detail to newly created situations is a question of *fiqh* that should be dealt with by the *fuqahā'*. If one understands the real nature of the *Sharī'ah*, one would think no more of passing on a sick person to someone who is not a physician than to turn over matters concerning Muslim personal laws to one who is not a specialist in the *Sharī'ah*, that is to say a *faqīh* or '*ālim* who specialises in *fiqh*. Otherwise, in both cases, the patient, whether he be an individual or a society, faces the danger of a graver malady and even death.

III

In conclusion, it may be added that the blind following of Western ideas in matters concerned with law, as in so many other domains, will never solve any basic problem of Islamic society. It is a form of *taqlīd* or blind following much more dangerous than the traditional type of *taqlīd* which has always been decried by Muslim sages over the ages. Only by accepting the validity of the *Sharī'ah* and especially of the personal laws promulgated by it and by relying upon these laws can Islamic society face the problems of the modern world. And only through the *Sharī'ah* can meaningful change be brought about. In fact the value of any change can only be gauged *vis-à-vis* a permanent truth. If we were to lose the *Sharī'ah*, we would lose that very thing for whose subsistence we are trying to 'reform' our present society. In such a case, our reformations would only become deformations. Thus we would only let loose forces which would disrupt the very basis of our society and open doors which would enable individual whims and fancies to exert themselves over the Divine Norm which alone gives meaning to human life.

4

The Immutable Principles of Islam and Westernised Education in the Islamic World

The introduction of Western educational systems into the Islamic world is one of the major elements which have brought tension and heterogeneity within the very matrix of Islamic society. This factor, in addition to the constant contact between many Muslim scholars and students with educational institutions in the Western world itself, has brought to the centre of the stage the crucial question of the relation between the immutable principles of Islam and philosophy, methods and contents of Western educational systems. This disparity, incongruence and usually open conflict between Islamic and Western educational systems and their aims must be examined and studied seriously by all those who are interested in the welfare of Islamic society and its future.

Two contending educational systems have created in the Muslim world today a chasm between a Western-educated minority and a majority which on both the popular and intellectual levels is rooted in traditional Islam. A generation of Muslims in many lands have become trained in a mode of thought, based on modern science and philosophy, which makes it difficult for them to understand the language of the traditional works in which Islamic wisdom is contained. One sees in many parts of the Muslim world two men belonging to the same country and even speaking the same language externally, but who do not understand each other because they are using different systems of reference and worlds of ideas. At the same time, for over a century, a large number of works have been produced by Western orientalists, many of whom have been hostile to Islam, and in fact have written on Islam not because of their love of the subject but in order to refute it. Yet these works, even the prejudiced and distorted ones, are the only sources available on Islam to those trained in the modern educational system and they appeal to many by what appears to be their 'scientific' method and language.

To this situation is added the need of different parts of the Islamic community such as the Sunni and Shi'ite to come to know each other better and, on a larger scale, to come to gain a more intimate knowledge of the other great religious traditions of the world. The problem of the encounter with other religions is a counterpart of the contact with modernism. A traditional Muslim who has not encountered the modern world need not think of Christian theology or of Hindu and Buddhist metaphysics. But once contact is made with the different forms of modernism there is in most cases an inner necessity to come to know other religions as well. In fact, such knowledge is often an antidote for the scepticism brought about as a result of the influence of modernism whereas in a homogeneous Islamic climate such knowledge would be in most cases unnecessary and redundant.

With these factors in mind, it is our belief that it is the function of those Muslim scholars who are concerned with Islamic studies in the West or in the context of modern eduational institutions within the Islamic world itself to be aware of the following goals and aims which concern the whole of the Islamic community and its future:

1 Islam is a living spiritual and religious tradition, not a dead religion which is simply of historical interest. The duty of Islamic scholars functioning in a modern context should be first and foremost to present to the modern world the many treasuries of wisdom which still exist in the Islamic tradition but which are half forgotten by a generation of modern Western-educated Muslims. This means translating the traditional truths of Islam into a contemporary language without betraying them. Such a difficult task requires one who himself firmly believes in Islam and has not become enamoured of the noise and clamour of modernism. It calls for a person who judges the world according to the immutable principles of Islam and does not seek to 'reform' (so-called) the God-given truths of Islam in the light of the transient and ephemeral conditions which are called 'the times'. Such a person must be free from a sense of intellectual inferiority *vis-à-vis* the West. On the contrary, he should consciously uphold and be proud of the Islamic tradition with all its intellectual and spiritual riches and not see Islam just as a simple rational faith devoid of a spiritual dimension as some have tried to make it.

At the same time, he must know the Western world well, know it well but not in a second-hand fashion that would make him take for new clothing what has already been discarded by the Western intelligentsia. He must know the inner forces that motivate the Western mind and have a clear grasp of the philosophical, scientific, religious, artistic and social life of the West in their religious and historical roots as well as in their present-day manifestations. Only a person who himself knows through first hand knowledge the intellectual life of

Islam and has mastered the contemporary medium of expression can hope to present in a fresh form and language the perennial wisdom which exists within the Islamic tradition. Only such a person can provide the necessary knowledge of Islam for a new generation that has been severed from this wisdom by having been trained in another mode of thought and expression and which at the same time is in desperate need of the saving truth contained in the Islamic message.

2 The study of Islam by orientalists has produced a large number of works which are studied by all interested in Islamic studies, not only in the West and in non-Muslim countries of Asia but even in those Muslim countries where a European language such as English or French is widespread. Unfortunately, Islam has not received favourable treatment in most of these works, even in comparison with other great religions of Asia such as Hinduism and Buddhism. Many factors such as the historical contacts between Christianity and Islam which have not always been friendly, the medieval fear of Muslims in Europe, the fact that Islam followed Christianity historically, the Semitic origin of Islam for the predominantly Indo-European people of the Western world, who are thus naturally more attracted towards Hinduism and other Aryan religions, all play a role in the unfavourable treatment which Islam has received and continues to receive from many quarters in the West, there being of course certain honourable exceptions. In fact, until quite recently many orientalists writing about Islam embarked upon this field not because they had a love for some aspect of it but because they had been somehow unwillingly pushed into it as philologists or missionaries.

The considerable amount of research done on Islamic studies by orientalists contains much of scientific and historical value, even if there are many elements in their works which are unacceptable from the Islamic point of view, and even if one finds in many cases distortions and misunderstandings in interpretation. Whatever the value of these studies may be, they cannot be refuted nor can their influence be annulled by simply denouncing orientalists or using the language of demagogy against them. What the orientalists have done is to study Islam for their own ends and needs. The duty of the Muslim scholars concerned with modern educational and academic institutions and set-ups is to provide a Muslim answer to the challenge of the orientalists in a language and method appropriate for such a task. Such an undertaking would also be of great interest to the world of orientalism itself. What is needed is a study of all domains of the Islamic tradition and civilisation by Muslim scholars who, while firmly believing in their own tenets, can deal with them in a scholarly manner so as to provide a response to the challenges to Islam posed by the works of many orientalists. Furthermore, they must couch them in language acceptable to those who are reared in the rationalistic and sceptical ambience of modern schools. Only an undertaking of this kind could curtail the influence of such works on those Muslims who are affected by their writings. Such an undertaking could at the same time help to present Islam and its culture and history to the outside world in its true colour.

3 Closely allied to the challenge to Islam of the study of these orientalists is the whole modern scientific, historical and philosophic attitude of which the approach and method prevalent among most orientalists is but a reflection. This immense challenge which Islam faces, as do all other religions, is to be seen today especially in the context of such ideologies and theories as evolution, psychoanalysis, existentialism, historicism and on another level dialectical materialism. It is not, of course, possible for a single scholar to be a specialist in all scientific disciplines and philosophical schools and to provide complete answers to all of the questions posed by these 'isms'. A complete response requires concerted effort on the part of a large number of Islamic thinkers working in harmony within the bosom of the Islamic tradition. Traditional Islamic wisdom possesses within itself the metaphysical doctrines which alone can provide the answers to such problems, but these answers need to be formulated and crystallised. These modern modes of thought in fact have come about for the most part as a result of forgetting metaphysical principles.

To present the traditional Islamic doctrines in a contemporary language would in fact itself contribute towards facing these and similar challenges posed by modernism. The very situation of Muslim scholars concerned with Islamic scholarship but in a Western-oriented university, whether it be located in the East or the West, places them in the forefront of this vital task to provide Islamic answers to the fashionable ideas of the times, some of which are pseudo-science parading in the dress of science and others purely and simply the fruit of the secularism of the past four centuries in the West. Also, by studying Islam as a living reality and emphasising the perennial nature of the truths contained in the Islamic tradition, such scholars can provide an antidote to the malady of historicism which is so prevalent today and which Islam opposes in its philosophical roots by refusing to admit that the truth can become incarnated in history.

4 Every religion by the fact that it enters into the world participates in the multiplicity which is characteristic of it and therefore is soon divided into different schools and perspectives. In fact, it is through the presence of these dimensions, providentially placed within a revelation, that it is able to integrate into its structure people of differing

psychological and spiritual temperaments. Islam is no exception to this rule, although it has displayed more homogeneity and less diversity than other world religions. One of the tasks of contemporary Islamic scholarship should be to study this diversity in Islam in the light of its unifying principles, to delineate the structure of the two great orthodox dimensions of Islam, namely Sunnism and Shi'ism, as well as the movements and sects which have diverged from them. It should make each one better known to the other.

Family feuds occur naturally within every family, but they are immediately put aside when the whole family group is endangered. In the present situation in the Islamic world, an intellectual and spiritual understanding between Sunnism and Shi'ism is essential, as is a firm comprehension of the total orthodoxy of Islam which consists of these two main branches. It is also important to make a critical study of the small religious groups who over the centuries have separated from the mainstream of Islamic religious life and to discover their relation to the main body of Islamic orthodoxy. Although such studies can take place and in fact have already taken place to a certain extent in traditional Islamic educational institutions such as al-Azhar, it is especially in the context of the modern world that the pertinence of such a dialogue becomes so evident. That is why some of the most ardent proponents of the renewal of dialogue between various schools of Islamic thought and jurisprudence are those Muslim scholars who have had an intimate experience of modern education and various Western modes of thought.

5 Also due to contact with the modern world, which both corrodes the homogeneous religious world view and at the same time facilitates knowledge of other religious traditions, the carrying out of a serious dialogue between Islam and other religions has become a necessity. Until now Muslims as a whole have been less interested in the study of other religions than either the Christians or the Hindus and Buddhists, perhaps because the presence of other religions was an already accepted truth in Islam before modern times. Of all the great religious traditions of mankind, Islam is the only one to have had contact before the modern period with nearly every important tradition, with Christianity and Judaism in the Western and central territories of Islam, with Zoroastrianism and other Iranian religions in Persia itself and in Iraq, with Hinduism in India, with Buddhism in north-western Persia and Afghanistan and with the Chinese tradition in Sinkiang. Also the principle of the universality of revelation is clearly stated in the Quran and has in fact been explored to a certain extent by some of the older Muslim masters such as Rūmī and Ibn 'Arabī. Therefore, in principle it is easier for Islam to make a sympathetic study of other religions and remain completely faithful to its own principles than is the case with

many other religions, which may find an acceptance of other traditions difficult from the point of view of their own accepted dogmatic and theological structure. However, in modern times few serious studies of other religions have as yet been carried out by Muslim scholars and few attempts have been made to penetrate the inner message of other religions. The feud between Muslims and Christians in the Near East since the nineteenth century, combined with the problems created by the partition of Palestine *vis-à-vis* the Jews during the past decades, have made the sympathetic study of these religions difficult, at least in the Arab Near East where the religious communities issuing from the Abrahamic tradition live so closely together. The same bitterness is felt among Muslims about Hinduism in so many regions of the subcontinent. Yet a study of other religions needs to be made by Muslim scholars not only for political expediency but in order to provide answers to those questions posed by secularism which cannot satisfactorily be dealt with save through the defence of religion as such. The best way to defend Islam in its integral nature today is to defend *religio perennis*, the primordial religion (*al-dīn al-ḥanīf*) which lies at the heart of Islam and also at the centre of all religions which have been sent to man by the grace of Heaven.

Of course to carry out all these tasks, to present the traditional wisdom of Islam in contemporary language, to answer the questions posed by the works of orientalists, to provide an answer to the challenges of modernism, to bring about closer understanding between the different groups of Muslims, and finally to provide a dialogue between Islam and other religions is a momentous undertaking.

It calls into play all the intellectual resources of the Islamic world. It requires a reassertion of the immutable principles of Islam within the matrix of Western educational systems. It also means the re-creation of an authentic Islamic educational system which would have its roots in the traditional Islamic schools and its branches extending to the domain claimed by modern ideologies and methods of education. An authentic and at the same time contemporary Islamic educational system would not shun these domains, nor would it surrender to the modern theories which claim to govern them. Rather, it would conquer these domains and make them its own. It would extend the branches of the tree of Islamic education so as to embrace these domains and disciplines. Putting aside the preservation of the Islamic religion itself, no task is more crucial in the present context of Islamic society than this reassertion of the immutable principles of Islam and their application to methods and fields of knowledge claimed by modern, Western education and learning. The degree of success of this task will decide the extent to which Islamic society and civilisation will continue to be Islamic in reality as well as in name.

Cultural and Intellectual Life

5

A Typological Study of Islamic Culture

To understand the life and thought of Islam and its civilisation, it is necessary to understand the diverse ethnic and cultural worlds into which the Islamic revelation descended and which Islam transformed and made its own.

One can speak of one Islamic culture with many different colours, 'zones' and variations or of several cultures within Islamic civilisation, depending on what is meant by the term 'culture', which is, in any case, a word of recent origin in the Islamic world and is utilised under the direct influence of the use of this term in Western languages. If we consider the spiritual and intellectual elements which determine the life of a traditional society, however, and define culture in such a way as to embrace these basic elements, then without doubt there is a single Islamic culture with distinct 'zones' or worlds contained within it, 'worlds' which are united by the spirit and sacred form of the tradition and separated by local ethnic, linguistic, geographical and other factors. A traditional civilisation, such as that of Islam, is dominated by a Divine Norm, by a 'presiding Idea' which leaves its profoundest imprint upon its earthly receptacles; yet each receptacle is given the freedom to develop its own innate possibilities within the tradition into which it is integrated and hence to give birth to a particular 'world' or 'zone' within the general matrix of the tradition in question. To study the typology of Islamic culture is to be concerned with the contours and features of these 'worlds', such as the Arabic, Iranian, Turkish, Malay and Black African, within the totality of Islamic culture and also to analyse the complex patterns which exist within each of these 'worlds'.

The first question which naturally arises in discussing the typology of Islamic culture is the criterion or criteria by which the various 'worlds' or types are distinguished and defined. Many factors could be enumerated which alone, or, more usually, in combination with each other, have been responsible for the creation of these cultural 'worlds' and which can be employed as criteria for their delineation and description. One could divide the Islamic world according to the religious schools followed by various communities, schools which for this purpose include not only the four *madhhabs* of Sunni law and Twelve-Imam Shi'ism, but also the various branches of Ismā'īlism and even smaller sects such as the Nuṣayrīs, the Ahl-i Ḥaqq, the 'Alawīs, etc. Considering the all-embracing character of the Divine Law and its pertinence to all aspects of life, and the sense of community created by belonging to a distinct school, without doubt the fact that a particular collectivity follows Shāfi'ī or Mālikī law or for even stronger reasons Twelve-Imam or other branches of Shi'ism imposes a notable cultural homogeneity over the community in question. That this factor becomes especially strong when it is combined with ethnic grouping and also with geographical isolation can be seen in many quarters of the Islamic world.

Likewise, the spread of a particular Sufi order, especially if it also possesses an extensive popular dimension and has played a role in the spread of Islam, can be considered another major factor of cultural differentiation, one which touches directly the 'spiritual style' of a particular 'world', and indirectly many other facets of its life. For example, the spread of the Mawlawī and Baktāshī orders in Ottoman Turkey and the Qādiriyyah and Tijāniyyah orders in several regions of West Africa has played a central role in giving a distinct spiritual and hence cultural flavour to the life of the traditional Islamic communities in these regions.

As far as the earthly vessel of the tradition is concerned, obviously the ethnic and racial characteristics of the peoples which have embraced Islam have been a most decisive factor in local cultural variations. These characteristics have affected language and literature, art forms of all kinds, including dress, ornamentation, various styles of calligraphy and architecture, music, etc. In fact, many students of Islamic history would probably simply divide Islamic culture into various types according to ethnic or linguistic criteria, as people usually speak about Arab or Persian or Malay Islam. In some cases the language and in others other ethnic features are considered as the overriding and determining factors. Yet, despite the great importance of such elements, they are not sufficient unto themselves and must be taken into account along with other elements of a both spiritual and historico-geographical nature.

History is obviously a most powerful factor not only in moulding the cultural identity of a region but also in providing local colour and differentiation within a vaster cultural pattern. The common historical experience and the type of awareness a particular community possesses of the past can be as powerful an agent in determining local cultural patterns as the factors mentioned above. The Egyptians have a different historical relation to the pharaohs from the Syrians, yet both groups belong to the Arabic zone of Islamic culture. Despite this unity, therefore, this awareness makes of Egypt a particular 'zone' within the larger Arab cultural world. In Persia, even those who speak Ādharī Turkish have a common historical experience and consciousness with the rest of the Persians of such figures as Cyrus or Darius, while the Bengalis or Sindhis who for centuries spoke Persian do not possess the same relation with the Achamaenian past. This element is certainly one of the factors which determine the Persian zone of Islamic culture, bind its members together and distinguish it from other regions of the Islamic world which share many other features with this 'world'.

Finally, the demographic and geographical characteristics must be taken into consideration. Those regions in which there has been over the centuries continuous ebb and flow between the nomads and sedentary peoples have gained certain profound common features, as also have those with a completely sedentary agricultural community. Moreover, geographical features which have caused isolation for long periods or submitted the population to special natural conditions have played a considerable role in local cultural variations. Some of the communities in far-away mountainous areas or in oases in the middle of deserts or those removed from major trade routes or on inaccessible islands or, on the contrary, those placed at the crossroads of trade or invasions have gained special cultural features which play a considerable role in their belonging to a particular type of Islamic culture. Some of the small religious communities in western Persia or northern Syria, or the cities lying just north of the Sahara or the borders of the Persian Gulf or Somaliland, all point to the importance of such factors. These and many other elements must be used separately as well as together to make possible the study of the complicated cultural patterns within Islamic civilisation, patterns which depict cultural 'worlds' all interrelated, yet distinct and possessing very complex relationships to the other 'worlds' contained within the matrix of Islam.

The historical process by which the various 'worlds' or 'zones' of Islamic culture came into being must be outlined briefly before each 'zone' is described because the effects of this process are inseparable from the elements which define and distinguish these zones. It is well known that the Arabs first united Arabia, then captured the southern provinces of the Byzantine empire and the whole of the Persian empire. The Arab world was, therefore, historically the oldest outlined 'zone' to come into being in Islamic civilisation. But it must be noted that the Islamicisation of certain parts of the Arab world such as North Africa went on concurrently with that of Persia and even of a certain number of black people of West Africa.

Once having become Islamic mostly by peaceful means and not by coercion as is usually asserted, the Persians became the main instrument for the spread of Islam over most of the rest of the Asian landmass at least as far as Malaysia. Although Sindh and some of the provinces of Central Asia were conquered directly by the Arab armies, the great saints of Persian origin such as those of the Suhrawardiyyah and Chishtiyyah, combining with an already totally Islamicised Persian language, carried Islam, on the one hand, to the farthest reaches of the subcontinent of India and, on the other, to the Turks of Central Asia and beyond. Some of these Turks, however, had already become members of the armies of the caliphs in Baghdad and embraced Islam in that city. But the fact that Persia became Islamic through the Arabs and Arabic culture and language and most of the rest of Islamic Asia through Persian elements is of great significance for the typology of Islamic culture during later centuries.

In China, where Islam made an inroad in what was called 'eastern Turkestan' and which has now come to be known as Sinkiang, the Persian elements, and especially the language, played an important role so that in many ways this 'zone' shares common elements with the Turkish and Indian worlds, although it naturally possesses many distinct features of its own.

The African world, however, received Islam almost completely from Arabic and Berber sources, the only exception being West Africa where Arabic and Persian elements were combined. But here also the spread of Islam took place almost completely without external coercion, although within the area itself there were wars between various tribes and states as elsewhere. The expansion of Islam came through Sufi saints and also through pious merchants of Arabic or Berber and later of local African origin. The emigration of Indian and Malay Muslims to Africa represents a much more recent and geographically restricted phenomenon.

In South-East Asia, which contains today the largest single concentration of Muslims in any geographical area of comparable size, contact with Islam was mostly through the sea and from the regions of Hadramawt and the Persian Gulf. For that reason, its character differs somewhat from the cultural 'flavour' of Islam as it spread overland to lands as near as Bengal and even Burma. In the Malay-Indonesian world the cultural imprint of Hadramawt left an indelible mark upon the later development of Islam, as did the composite nature of all that came from the Persian Gulf in which Arabic and Persian elements were mingled in a rather unique blend with other local ingredients. The role of Arab traders and scholars in that region persisted over the centuries.

Finally, it was the Ottoman Turks who not only completed the 'Turkification' of Anatolia but also carried Islam to the Balkans. There, all that remains of Islamic culture is inextricably bound to the

Turkish world, and the whole phenomenon of Islam in Eastern Europe cannot be studied separately from the cultural patterns of the Turkish part of Islamic culture.

When scholars discuss the actual 'zones' of Islamic culture some historians such as Toynbee have spoken of two basic poles of civilisation (the Arabic, and the Iranic) while others such as V. Monteil – to cite just one example – have divided the Islamic world into five 'zones': the Arabic, the Iranian, the Turkish, the Malay and the Black African. Although both these divisions have their shortcomings, and leave many questions unanswered, they can serve as possible points of departure for a study of the typology of Islamic culture. The Arabic and Iranic poles can be kept in view when considering the larger perspective of Islamic civilisation and the processes which caused the spread of Islamic culture. The five 'zones' taken into consideration are based upon the long historical processes which have been at play in each region of the Islamic world.

The Arabic 'zone' of Islamic culture is usually defined only linguistically, namely as that part of the Islamic world whose people use Arabic as their mother tongue. It includes what in a political sense today is called the Arab world and embraces certain states such as the Sudan, Somaliland and Mauritania not all of whose people can be called Arab in whatever way such a term is defined. The vast Arabic 'zone' of Islam, stretching from Iraq to Mauritania, can itself be subdivided into several very distinct sections. First of all, one can clearly distinguish between an eastern and a western Arab world with the line drawn somewhere in the desert separating eastern and western Libya. In the eastern part or *al-Mashriq*, the Hejaz and Najd, the birthplace of Islam, form to this day a distinct unit with a still dominant nomadic cultural pattern which stretches into southern Jordan, Syria and Iraq. The Levant states form another distinct area, united by geographical similarities, common historical experience, especially domination by the Ottomans, and even an almost uniform Arabic dialect.

Egypt, in many ways the centre of the Arabic 'zone' of Islamic culture, is also quite distinct and different from other regions. The very physiognomy and anatomy of its people as well as habits and morals reflect an ancient past which became totally Islamicised and Arabised and later in its history even underwent a notable Turkish influence, which is reflected in certain aspects of her art and daily habits.

Also quite distinct in the eastern part of the Arab world are the southern regions of the Arabian peninsula. The Yemen, which was the only land of this region to have embraced Islam peacefully, has continued its long sedentary, yet purely Arabic, cultural patterns which are reflected in its distinct architecture and city planning. It represents a cultural 'zone' which is easily distinguishable from other parts of

Arabia through the visual aspects of its art as well as the intellectual and literary expressions of its people. Likewise, Hadramawt and Aden as well as Muscat and Oman have over the ages formed a distinct cultural 'zone' related on the one hand to their Arabic background and on the other to the Indian Ocean, with which they have always been closely associated.

As for Iraq, it too represents a unique section of the eastern part of the Arab world. Half Sunni and half Shi'ite, it includes important non-Arab minorities, especially the Kurds and Persians but also the Assyrians, etc. It is heir to the great civilisations of ancient Mesopotamia and during the past few centuries had the strange historic experience of being located between two powerful empires, the Ottoman and the Safavid, sometimes ruled by one and sometimes the other. For these and other reasons, Iraq, too, is a distinct area within the eastern Arabic 'zone' of Islamic culture.

The western part of the Arab world, or the region traditionally known as *al-Maghrib* and stretching from Libya to the Atlantic, has always been a distinct region. Evidence for this lies in the dialect of Arabic spoken in the area, the style of calligraphy, architecture and city planning and the presence of Berbers who have mixed with the Arabic population to create a unique synthesis. Even the use of the Arabic numerals as known in the West, rather than the earlier 'Indian numerals' (*al-arqām al-hindiyyah*) which are used in the eastern lands of Islam, is limited within the Islamic world to the region of the Maghrib. There is, however, much of purely Arabic origin in this region which is in many ways less tainted by non-Arabic influences than farther east. A city like Fez is more Arabic in character than any city found outside the Hejaz, while the completely white towns and villages which characterise this region reflect the sepulchral beatitude associated with the purity of the soul of the Holy Prophet.

Within the Maghrib, there is again a distinction to be made between the area stretching from western Libya to eastern Algeria and the territory west of this area from Tlemcen to the Atlantic coast, including the whole of Morocco, which alone is called Maghrib today. Furthermore, southern Spain or Andalusia also belonged to this region before it left Muslim hands, and in fact to this day Andalusia possesses profound cultural links with Morocco. In this farthest region of the Maghrib, or what is traditionally called *al-Maghrib al-aqṣā*, a profound homogeneity has been imposed by a long common history dominated by the rule of families from the household of the Holy Prophet, continuous interaction with the nomadic elements and a unique mixture with the Berber population. In addition, many aspects of Islamic art such as architecture, gardening, calligraphy, and the like, achieved an outstanding level of development, while the preservation of some of the earliest phases of Islamic culture, such as male dress reflecting the early Medina models, has contributed to this cultural unity. Even the cuisine in this area is quite distinct and reflects the long development of the culinary art in Andalusia and Morocco itself.

Throughout the Arab world there are also local cultural areas marked by ethnic, linguistic or religious bonds of special nature. In North Africa the Berber areas are noted for being of particular cultural importance. They possess their own distinct language and artistic expressions as well as physical features which show them forming a cultural zone of their own. Other groups at the edge of the Sahara are also to be noted such as the Tuareg, who inhabit southern Algeria but who, like the Berbers, roam over much wider areas.

In the Arab East, there are first of all the special religious communities such as the Nuṣayrīs and 'Alawīs of Syria who have also been isolated geographically over the ages and the Druzes, who form a distinct community, not only for religious regions but also for ethnic ones. Many such small communities which possess cultural patterns of their own within the greater matrix of Islamic culture are to be found throughout the Near East. To these may, in a sense, be added the Christian Arab communities of Egypt, Syria, the Lebanon, Jordan, etc., which although not Islamic have become integrated into the mosaic of Islamic culture as also have the traditional Oriental Jews, who have lived over the centuries in the bosom of the Islamic world.

Within the Arab world, therefore, which is itself one of the major 'zones' of Islamic culture, one can detect first of all the major division of the East and the West and then, within each area, the more local areas mentioned above. But this whole area is united beyond local cultural variations by the usage of the Arabic language as its mother tongue and by an adherence to the Quranic revelation which appears as almost 'racial', in the sense of being connected with the history of the Arabs as a people. Strangely enough this sense of belonging to the Arab race is felt much more through the usage of the Arabic language than by tracing actual genealogies so that, in this part of the Islamic world, language considerations dominate completely racial and ethnic ones and to a large extent determine them, thanks most of all to the special spiritual power granted to this language by the fact that it was chosen as the vehicle for the revelation of Islam.

The second important zone of Islamic culture, namely the Iranian, represents an even more diverse field than the Arabic one. It is characterised by its Indo-Iranian linguistic and ethnic character and by the dominance within it of Persian Islamic culture and for a long time of the Persian language itself. The centre of this world has always been the Iranian plateau stretching from Iraq to Central Asia. It was here that classical Persian Islamic culture was nurtured and from which it spread to many lands near and far. This 'zone' of Islamic culture includes first of all present day Iran or Persia, but also Afghanistan, Tajikistan and certain parts of Pakistan and Caucasia. This area, which corresponds to the homeland of traditional Persia, is heir to a single historical experience, uses the same Persian (or *Darī*) language and possesses nearly the same artistic traditions. Its music and poetry belong to the same world and even its cuisine reflects the same cultural ambience. Iran itself is culturally homogeneous and tightly knit and its links with the areas adjacent to it, which for so many centuries formed parts of the same whole, remain profound. It can also be distinguished from the rest of this cultural area through the fact that it is predominantly Twelve-Imām Shī'ite, while the rest of this 'zone' is mostly Sunni. The effect of Shī'ism may be detected far beyond what is usually understood as the religious domain and is to be seen in most facets of the cultural life of present day Persia. What in fact distinguishes Persia and Afghanistan culturally today is the fact that one is mostly Shī'ite with Sunni minorities and other Sunni with a Shī'ite minority.

At the periphery of this area, one can detect other regions of Iranic origin but with distinct local characteristics usually defined linguistically or ethnically or both, such areas as the Kurdish world, which stands as a cultural region of its own located within and between the larger Persian, Iraqi and Turkish worlds. The Kurds are among the purest of Iranian ethnic groups, and precisely because of having remained, through their isolation, relatively unaffected by external forces have preserved their original identity. As examples of other groups of a similar nature one might cite the Baluchis who live in both Iran and Pakistan, and the Pushto-speaking people who live in both Afghanistan and Pakistan.

In the Iranian cultural world, as in the Arabic, there are also numerous small cultural units associated with communities which have either become isolated geographically or belong to particular religious schools or sects. Besides the non-Islamic groups which present a case similar for the most part to what is to be found in the Arab world, there are also such groups as the Ahl-i Ḥaqq and the 'Alī-allāhīs spread in various mountainous regions of Persia and the recently converted population of Kafiristan, now renamed Nuristan, in Afghanistan.

Also of particular interest as a distinct cultural zone in this region is the whole area around the Persian Gulf, both the Persian and the Arab sides. Due to long periods of close association and submission to various forms of influence from both India and Africa, the people inhabiting the areas around the Persian Gulf have developed distinct cultural features of their own. Their art and architecture have become quite distinct. They have adopted in their popular religious practices certain African and Indian themes not to be met with anywhere else in either the Arab world or Persia. And even their physiognomy reveals Arabic, Persian, Indian and Black African blood blended in a unique fashion. However one considers it, there is no doubt that the whole area around the Persian Gulf represents a cultural area that is unique although it is of course inseparable from the Persian world on the one hand and the Arabic one on the other.

The rest of the 'Indo-Iranian' world embracing Pakistan, parts of India, Bangladesh, and sections of Sri Lanka can be characterised for the most part as so many zones in which Islam carried by Persian cultural elements has transformed the underlying Hindu culture. Moreover, each zone can in general be distinguished linguistically and geographically. For example, there is Sindhi Islamic culture, a Punjabi one, or a Gujarati, Kashmiri or Bengali one. In this vast and diverse world, the typology of Islamic culture can be studied mostly in the light of linguistic and geographical criteria and the degree to which Islam has penetrated each area in question. For example, the influence of Islam in the north was much greater than in the south, and even in the north, in certain areas such as Bengal, a significant Islamic culture has come into being, while in other areas, such as Rajasthan, its diffusion was more limited and has not caused a flowering of a major new branch of Islamic culture.

In nearly all the areas in the Indian world which fell under the sway of Islamic culture, the influence of the religion of Islam itself and of Persian literature was central. Many of the forms of Islamic literature created in the subcontinent, such as Sindhi, Punjabi, Kashmiri, Bengali, Gujarati, etc., were modelled consciously upon Persian, while the major new Islamic language which came into being in the subcontinent, namely Urdu, is again the fruit of the wedding between the Indic languages and Persian with some Turkish elements added. But strangely enough, this language, which was born around the Delhi area, did not remain geographically bound as did other Islamic languages of the subcontinent. With the founding of Pakistan, it became the official language of the new Islamic state and shifted its major focus of life farther west. Despite its paramount importance for the understanding of Muslim culture in the subcontinent, therefore, it cannot be used in the same way as can the more local languages as indices of local cultural areas within the vast tapestry of Islamic culture in the Indian subcontinent.

It is also necessary to draw attention to smaller religious groupings in the subcontinent as in the Arab and Persian worlds. Of particular importance in this respect is the Twelve-Imām Shi'ite community in India and Pakistan, which has given a distinct cultural colour to certain areas such as Lucknow. Also within the Ismā'īlī community, both the Āgā Khānids and the Dā'ūdīs are closely knit communities with special cultural characteristics which set them apart as distinct cultural entities within the larger Islamic community. To a lesser extent the same may be said of members of some of the more popular Sufi orders in India, such as the Chishtis, who have created communities of their own, again with easily discernible cultural features.

If the bi-polar concept of Islamic civilisation can be accepted, then the Turkish world belongs culturally to the 'Iranic' zone of Islamic civilisation. But it is itself a vast and variegated cultural field embracing many areas and people and displaying great diversity. The contact of the Turks with the Islamic world goes back to the first/seventh-century Arab conquests of Central Asia. Even before that period the Turks had close contact with the Sassanids and various Iranian peoples in neighbouring areas. The Uighur alphabet was taken by the Turks from the Soghdians and itself helped to spread diverse cultural currents among the Turkish tribes. By the second/eighth century, Islam had become solidly entrenched in Transoxiana, the Arabs having advanced as far as the Pamir mountains and T'ien-Shan.

The Arab armies also advanced through Caucasia and made contact with the Turkish Khazars in the Volga valley, some of whom embraced Islam peacefully. Even farther north, by the third/ninth century, the Bulgars had also embraced Islam through contact with Khwarazm. This region itself became a source of slaves for the Islamic world, and the presence of Turkish slaves led finally to the establishment of even slave dynasties in various Islamic lands, such as the Ghaznawids and the Mamluks. The latter continued to draw from the Turkmen and Qipchaq Turks for slaves and only later turned to Circassia. As for Transoxiana itself, and the lands beyond, the Islamicisation of Turks advanced steadily so that by the tenth/sixteenth century nearly all the Turks of Eurasia were Muslims. Islam, which spread mostly by means of Sufi saints, replaced Shamanism, Buddhism, Manichaeism and Christianity among the Turks and made of the Turkish speaking people one of the most important components of the Islamic world.

The people who speak various forms of Turkish do not, however, compose a single cultural zone. Those of Central Asia and Transoxiana in which the Turkish ethnic element and Persian cultural factors are profoundly intermingled, form a distinct cultural zone marked also by the presence of strong nomadic elements. The figure who more than any other, in fact, unites the Turks and Persians spiritually and culturally is Jalāl al-Dīn Rūmī, who came from the region of Khorasan where the two zones of Islamic culture, namely the Persian and the Turkish, meet. The Central Asian region also contains Mongolian elements not to be encountered in other Turkish 'zones' of Islamic culture.

The most notable cultural region in the Turkish-speaking world is of course Turkey itself, the heartland of the Ottoman Empire and the major bridge between Europe and Asia. This area which includes not only Turkey but also certain adjacent territories such as the border lands of Syria, parts of Cyprus and certain areas in Greece near the Turkish border, is characterised by a wedding between Islam in its Turkish form with all that was inherited from the Byzantine past. In literature and music as well as many of the plastic arts, it is closely wedded to the Persian world, while it displays distinct features of its own such as its architecture and city planning. This region is also marked by the presence of a large number of 'Alawīs in its eastern half, which is to be distinguished in this respect as a cultural area, although completely integrated in other aspects into Turkish cultural patterns.

A region which is also of Turkish character, but different in type from both Turkey and Central Asia, is Caucasia. This region is composed again of Turkish and Persian elements as well as Armenian and Georgian ones. In its ethnic composition as well as in the flavour of its artistic life, it denotes a distinct cultural area linked with both the Persian and Turkish 'zones' which constitute its tie with the rest of the Islamic world.

The Muslim areas in the Balkans, especially in Yugoslavia and Albania, although ethnically different, have been deeply impregnated with the Turkish form of Islamic culture. The spread of various Turkish Sufi orders among them, the adoption of the Ḥanafī school of law like the Turks, the modelling of much of their religious literature upon Turkish, their emulation of Turkish mosque architecture and many other elements have caused this area of Islamic culture in the Balkans to be closely associated over the ages with the Turkish world.

At the other end of the Islamic world a similar phenomenon is also to be observed. Chinese Islam has always been in direct contact with the Turkish world and Muslims in fact saw it over the centuries as an extension of this world, calling the land of the Chinese Muslims in western China 'eastern Turkestan' (*Turkistān-i sharqī*). There were also Muslim settlements in Canton as early as the second/eighth century and Arab (*Ta-shi*) and Persian (*Po-se*) traders were well known in that province by that time, having reached China by the sea route. But the major Islamic community was the one which stood at the end of the silk road in western China and was connected to the rest of the Islamic world through the long land route. This particular area of Islamic culture has remained quite distinct over the ages, having produced its own remarkable but little studied literature and having kept at the same time close contact with the main strands of Islamic literature. The Chinese Muslims often read the Holy Quran with Persian commentaries, knew Sa'dī well and also cultivated the study of Turkish. At the same time, for instance in their architecture, they adopted distinctly Chinese elements into their culture.

The Malay cultural world, stretching from Malaysia and Indonesia to the southern Philippines, is another vast and diverse cultural 'zone' within the Islamic world, somewhat more ethnically homogeneous than some of the other areas but nevertheless displaying extensive variations. Islam already possesses a long history in much of the region while the process of Islamisation is still going on in some of the interior areas. The religion first came to this part of the world in the seventh/thirteenth century when Indian Islamic elements reached Sumatra. In the ninth/fifteenth century, Islam began to spread into Java, gradually replacing a Hindu-Buddhist empire which was falling apart but which has left its impact upon the cultural life of parts of Indonesia to this day. The spread of Islam there took place essentially through the activity of saints and tradesmen. Its earliest centres of strength were Malacca and, from the tenth/sixteenth century, Acheh. More and more Arab traders began to reach the area spreading Islam farther east to Borneo, the Sulu Islands, the Moluccas and the Philippines. Relations with the Arab world intensified, especially with the region of Hadramawt, which has left a special mark upon the area. Moreover, in the eleventh/seventeenth century strong currents of Sufism from the Persian world penetrated the region with Sumatra and the southern part of the Malay peninsula serving as the base from which most of these influences spread to the other islands.

What came into being as a result of these complex forces is a cultural 'zone' that is in many ways unique in the Islamic world. The Malay-Indonesian complex adopted *Shāfi'ī* law but the law remained for the most part confined to family law while other *Sharī'ite* institutions found in most other parts of the Islamic world were never developed. In certain regions, the adoption of Islam began from the esoteric dimension and moved toward the exoteric but the process has not as yet embraced the whole of society. Even the traditional schools (*madrasahs*) have been more like Sufi centres (*khānaqāhs*) than schools for formal religious learning. There is also much that is peculiar to this world in its art. Music and the plastic arts and even the dance and theatre have survived from the Hindu, Buddhist and even the more ancient indigenous past in forms which, while traditional, have not become completely Islamicised. This is to be seen even in mosque architecture, which embraces a great deal of local style rather than the universal principles of Islamic architecture found throughout the rest of the Islamic world. Since the thirteenth/nineteenth century, however, when a more intimate contact was created with Arabia and Mecca, thanks mostly to the rite of pilgrimage which plays a specially crucial role in Malay Islam, a new wave of Islamicisation of form set in. Many local practices, including calling the prayers with a drum, still continue.

This region possesses numerous languages, of which Malay is by far the most important and has now become the national language of both Malaysia and Indonesia, although in Indonesia it is written in the Latin alphabet. In Malaysia both the Arabic and Latin alphabets are used. This language became deeply impregnated with Arabic terms and influenced by *genres* of classic Islamic literature, both Arabic and Persian. It remains a central cultural factor of this world, complementing the ethnic and artistic traits which also bind the people of the Malay world together.

It is noteworthy to add that Malaysia differs somewhat from Indonesia in that it has a large Indian and Chinese population which is non-Islamic while Indonesia is nearly 90 per cent Muslim. But this fact is of only recent historic origin, most of the non-Muslim population of Malaysia having been brought to this region by the British since the last century. Despite these minorities, therefore, Malaysia and Indonesia possess a profound cultural unity among themselves and with Muslims farther east. This unity is based on a common background which persists despite the politico-ethnic changes caused by the presence of the British and the Dutch in the area during the past few centuries.

In the Malay world Singapore occupies a rather special cultural climate which again has deep historical roots. For two centuries at least, Singapore has been the centre from which many Malay pilgrims have journeyed to Mecca, where people from the whole region near and far have met to exchange ideas and where many eminent Muslim scholars from Hadramawt, as well as from India, have resided and have provided Islamic education at the highest level. The metropolitan atmosphere of Singapore thus affected the whole area. In fact it was the centre from which major Islamic movements that influenced Malaysia as well as Indonesia originated early this century. It remains to this day a specially cosmopolitan cultural area where many religions meet but where also the deepest contacts are preserved with the main centres of the Islamic world.

The world of Black Africa has been in contact with the Islamic world since the days of the Holy Prophet and possesses some of the oldest living Islamic communities. Yet it is also the area where Islam has been growing the most rapidly during the past century and where some of the newest Islamic communities are to be found. The world of Black African Islam represents bewildering cultural diversity and variety in conformity with the tribal structure of the people of this continent. Yet there is a serenity and a contemplative quality in Black African Islam which is found everywhere and which unifies African Islam despite all the variety encountered over the vast stretches of this continent where Islam has spread.

Besides the small number of Muslims who had migrated to Ethiopia in the earliest Islamic period, properly speaking the first Islamic community of Black Africa is without doubt that of the Sudan, where the Arabs first conquered the Nubians and then the Funj. The latter, who had migrated northwards, became gradually Islamicised by the Sufis in the eighth/fourteenth century. Sudan is, however, the only Black African country where the process of Islamicisation and Arabisation went hand in hand and where today Arabic is the official language. It therefore represents a unique synthesis in Africa and possesses special cultural traits due to this fact.

Another distinct Islamic cultural area with a long Islamic history is that embracing the east coast, including Somaliland and Zanzibar. Mogadishu is said to have been founded by immigrants from al-Aḥsā, and Zanzibar received a major wave of immigration from Shiraz and the ports of the Persian Gulf in the early centuries of Islamic history. The region has always preserved a close link with the Arab and the Persian cultural worlds and is also closely associated with the cultural climate of the Indian Ocean. In Somaliland the role of the nomadic Somalis in the spread of Islam in East Africa is particularly important. By the tenth/sixteenth century these nomads had adopted Islam and henceforth carried it with them to adjacent regions.

Until the building of roads by Europeans in the thirteenth/nineteenth century, the influence of Islam in East Africa remained confined mostly to the coastal region. It was in fact here that the Swahili (literally coastal) language, which is a synthesis of Bantu, Arabic and Persian, came into being. It is today the most important Islamic language of East Africa and plays a major role in the cultural life of the region. But from the thirteenth/nineteenth century onwards Islam has been spreading inland, aided also by the migration of many Indo-Pakistanis who have brought the cultural traits of their homeland as well as Twelve-Imām Shi'ism and Ismā'īlism into the region. Today, while Somaliland, Zanzibar and Eritrea are predominantly Muslim, there are important Muslim minorities in Uganda and Tanganyika consisting of both local Black African Muslims and immigrants from the Indo-Pakistan world, so that a unique cultural climate is created in the region.

From the point of view of population, the main concentration of Muslims in Africa is to be found not in the east but in West Africa where Islam is also over a thousand years old, having spread there from the third/ninth century on by traders following the southern route of the Sahara as well as by Sufi saints. Soon, major Islamic centres were established south of the Sahara and certain cities such as Timbuktu became prominent centres of religious learning and Arabic scholarship. By the fifth/eleventh century several Muslim states were established in West Africa and the people of this region gradually became known to the Arabs as the *takārīr* (pl. of *takrūr* from Tokolor). The great kingdom of Mali came into being with its most famous ruler Mansa Mūsā (eighth/fourteenth century) having gained fame throughout the Arab world. This period of Mali dominance was followed by the rise of the Songhay, who replaced the power of Mali. The Kanem-Bornu in turn entered the stage of Islamic history. They claimed descent from the Umayyad caliphs and held that the descendants of the Umayyads lived among them. They, like many states which were to follow, held close relations with Morocco, Tunisia and Egypt.

Other important African tribes of the West gradually embraced Islam. The Fulani were among the main propagators of Islam and produced '*ulamā*' who carried Islam to Kano. The Hausa became Islamicised from the eighth/fourteenth century onwards while the Yoruba entered Islam in the tenth/sixteenth century and the Bambara became a Muslim power in the upper Niger in the eleventh/seventeenth century. The pattern throughout West Africa has been the creation of local cultural units, based upon tribes or tribal units which have embraced Islam and which have often reached regional political prominence. Among some of the main groups, such as the Fulani and Hausa, there have moreover been constant phases of Islamic renewal; numerous charismatic figures have appeared leaving the profoundest religious and cultural effect upon their followers. The figure of 'Uthmān dan Fodio in the twelfth/eighteenth century is one among many; he typifies a basic feature of African Islam which is also seen in the Sudan, Somaliland and elsewhere.

In certain regions of West Africa, such as the Senegal, there was a major renewal and further penetration of Islam in the thirteenth/nineteenth century thanks to the spread of the Sufi orders. In the Senegal, the Moroccan order of the Tijāniyyah spread rapidly during the last century. So did a special offshoot of the Qādiriyyah called the Murīd movement and associated with the name of its founder, Aḥmad Bamba. These orders are so widespread in the Senegal that they may be said to have lent a special cultural texture to that region.

Islamic communities are also to be found in most other African countries, such as the Congo, where they follow the same pattern as in East and West Africa except that there they remain as minority forces living alongside Christianity and the older African traditions. In South Africa, however, there exists a special situation in that the country has a rigorous and active Muslim population which is not composed primarily of local African tribes or townsmen but of a mixture of eleventh/seventeenth century Malay and thirteenth/nineteenth century Indian immigrants in close contact with the cultural world of the Indian Ocean. There are also branches of many Sufi orders of the subcontinent within the community. The South African Muslim community is, therefore, a unique cultural blend but one which remains in close relation with both the rest of African Islam and the major centres of the Islamic world.

Altogether, Islamic culture in Africa displays a keen awareness of the tribal and regional particularities of the peoples which have embraced Islam and can be divided into various areas in accordance with the major ethnic groups which practise Islam. It has penetrated the soul of Black Africans most profoundly; yet it has not been the cause of a levelling process. Many local practices, as long as they are not contradictory to the *Sharī'ah*, have been allowed to continue. As for the *Sharī'ah* itself, its domain of application has been mostly family law and all that concerns the relations between individuals. Despite local cultural diversities, however, it needs to be emphasised that a profound unity dominates Black African Islam; this can be seen not only in the qualities displayed by Black Muslims in their behaviour and character, but also in Islamic architecture and decoration, which possess a remarkable unity throughout this vast region despite the ethnic and historical differences of the peoples who have embraced Islam in Black Africa.

A thorough study of the different 'types' of Islamic culture would need to include also older, smaller minorities in such countries as the Soviet Union, Finland and the West Indies and the newly formed and usually growing minorities in Western Europe, Australia, various countries of the American continent, Korea and Japan. It would also need to consider the transformations which Islamic culture is undergoing under the pressure of modernising and Westernising forces within and outside its borders. But these are subjects which must of necessity be excluded from so brief a discussion as this on so vast a subject. Suffice it to say, however, that despite its many 'types' and division into many 'zones' Islamic culture displays an undeniable unity which is the result of the spirit and form of the Islamic revelation and ultimately of the Divine Unity itself. In the same way that the whole created order is the theophanic reflection of the One in the mirror of multiplicity, so are the various 'faces' of Islamic culture so many human echoes of the one Message which is itself beyond the human and which alone bestows upon the activity of a human collectivity the purposes and values which make it worthy of being called a culture in conformity with the noble destiny of man.

6

A Panorama of Classical Islamic Intellectual Life

Islam spread more rapidly than all other religions of which there exists a historical record. Only a century after its inception in Mecca, the new religion was dominant over the Pyrenees in the west and the steppes of Central Asia in the east. Moreover, to the same degree that its expansion was rapid, the consolidation of this newly conquered domain into a new world civilisation was profound and permanent. Islam developed its characteristic art within a century of its birth and its own learning and arts and sciences a hundred years later. By the end of the third/ninth century, the intellectual life of Islam had reached one of the peaks of its activity and Islamic civilisation had itself become, through the assimilation of the heritage of many previous civilisations, the new focus of intellectual life in the world.

The lands which became rapidly consolidated into the Islamic world contained centres where most of the philosophical and scientific life of previous ages had been carried out. The intellectual activity of Athens had long ago been transferred to Alexandria and adjacent schools such as that of Pergamon; and then through channels of eastern branches of Christianity such as the Monophysites and Nestorians this heritage had already become planted upon the soil of what was later to become the heart of the Islamic world, in such centres as Antioch, Edessa and Nisibis. The more esoteric aspect of the Graeco-Alexandrian tradition connected with neo-Pythagoreanism and Hermeticism had also become established in the same region in the cult of the Sabaeans of Ḥarrān who in their religious and intellectual life combined the Hermetic-Pythagorean ideas of Alexandria with astronomical and astrological ideas drawn from late Babylonian and Chaldaean sources.

Besides the intellectual heritage of the Mediterranean world, that of the Persians and Indians also became available to the Muslims. Already during the Sassanid period the Persian king, Shāpūr I, had established a school in Jundishapur to rival that of Antioch. In this school Persian and Indian learning, written mostly in Pahlavi and Sanskrit, became as significant as the Graeco-Alexandrian learning in Greek and Syriac. This school became important especially in medicine and astronomy and by the seventh century it was probably the most important medical centre in the world, combining the scientific traditions of the Greeks, the Persians and the Indians.

All these centres and many others became a part of the Islamic world, and their activity in fact continued in certain cases for several centuries after the Islamic conquests, in the hands of the Christians, Jews, or Zoroastrians who now became minorities with recognised rights in the new world civilisation.

The very fact that these minorities as 'people of the book' were allowed to survive in the new order itself made the transmission of the pre-Islamic sciences to Muslims much easier. When the time came for Islamic society to take cognisance of the presence of this heritage and to integrate it into its own perspective, there were translators and men of learning already present within its own borders. The scholars belonging to these minority religious communities, or having recently embraced Islam, knew either Greek or Syriac if they were Christians or Sabaeans and Pahlavi if Zoroastrian. They were also masters in the sciences in question as well as being well versed in Arabic, which by now was not only the religious language of Islam but also the language of discourse and learning of Islamic civilisation. When the need for pre-Islamic learning was felt by Muslims, the means to acquire it was ready at hand.

But neither the presence of centres of learning nor the availability of scholars and translators would be sufficient to explain the remarkable enthusiasm and determination with which the Islamic world set out to make the knowledge of the ancients its own. This can be particularly appreciated when one realises that the Byzantine civilisation whose tongue was in fact Greek did not display the same amount of interest in the sciences of the ancient world. Islamic civilisation set out deliberately and through concerted effort to master Greek, Persian and Indian learning and science when it was the most powerful nation on earth and had no military, political or economic motive for turning attention to these sciences.

The main reason must therefore be sought in the characteristics of the Islamic revelation itself. Islam is a religion based on knowledge – and not on love, as is for example Christianity – a knowledge in which the intellect (*al-'aql*) itself plays the positive role of leading man to the Divine. Islam also considers itself the last religion of humanity and, by virtue of this very fact, a return to the primordial religion (*al-dīn al-ḥanīf*) and the synthesis of all religions that have preceded it. These two characteristics taken together made it both possible and necessary for Muslims to come to know the learning of earlier civilisations and to assimilate those elements which harmonised with its world view into the Islamic scheme of things.

Being essentially a 'way of knowledge', Islam could not remain indifferent to any form of knowledge. From the point of view of knowledge, a doctrine or idea is either true or false; it cannot be brushed aside and ignored once its existence is known. Plato and Aristotle had expressed views about God, man and the nature of things. Once known, their views could not be simply ignored. They were either true, in which case they should be accepted into the Islamic scheme of things considered in its universal sense, or they were false, in which case they should be refuted. But in either case they had to be studied and better known.

In considering itself as the last religion of man, Islam has always believed that all that confirms its truths – which can be ultimately summarised in the axial and central doctrine of Unity (*al-tawḥīd*) – is 'Islamic' and legitimately its own. Moses and Christ are stars in the firmament of Islam irrespective of their role in Judaism and Christianity. Seen in this light, all that affirmed 'unity' in both its metaphysical and cosmological sense in the pre-Islamic sciences and philosophies belonged legitimately to Muslims, and the Islamic intellectual elite did not feel any religious inhibitions in making these ideas its own. This was especially true since Muslims, like Philo before them and certain Christian theologians in the West during the Middle Ages and the Renaissance, such as those who spoke of the 'atomism of Moses', considered philosophy and the sciences to have been derived from revelation, from 'the niche of prophecy', to use the Quranic terminology.

The figure of Hermes is particularly significant in this connection as we shall have the occasion to discuss in detail in Chapter 9. Already the Hermes associated with the Alexandrian school of alchemy and the *Corpus Hermeticum* symbolises the synthesis of Greek and Egyptian traditions of science and cosmology. In Islam, Hermes became identified with the antediluvian prophet Idrīs, mentioned in the Quran, and the Hebrew Enoch. The figure of Hermes was, moreover, elaborated to include three different figures, each associated with an aspect of the arts and sciences. Hermes Trismegistos as known in the West comes not from Alexandrian but from Islamic sources. Through the three Hermes, considered as the founders of science and philosophy and the first associated with the prophet Idrīs, Islam was able to legitimise the incorporation of the intellectual heritage of previous civilisations into its own world view, to the extent that this heritage was itself compatible with the genius of the Islamic revelation.

The immediate source of the spark which ignited the fire of intellectual activity and translation of Greek, Syriac, Pahlavi and Sanskrit texts into Arabic, more than any possible utilitarian motives to benefit from medicine and astrology, was the debates held in Damascus, Basra, Kufa, Baghdad and other Muslim cities between Muslims and scholars and theologians of other religions. Often these debates were held in the presence of the caliphs or religious authorities, especially the Shiʿite Imāms. In these debates, where open discussion was usually permitted, the Muslims found themselves on the defensive before the weapons of logic and philosophy with which their adversaries were armed. Soon the Muslims realised that in order to defend the tenets of the faith itself they had to arm themselves with the same weapons. The challenge of a theologian like John the Damascene could only be answered with a theology of similar intellectual content. Therefore, the Muslims sought to master the logic and philosophy of other religious communities especially the Christians, who were thoroughly acquainted with Greek philosophy and logic. This movement not only led to the concerted effort to translate, leading to the founding of such vast institutions as the 'House of Wisdom' (*Bayt al-ḥikmah*) of al-Ma'mūn in Baghdad, whose specific function was translation of works into Arabic, but it was also instrumental in the particular way in which Muslim theology was formulated, as we see in the case of the Christian hypostases and the Islamic Divine Attributes.

The golden age of translation lasted for a period of nearly 150 years from about 150/767 to 300/912. During this period a large number of basic Greek texts in philosophy and the sciences in the most general sense were rendered into Arabic, sometimes directly from the Greek, at other times through the intermediary of Syriac. Special attention was paid to the works of Aristotle and his commentators, of which there are more translations in Arabic than in European languages, and also to classical mathematical and astronomical treatises such as those of Euclid, Archimedes and Ptolemy. Medico-philosophical treatises, especially those of Galen, were also translated extensively, as were many works in the occult sciences whose original Greek or Syriac version is lost. In fact Arabic is today a most valuable source of knowledge for Greek philosophy and science, especially of the later period, precisely because of the large number of texts translated and preserved as well as the high quality of many of the translations. Altogether, from the point of view of quality and quantity alike the transmission of the learning of the ancient world to Muslims through the medium of Arabic is one of the most startling phenomena of cultural history; for not only was it instrumental in bringing into being Muslim sciences and philosophy but also it indirectly played a vital role in the creation of medieval and Renaissance science and philosophy in the West and even influenced China and India.

The greatest translators belong to the Abbasid period, the most important being Ḥunayn ibn Isḥāq, who founded a school of translation known for the exactness and fluency of its renderings. Almost as significant was Ibn Muqaffaʿ, a Persian convert to Islam from Zoroastrianism, whose translations from the Pahlavi helped to found the new philosophical and scientific style of prose that was being established in the Arabic language. But even before the Abbasid period, translations had been made and contact established between Islamic religious circles and pre-Islamic forms of learning. The figure of Imām Jaʿfar al-Ṣādiq, the sixth Shiʿite Imām, and his interest in the pre-Islamic sciences have often been taken by modern scholars as being apocryphal tales not to be accepted seriously. More recent research, however, has revealed that there is no reason whatsoever for doubting these traditional claims or for denying the link between the Imām and Jābir ibn Ḥayyān, the father of Islamic alchemy. It is most likely that the great flowering of interest in the pre-Islamic sciences during the Abbasid period goes back to earlier contacts during the late Umayyad era when, from the inner process within Islam itself, there grew the possibilities of contact with the pre-Islamic sciences and their legitimisation and integration into the Islamic tradition. It is in fact upon the properly Islamic basis of the first century AH, to which was added the heritage of the ancient world through the movement of translation, that Islamic intellectual history began to elaborate and manifest itself from the second/eighth century onwards.

The earliest intellectual activity in Islam is concerned with those Islamic sciences which are properly speaking known as 'transmitted' (*al-ʿulūm al-naqliyyah*) such as Quranic commentary, the traditions of the Prophet (*Ḥadīth*), questions concerning the Sacred Law of Islam, theology (*kalām*), as well as the sciences dealing with language, prosody, etc. This whole group of sciences is usually distinguished in the Islamic classification of the sciences from the 'intellectual sciences' (*al-ʿulūm al-ʿaqliyyah*), such as philosophy and mathematics, which, in contrast to the first group, need not be learned through transmission and may be acquired through the innate intelligence possessed by man.

During the first Islamic century, while the efforts of most men of learning were concentrated in the domain of the religious sciences, particularly the Quran and *Ḥadīth*, in Kufa and Basra there began to develop contending schools of grammar which soon turned to different philosophies of language, the first more inclined towards Aristotelian and the second toward Stoic logic. Some of the earliest philosophical and metaphysical ideas in Islam are to be found in these early schools of grammar, and this type of philosophical analysis of language and rhetoric in fact continued throughout the Islamic period and was especially developed among some of the Andalusian Muslim thinkers, such as Ibn Ḥazm of Cordova. The metaphysical significance of the sounds and letters of the Arabic language, the sacred language of Islam, is also important in the esoteric and mystical aspects of Islam contained within Sufism and also Shī'ism. This aspect of the Islamic tradition left its influence upon men like Raymond Lull and others in the West who were interested in the esoteric significance of language.

Of the transmitted sciences the one that is closest to the mainstream of Islamic intellectual history, particularly in the fields of philosophy and the sciences, is *kalām*, usually translated as theology, although the significance of theology in Christianity and of *kalām* in Islam is not by any means the same. The science of *kalām* has its roots in the earliest debates in the Islamic community on the questions of free will and predestination, the created or uncreated nature of the Quran, the relation of faith to works, the definition of who is a believer, etc. Concerning these basic religious questions, there arose different groups during the first century AH such as the Murji'ites, Qadarites and Khawārij, each of which sought to answer one of these questions in such a particular way that it became known as a community possessing a distinct and definable opinion *vis-à-vis* the majority of Muslims.

From these early movements there grew the first systematic theological school, named the Mu'tazilah and founded by Wāṣil ibn 'Aṭā'. This school, which gained ascendancy during the caliphate of al-Ma'mūn and continued to be influential up to the fifth/eleventh century in Baghdad and after that for many centuries among the Zaydīs of the Yemen, sought to preserve Divine Unity from all that would blemish its transcendence. But in so doing it chose a rationalistic interpretation of the Divinity which tended to make God more into a philosophical abstraction than a Reality Who is the fountainhead and basis of revealed religion. The Mu'tazilites proffered five main principles upon which their different followers agreed and for which they have become celebrated. These are: the Unity of God, His Justice, promise of reward and threat of punishment for good and evil acts, belief in the possibility of a state between belief and unbelief, and finally emphasis upon ordering the good and prohibiting the evil. The main Mu'tazilite figures such as Naẓẓām and 'Allāf were powerful logicians and dialecticians, men to be reckoned with in the history of Islamic theology. It is they who for the first time developed the theory of atomism which is peculiar to *kalām* and which was later developed extensively by the Ash'arites.

The most significant influence of the Mu'tazilites was, however, probably in providing an atmosphere in Sunni Islam more conducive to the reception of the philosophical and scientific heritage of pre-Islamic days. It is not accidental that their period of ascendancy in Baghdad coincides with the height of activity in translation of works into Arabic. There are also certain similarities, although there is not in any way identity, between the Mu'tazilites and Shī'ite theologians. The latter in turn were more sympathetic to the Hermetico-Pythagorean tradition and Graeco-Alexandrian philosophy in general than the Sunnis, not for any rationalistic reason but because of the more esoteric character of Shī'ism, which permitted the integration of certain esoteric forms of Graeco-Alexandrian science and philosophy into its perspective. In its support of the cause of coming to know and to understand this pre-Islamic heritage, however, Shī'ism was favourable to the climate created by the Mu'tazilites in Baghdad, although in other fundamental questions such as the meaning and role of the Imām the two differ completely.

At the end of the third/ninth century, the dominance of Mu'tazilite *kalām* in Sunni circles was challenged by the new theological schools of Ash'arism founded by Abu'l-Ḥasan al-Ash'arī and developed by his disciple Abū Bakr al-Bāqillānī. This school, which opposed the rationalistic tendencies of the Mu'tazilites, sought to re-establish the concrete presence of God by charting a middle course between *tashbīh* and *tanzīh*, or considering God to have anthropomorphic qualities on the one hand, and abstracting all qualities from Him on the other. It thus depicted a conception of the Divinity much closer to the ethos of Islam and for this reason soon began to replace Mu'tazilite *kalām*. Of course a sizeable and significant element of the Islamic community was opposed to all forms of *kalām* as a human intrusion into the Divine Order. But, to the extent that *kalām* continued to be pursued in the Sunni world, Ash'arism replaced Mu'tazilism and has continued to be dominant to this day. The school of the Māturīdites, which sought a more intermediate course between the demands of reason and the *dicta* of revelation, was never able to gain a great deal of popularity although it was able to survive on its own. Shī'ite theology, however, took the opposite direction from Ash'arism and became more and more sympathetic to gnosis (*al-ma'rifah* or *'irfān*) and theosophy (*al-ḥikmah*), while Ash'arism became the arch-opponent of philosophy (*falsafah*) and all the theosophical and philosophical schools which were based on a systematic and rational – although not rationalistic – approach to knowledge.

The significance of Ash'arite *kalām* in Islamic thought, besides the role it played as the opponent of philosophy and therefore the force that often caused the philosophers to take particular positions and answer particular questions, was its development of the theory of atomism already begun by the Mu'tazilites. There is an 'atomic' element in the Semitic, nomadic mentality which is clearly reflected in the Arabic language. There is the tendency of going from one truth to another by an intuitive jump rather than by a continuous process. The Arabic sentence itself reflects this fact; the subject and the predicate are connected, not by a copula as in Indo-European languages, but by an invisible link which must be grasped intuitively. This 'atomism' was bound to make itself manifest on the level of thought as well, even though Ash'arism was not by any means exclusively Arabic. Some of the greatest Ash'arite theologians, such as Imām al-Ḥaramayn al-Juwaynī, Abū Ḥāmid al-Ghazzālī and Fakhr al-Dīn al-Rāzī, were Persians. But here it became a matter of 'mental style' that spread through Islam beyond the confines of those who were racially Arabs.

The atomism of *kalām* divides all sensible reality into atoms or units (technically 'parts that cannot be divided', *juz' lā yatajazzā*) which unlike the atoms of Democritus possess neither length nor any other dimension. The atoms of *kalām* are units without length or breadth but combine to form bodies possessing dimensions. It is a particular form of atomism for which both Buddhist and late Greek origins have been posited without any great certainty, but which in any case differs from the classical atomism of Democritus and Lucretius.

The Ash'arites, moreover, divide time, space and motion into atomic units as well. As a result the nexus between cause and effect is denied by them. If there is no substantial continuity between things, as well as between moments of time and points of space, how can there be causality? The whole cosmic matrix was segmented and atomised. To fill this 'gap', the Ash'arites appealed to the Divine Will. For them it is the Divine Will which relates two moments of existence together and gives homogeneity to the world about us. According to this voluntarism, fire appears to 'cause' heat. It is however only the mind which by observing the phenomenon of heat connected with fire thinks that one causes the other. Actually it is God Who wills the fire to be hot; He could will that it be cold tomorrow without there being any logical contradiction whatsoever. Miracles are in fact called *khāriq al-'ādah*, that which breaks the habit of the mind to connect two phenomena together as cause and effect. One sees here arguments very similar to what Hume was to offer many centuries later in order to destroy the validity of causality, without, however, positing the Divine Will as the nexus between two phenomena which the mind conceives as cause and effect. In fact, some of the examples of Hume are the same as those of the Ash'arites, making one think that perhaps he had become acquainted with them through certain Latin sources.

Not being bound by Aristotelian physics, the Ash'arites were free to develop what one might call a 'philosophy of nature' of their own based on this conception of the discontinuity of things. Within this scheme they developed ideas which are of great interest in the history and methodology of science and appear particularly attractive today when in sub-particle physics a similar situation exists and causality in the classical sense is denied. Strangely enough, the Ash'arite theologians, with a few exceptions like Rāzī, were not interested in the sciences of nature at all. Their aim in developing this atomism was to break the hold of reason upon the understanding of reality and to open the human mind to the possibilities of understanding the verities of revelation. They were not concerned with the development of the sciences but ironically enough developed theories about time, space, motion and causality which were fecund in the later development of physics and which appear as particularly of interest in retrospect.

In Islamic civilisation, disciplines are clearly defined and, although we can speak of the 'philosophy' of *kalām*' in English, when Muslims speak of philosophy (*al-falsafah*) or theosophy (*al-ḥikmah*) they refer to particular schools with well-defined methods and ends and very distinct from *kalām*. Islamic philosophy, properly speaking, began in the third/ninth century after the translation of philosophical texts into Arabic and their gradual elaboration and assimilation by Muslim thinkers. Traditional Islamic sources mention Abu'l-'Abbās Īrānshahrī as the first person in Islam to have devoted himself to philosophy. He, like his successors such as al-Fārābī, believed that the original home of philosophy was the East and that in reviving interest in philosophy he had brought philosophy back to its original abode. Besides a few segments cited in later texts, no writings of this mysterious figure have survived, and so we have to turn to al-Kindī, the Latin Alkindus, as the first Muslim philosopher who left behind an appreciable corpus, and who must be credited with founding the Peripatetic (*mashshā'ī*) school of Islamic philosophy, almost the only Islamic school which became known in the Latin West.

Al-Kindī, in contrast to most Muslim philosophers who were Persians, was an Arab of aristocratic descent. He was born in Basra c. 185/801, studied there and in Baghdad, where he later became famous at the court of the caliphs, and finally died in the same city c. 252/866 after falling from grace at court. Having received the best education of his day and been amidst the current of the intellectual life of the Abbasid capital at the very moment when the great wave of translation reached its peak, al-Kindī helped more than any other figure to establish the Peripatetic school of Islamic philosophy, a school which is based on Aristotle as seen mostly through the eyes of his Alexandrian neo-Platonic commentators and interpreted according to the unitary principle of Islam.

This Peripatetic school combined neo-Platonic and Aristotelian teachings, partly because of the unitary vision of philosophy held by Muslim thinkers and also partly due to the fact that Muslims considered the last parts of the *Enneads* of Plotinus to be the *Theology* of Aristotle and took the epitome of Proclus' *Elements of Theology* to be *Liber de Causis*, attributed again to the school of Aristotle. There thus developed a neo-Platonic interpretation of Aristotelian metaphysics centred upon the doctrine of the One and the emanation of the intellects and grades of being from it, a new synthesis which is not found with the same accent and colour in any school of Greek philosophy. This is especially true because the Muslims emphasised being and the distinction between the Necessary Being, or God, and the contingent beings which comprise all things in the Universe, and they stressed the contingent nature of these things.

Strangely enough, in the development of this elaborate metaphysical and philosophical system, al-Kindī held certain views which are particularly his own and which were not followed by the later Peripatetics. He believed in creation *ex nihilo*, more in line with Muslim theologians than philosophers, and had a conception of the classification of the sciences more akin to certain Latin scholastics than to his fellow Muslim Peripatetics. He was also deeply impregnated with neo-Pythagoreanism, more than later Peripatetics, although in Islam, in contrast to the Latin West, the Aristotelian and Pythagorean-Platonic tradition did not remain completely distinct; most of the famous Muslim Peripatetic philosophers were also master musicians and some were outstanding mathematicians.

In many other domains, however, al-Kindī began avenues of thought which were followed by later Muslim thinkers. Like them, he was as much interested in the sciences as in philosophy and is therefore like the other Muslim Peripatetics a philosopher-scientist rather than just a philosopher. Also like later thinkers, he was intensely interested in the harmony between philosophy and religion, although the path he trod was not pursued by his successors. He also set the tone for philosophical and scientific inquiry and is credited with a statement which characterises the method and spirit of nearly all the members of this school: 'We should not be ashamed to acknowledge truth and assimilate it from whatever source it comes to us, even if it is brought to us by former generations and foreign peoples. For him who seeks the truth there is nothing of higher value than truth itself; it never cheapens or debases him who reaches for it, but ennobles and honours him.'[1]

Al-Kindī left behind an enormous corpus of nearly 270 works on practically every domain of knowledge from logic and philosophy to metallurgy, pharmacology and the occult sciences. Most of this vast corpus has been lost while a few of the basic works such as *Fi'l-falsafat al-ūlā* (*On First Philosophy*) and *Risālah fi'l-'aql* (*On the Intellect*) survive in Arabic and also a few in Latin and Hebrew. Yet al-Kindī was extremely celebrated among Muslims as well as among the Latins. His fourfold division of the intellect based on the commentary of Alexander Aphrodisias upon the *De Anima* of Aristotle and contained in the treatise on the intellect was not only very influential in Islamic philosophy but through the translation of this treatise into Latin as *De Intellectu* came to be well known in the West. Al-Kindī was regarded throughout the Occidental Middle Ages as one of the judices of astrology and during the Renaissance Cardanus considered him to be one of the twelve most important intellectual figures of human history.

The new intellectual perspective of Muslim Peripatetic philosophy begun by al-Kindī was established on a firm basis by Abū Naṣr al-Fārābī, the Latin Alpharabius, whom some consider more than al-Kindī to be the real founder of Islamic philosophy. By now the centre of Islamic civilisation, especially its intellectual aspect, was shifting to a certain extent to Khorasan, where the new Persian language and culture was also being created. It is in this region that Fārābī was born c. 257/870 and where he received his earliest education. Later he came to Baghdad both to learn and teach and finally he migrated to Syria, where he died in 339/950. Fārābī is entitled the 'Second Teacher', after Aristotle, whom Muslims bestowed with the title of the 'First Teacher', to be followed in this tradition by St Thomas and Dante. In this context 'teacher' denotes more than anything the function of clarifying the limits and boundaries of the domains of knowledge and classifying and ordering the sciences, a task that Aristotle achieved in the context of Greek civilisation and Fārābī performed for Islam. Fārābī is the author of the first influential work on the classification of the sciences, which was twice translated into Latin as *De Scientiis* and played a share in determining the curricula of a 'liberal arts' education in both East and West during the Middle Ages.

Fārābī was also a 'second Aristotle' in the sense that he commented upon the works of the Stagirite, especially the *Metaphysics* and the *Organon*, making the meaning of these works fully available to Muslim circles. He wrote, moreover, many works on logic himself and must be considered the father of this science among Muslims. Much of the exact philosophical and logical terminology in Arabic is due to this genius who was also the master of many tongues.

Fārābī must also be considered the founder of political philosophy in Islam. In this domain he relied upon the political ideas of Plato's *Laws* and *Republic* rather than the *Politics* of Aristotle, although his discussion of the virtues is akin to Aristotle's *Ethics*. Fārābī sought to harmonise the Platonic conception of the philosopher-king and divine *nomos* with the Islamic prophet-ruler and Divine Law or *Sharī'ah*. His attempt was significant enough to have left a mark upon nearly all later speculation in this domain, such as in the writings of Averroës, who also commented upon Plato's *Republic*. Fārābī's major political work, *Ārā' ahl madīnat al-fāḍilah* (*Treatise on the Opinions of the Citizens of the Ideal State*), remains the most popular and influential work of its kind in the history of Islamic philosophy.

Ibn Sīnā, or Avicenna as he is known in the West, crowned over two centuries of philosophical thought with an expression of Peripatetic philosophy which was so complete and profound as to leave its effect upon all later Islamic thought. Wherever and whenever the arts and sciences have been cultivated in Islam, his spirit has hovered over them as their 'guardian angel'. More than that, he may in many ways be considered as the founder of scholastic philosophy in its systematic formulation.

Avicenna was born near Bukhara in 370/980 into a family devoted to learning. By the age of ten he had mastered the religious sciences, by sixteen was a well-known physician, and by eighteen, thanks to the commentary of Fārābī, had overcome all the difficulties in understanding the *Metaphysics* of Aristotle. His precocity is proverbial in the East even today. From the age of twenty-one until his death in 428/1037, he wandered from one court in Persia to another as physician and even vizier, spending most of this period in Isfahan and Hamadan, where he finally died. During this turbulent life his intellectual activity continued unabated. Sometimes he even wrote on horseback while going to a battle. The result was over 220 works, which include the *Kitāb al-shifā'* (*Book of Healing*), the largest encyclopedia of knowledge ever written by one man, and the *Canon*, which became the best known medical work in East and West and gained him the title of 'Prince of Physicians'.

The universal genius of Avicenna, the greatest of the philosopher-scientists in Islam, left hardly any field untouched. In metaphysics, he established the ontology which characterises medieval philosophy and left a profound mark upon St Thomas and especially Duns Scotus. The distinction between the Necessary and contingent being and between existence and essence or quiddity, the identity of the act of intellection with existence in the generation of the heavenly intelligences, and the emphasis upon the role of the tenth intellect as the illuminator of the human intellect in the act of knowledge are outstanding features of this most perfect formulation of Muslim Peripatetic philosophy elaborated by Avicenna.

Of no less significance is his study of natural philosophy. There, although continuing the Aristotelian tradition of hylomorphism, he continued the criticism begun by John Philoponus against Aristotle's theory of projectile motion and developed the impetus theory and the concept which later became known in the West as *inclinatio* and which is the father of the fundamental concept of momentum in modern physics. His geological studies contain many original features and in fact under the name of *De Mineralibus* the section of the *Book of Healing* on geology and mineralogy came to be considered in the West for centuries as a work of Aristotle. It is in fact only in the section on natural philosophy in the *Book of Healing* that the study of all the three kingdoms, carried out so brilliantly in the case of animals and plants by Aristotle and Theophrastus, was brought together for the first time. The *Canon* also contains both important medical theories and new observations on medical cases as well as studies of the pharmaceutical properties of plants.

In addition to these and many other philosophical and scientific contributions, Avicenna toward the end of his life wrote a series of works intended for the 'elite' in which he sought to expound what he called the 'Oriental Philosophy'. Although some of this corpus is lost, enough survives to enable us to reconstruct the contours of this philosophy, or rather theosophy (*al-ḥikmah*), which he contrasted with the Peripatetic philosophy meant for the multitude. In this 'Oriental Philosophy' the role of the intellectual intuition and illumination (*ishrāq*) becomes paramount; philosophy turns from the attempt to describe a rational system to explaining the structure of reality with the aim of providing a plan of the cosmos with the help of which man can escape from this world considered as a cosmic crypt. Henceforth, in the East the primary role of philosophy became to provide the possibility of a vision of the spiritual universe. Philosophy thus became closely wedded to gnosis as we see in the Illuminationist (*ishrāqī*) theosophy of Suhrawardī over a century after Avicenna.

Curiously enough, this aspect of Avicenna's works did not became known in the West and this fact is the major cause of the great difference existing between Islamic and Latin Avicennism. In the East, Avicenna provided the first step in the journey towards illumination and even his Peripatetic philosophy became integrated by later philosophers and theosophers into a greater whole in which the development of the rational and logical faculties itself becomes a preparation for illumination. In the West, his philosophy became influential at Oxford and Paris from the twelfth century AD and influenced many figures such as Roger Bacon, who preferred him to Averroës, or St Thomas, whose third argument for the proof of the existence of God is based on Avicennan sources, or Duns Scotus, who used Avicenna as the 'point of departure' for the theological system that challenged Thomism in the fourteenth century. Altogether, however, in the West the influence of Avicenna was not as great as that of Averroës and it is not possible with full justice to speak of a definite 'Latin Avicennism' as one speaks of 'Latin Averroism'. But there is definitely an 'Avicennising Augustinism', to use the term of E. Gilson,[2] one of whose best known exponents was William of Auvergne. But the latter was especially insistent on emptying the Avicennan cosmos of the angels who play such an important role in Avicenna's ontology, cosmology and noetics. In doing so, he helped to secularise the cosmos, which was still sacred in Avicennan philosophy, and indirectly prepared the background for the Copernican revolution, which could only take place in a secularised cosmos. The difference in the interpretation of Avicenna in East and West is one of the factors that indicate the parting of ways between Islamic and Christian civilisations after the Middle Ages after centuries during which they followed a parallel course.

Besides the predominant Muslim Peripatetic school which reached its culmination with Avicenna, there were other philosophical and religious schools that must be considered. From the second/eighth century, neo-Pythagorean and Hermetic philosophy were cultivated in certain circles, sometimes combined. Followers of these schools differed from the Peripatetics in their apophatic theologies, interest in immediate rather than distant causes in natural philosophy, attraction towards Stoic rather than Aristotelian logic with its emphasis on the disjunctive syllogism, interest in Hippocratic rather than Galenic medicine, and of course their special devotion to mathematical symbolism and the occult sciences. In the case of the mathematical neo-Pythagorean philosophy its best known exposition is found in the *Epistles* of the Brethren of Purity, a collection of fifty-two treatises which exercised a widespread influence throughout the Islamic world. Being from a general Shi'ite background, these treatises were later adopted by the Ismā'īlīs, who came to develop a philosophy of their own distinct from the Peripatetics, a philosophy which included the thought of such figures as Abū Ya'qūb al-Sijistānī, Abū Ḥātim al-Rāzī, and several other figures. It reached its peak with Nāṣir-i Khusraw who, in contrast to the early Peripatetics, nearly all of whom wrote in Arabic, composed his philosophical works in Persian.

As for Hermeticism, it was naturally associated with alchemy. The first well-known Muslim alchemist, Jābir ibn Ḥayyān, wrote many treatises on Hermetic philosophy and was opposed to Aristotelian natural philosophy. Interestingly enough, his corpus, too, was adopted by the Ismā'īlīs who in fact added to it works of their own authorship but attributed to Jābir. Other famous alchemical texts such as the *Emerald Table* and the *Turba Philosophorum* also belong to the same Islamic Hermetical and alchemical tradition based on earlier Alexandrian, Byzantine and Syriac sources. And the *Picatrix* so well known in the West is a translation of the *Ghāyat al-ḥakīm* (*Aim of the Wise*) of al-Majrīṭī, the Andalusian scientist and alchemist of the fourth/tenth century or his school. All of these texts contain an exposition of a Hermetical philosophy which was a rival to the better known Peripatetic school. In the West also, the translation of these and other texts brought into being Latin alchemy and Hermeticism which throughout the Middle Ages and the Renaissance, from Lull to Paracelsus and

Fludd, provided a strong rival for Aristotelianism. Of course occasionally there was a parallelism rather than opposition and Peripatetic and Hermetico-occult sciences were combined. In fact, the first introduction of Aristotle's natural philosophy into the West came through the astrological work of Abū Ma'shar, the Latin Albumasar, which in the translation of John of Seville was known as *Liber introductorius maior*. The earlier interest of the Latins in Islamic science had caused Adelard of Bath to translate a shorter work of Abū Ma'shar into Latin, which prepared the ground for the wide reception of the larger astrological work through which Aristotelian physics reached the West twenty years before any of his specific works on natural philosophy became known in Latin.

The tradition of 'anti-Aristotelian' philosophy, particularly in physics, is to be found among other Muslim philosophers and scientists of the period. Among the earliest of these is Muḥammad ibn Zakariyyā' al-Rāzī, so well known in the West as Rhazes, who was born c. 251/865 and died in 313/925. Rāzī, who was an alchemist, physician, musician and philosopher, was much more respected by Muslim and also Jewish philosophers for his medicine, in whose clinical aspect he was the foremost medieval authority, than for his philosophy. But his philosophical ideas, although not of great importance in the later tradition of Islamic philosophy and criticised by many Ismā'īlī thinkers such as Abū Ḥātim al-Rāzī, have recently attracted much interest because of the unique views Rāzī holds concerning many questions.

Rāzī was not a follower; he considered himself as a master on equal footing with Plato and Aristotle. For this reason also he felt free to criticise them. In certain fields, especially ethics and cosmology, there are evident in him elements of pure Platonism untouched by neo-Platonic influences. In cosmology, he posited five eternal principles which present similarities to the *Timaeus* but reveal even more affinity with Manichaean cosmogony and cosmology. But in any case Rāzī was opposed to Aristotelian physics and often criticised the Stagirite for his views on natural philosophy. He had a particular love for Galen and a remarkable acquaintance with his works. He wrote specifically of his preference for Galen over Aristotle. He also opposed the general view of Muslim philosophers on the necessity of prophecy, whose existence he did not deny but whose necessity he did not accept. This was in fact the main reason why he did not have any appreciable influence upon later Islamic philosophy, which is essentially 'prophetic philosophy'.

Another great scientist, Abū Rayḥān al-Bīrūnī (362/973–c. 442/1051), who was an admirer of Rāzī but opposed to his 'anti-prophetic' philosophy, likewise wrote against Aristotelian natural philosophy. Bīrūnī, whom some consider as the most outstanding Muslim scientist, was more of a mathematician, historian and geographer than a philosopher in the usual sense, and it is through his scientific works that his philosophical views must be sought. This remarkable thinker combined the mind of mathematician and historian. He was the author of the first scientific work on comparative religion, the incomparable *India*, as well as the real founder of geodesy, and the author of one of the most elaborate astronomical treatises in the history of this science. It is in these works, and especially in a series of questions and answers exchanged with Avicenna, that Bīrūnī reveals his acute sense of observation and analysis which made him oppose certain tenets of Aristotelian physics such as the concept of 'natural place'. He in fact wrote openly on many subjects which were against the prevalent natural philosophy, such as the possibility of elliptical motion of the planets and the movement of the earth around the sun and remarked justly that the helio- or geocentric question was one to be solved by physics and theology and not astronomy alone, where parametrics could be measured the same way whether the sun or the earth was placed at the centre.

Ibn al-Haytham, the Latin Alhazen (c. 354/965–430/1039), who was a contemporary of Bīrūnī, was likewise a critic of Peripatetic philosophy in many ways. The author of the best medieval work on optics, which influenced Witelo and Kepler, Alhazen was also a remarkable experimental physicist and astronomer. He must be credited with the discovery of the principle of inertia in physics and with placing the science of optics on a new foundation. His mathematical study of the *camera obscura*, the correct explanation of the course of light in vision as opposed to the Aristotelian view, the explanation of reflection from spherical and parabolic mirrors, the study of spherical aberration, belief in the 'principle of least time' in refraction, and application of the rectangle of velocity long before Newton are among his outstanding scientific accomplishments.

But even more important in the long run for the philosophy of science was Alhazen's insistence upon the crystalline nature of the spheres. In Greek science, while the Aristotelians insisted that the aim of science was to know the nature of things, the mathematicians and astronomers generally believed that their aim was to 'save the phenomena'. The Ptolemaic spheres were convenient mathematical inventions that aided calculation and had no physical reality. Perhaps the most important heritage that Islamic science bestowed upon the West was to insist that the role of science including the mathematical must be the search for knowledge of the reality and being of things. The emphasis upon the crystalline nature of the spheres by Alhazen was precisely a statement of this belief. Physics in Muslim eyes was inseparable from ontology. This quest for the real in mathematical physics and astronomy was so thoroughly adopted in the West that even during the scientific revolution no one doubted that the role of physics was to discover the nature of things. Newton was actually following a philosophy of physics that Alhazen and other Muslim thinkers had bestowed upon all sciences of nature, not only the Aristotelian but also the mathematical and geometric sciences of Euclid, Ptolemy and their successors. The modern debates between the points of view of Meyerson, Cassirer, Northrop and the positivists and the analysts reveals in retrospect the significance of the realism imparted to mathematical physics by Alhazen and certain other Muslim thinkers.

During the fifth/eleventh century changed political and social conditions, brought about by the reunification of much of the Islamic world by the Seljuqs, favoured Ash'arite theology over philosophy and the 'intellectual sciences'. The new university system which had come into being, and in fact which served as a model for the earliest medieval universities in the West, now began to emphasise the teaching of theology or *kalām* – in some places almost exclusively – and attacks began to be made by outstanding theologians on the philosophers of the Peripatetic school. In fact, so many debates were held between the theologians and the philosophers that methods and arguments of *kalām* entered into the domain of philosophy itself, and even in Latin philosophical texts reference is often made to the *loquentes* of the three revealed religions, *loquentes* being derived from its root in a manner parallel to the derivation of *mutakallim* (i.e. scholar of *kalām*) and having the same meaning.

Of the theologians who were most influential in determining the future intellectual life of Islam, Ghazzālī and Fakhr al-Dīn Rāzī are particularly significant. Many modern scholars have considered Ghazzālī as the most influential figure in Islamic intellectual history. He is certainly one of the most important. Coming at a decisive moment in the history of Islam, he imparted a direction to it which has persisted ever since, especially in the Sunni world. Ghazzālī was both a Sufi and a theologian, and he criticised rationalistic philosophy in both capacities. On the one hand he sought to curtail the power of reason and make it subservient to revelation; on the other he tried to revive the ethics of Islamic society by breathing into it the spirit of Sufism and by making Sufism official in the religious schools and universities. He was eminently successful on both accounts.

Ghazzālī was not in any way opposed to logic or the use of reason and in fact composed treatises on logic. But what he did oppose was the claim of reason to comprehend the whole truth and to impose its partial views even in domains where it had no authority to assert itself. Therefore, while making use of reason he sought to criticise the rationalistic tendencies in Peripatetic philosophy. To this end he first summarised the views of the Peripatetics, especially Avicenna, who was the foremost among them, in a work called *Maqāṣid al-falāsifah* (*The Purpose of the Philosophers*), which was translated into Latin and through which Latin scholastics came to consider the author whom they called Algazel as a Peripatetic. Then he began to criticise these views in his *Tahāfut al-falāsifah* (*Incoherence of the Philosophers*), a work which broke the back of rationalistic philosophy and in fact brought the career of philosophy, as a discipline distinct from gnosis and theology, to an end in the Arabic part of the Islamic world. The response of Averroës to Ghazzālī was like an Indian summer for this early Peripatetic school and did not exercise any appreciable influence upon the later course of Islamic philosophy and thought. Ghazzālī also composed numerous works on Sufism of which the monumental *Iḥyā ulūm al-dīn* (*Revivification of the Sciences of Religion*) is the most notable and remains to this day the outstanding work on Sufi ethics.

The second theologian, Fakhr al-Dīn Rāzī, who like Ghazzālī hailed from Persia, continued the attacks of Ghazzālī by selecting a single work, *al-Ishārāt wa'l-tanbīhāt* (*The Book of Directives and Remarks*) of Avicenna, and criticising it thoroughly. This most learned of theologians applied his immense learning to criticising and demolishing the philosophical synthesis of Avicenna, of which the *The Book of Directives and Remarks* is perhaps the most concise testament. But by now the *kalām* applied to criticise the philosophers had itself become philosophical and was far removed from the simple assertions of al-Ash'arī. In fact, with Rāzī and later theologians like him a philosophical *kalām* developed which along with Sufism, mostly replaced philosophy in the Sunni world and especially in the Arab world, and was also of much influence among the Muslims of India.

Meanwhile during the fifth/eleventh and sixth/twelfth centuries, a great deal of intellectual activity took place in the Islamic West, that is in Andalusia, Morocco and the surrounding regions, which is of particular significance for the history of European philosophy, and in the domain of Sufism for the whole later intellectual history of Islam. Both Ash'arite theology and Peripatetic philosophy reached the Islamic West much later than their birth in the East. In fact we do not encounter any eminent representatives of either school in Andalusia until the sixth/twelfth century. The first outstanding theologian and philosopher of Andalusia was Ibn Ḥazm (383/993–456/1064), who developed an independent school of theology which he combined into a whole with law and the philosophy of language. This synthesis reflected all of the manifested and externalised aspects of the Divine revelation into a unity. Ibn Ḥazm also composed the first systematic work on religious sects and heresiography, for which he has been called the first 'historian of religious ideas'. He is also the author of the famous *Ṭawq al-ḥamāmah* (*Ring of the Dove*), which is a beautiful expression of the Platonic philosophy of love in its Islamic form.

In the sixth/twelfth century a religious reformer, Ibn Tumart, who was deeply influenced by Ghazzālī, began a movement which resulted in the establishment of the Almohads and the flowering of philosophy in the Islamic West. Before this period, there had occasionally been Sufis who had taught cosmological and metaphysical doctrines, such as Ibn Masarrah, who developed a particular form of cosmology based on 'pseudo-Empedoclean' fragments, a cosmology in which bodies themselves possess different degrees of existence. This cosmology was to have an influence upon the Jewish philosopher Ibn Gabirol, who in his *Fons vitae* employs a similar scheme, and also upon the master of Islamic esotericism, Ibn 'Arabī.

But the regular cultivation of philosophy began with Ibn Bājjah after the Almohad conquest. Ibn Bājjah, who was well known to the Latins as Avempace, is best known for his *Tadbīr al-mutawaḥḥid* (*Regime of the Solitary*), a philosophical protest against worldliness which terminates with the philosopher's reaching illumination in solitude. In contrast to Fārābī and also Averroës, Avempace did not develop a political philosophy devoted to the creation of the ideal state, but saw the role of philosophy as helping the individual to reach inner illumination. Avempace also wrote a commentary upon Aristotle's *Physics* in which he continued the criticism of John Philoponus and Avicenna against the Aristotelian theory of projectile motion, but in another vein. He also proposed what can be interpreted as the first new medieval quantitative relationship to describe this type of motion. He therefore represents, as Moody has shown,[3] an important development in medieval dynamics and influenced the late medieval physics which was developed by such men as Bradwardine, Oresme and Nicolas of Autrecourt. The *Pisan Dialogue* of Galileo contains the 'impetus theory' coming from Avicenna through the Latin critics of Aristotle and a dynamics which has appropriately been called 'Avempacean'.

Ibn Ṭufayl, Avempace's successor on the scene, was both a philosopher and a physician, like many a Muslim philosopher before and after and also like some of the Jewish philosophers such as Maimonides who were so close to Muslims during this period. His *Ḥayy ibn Yaqẓān* (*Alive Son of the Awake*), which served as a model for the *Robinson Crusoe* story and was the inspiration for some of the early Quakers as well as the source of Leibniz's *philosophus autodidactus*, is a philosophical romance whose end is mystical illumination and ecstasy. Although the title of this work is the same as that of Avicenna and although Ibn Ṭufayl follows the tradition established by Avicenna of writing philosophical narratives in which philosophical situations are depicted in a symbolic language, the two works are not identical. Avicenna in his philosophical narratives, or recitals as Corbin calls them,[4] was preparing the ground for his 'Oriental Philosophy' where the angel acts as the instrument of illumination; Ibn Ṭufayl was seeking to demonstrate that ultimately revealed religion and philosophy derive from the same truth, if the philosopher withdraws from society to meditate by himself. Ibn Ṭufayl's emphasis upon the 'inner light' shares this important element with the Avicennan cycle of narratives, that it shows the ultimate goal of true philosophy to be a knowledge which illuminates; but there is an element of 'utopianism' in Ibn Ṭufayl and a tendency, within the limits of medieval Islamic philosophy, to seek to reach the Divine outside the cadre of revealed religion.

The last and most celebrated of the Andalusian philosophers, Ibn Rushd or Averroës, was more influential in the West than in Islam. He was born in Cordova in 520/1126 to a distinguished family of jurists and received the best education possible in law, theology, philosophy and medicine. He served as chief judge of religious courts in Seville and Cordova and was court physician in Marrakesh. At the end of his life, because of a change in the political climate of Andalusia, he fell from grace and died a lonely figure in Marrakesh in 595/1198.

While the earlier Muslim Peripatetics developed elaborate philosophical systems for which they are known, Averroës devoted himself most of all to commenting on the works of Aristotle. Without the inclusion of small treatises on Aristotelian themes and doubtful commentaries, there are thirty-eight commentaries by Averroës on the works of Aristotle, five of which were written in three forms: long, medium and short. In fact Averroës became known in the West as *the* commentator of Aristotle *par excellence*. It is by this title that St Thomas refers to him, and Dante mentions him as the person who wrote the great commentary (*il gran commento*). Through his eyes the West came to know Aristotle, and the figure of Averroës was never separated from that of the Stagirite throughout the Middle Ages. Averroës also wrote certain independent philosophical works such as the *Tahāfut al-tahāfut* (*Incoherence of the Incoherence*), an answer to Ghazzālī's *Incoherence of the Philosophers*, and *Faṣl al-maqāl* (*The Harmony between Philosophy and Religion*), in which like other Muslim philosophers but in his own way he sought to harmonise reason and revelation by giving each its due as an independent way of reaching the truth, but not according to the 'double truth' theory which is a misconception of his teachings by Latin Averroists. He also wrote on political philosophy, following upon the path of Fārābī, and commented upon Plato's *Republic*.

Averroës became known to the West in two different periods. He was 'twice revealed', to quote the statement of Wolfson.[5] He was once translated in the twelfth century and then again during the Renaissance. The movement, begun early in the twelfth century in Toledo, to translate Arabic works into Latin under the direction of the Bishop of Toledo, had incited such interest that less than twenty years after the death of Averroës his works began to be translated by such men as Hermann the German and Michael Scot, and the translations became rapidly disseminated. As the result of a misunderstanding of the Islamic background of his philosophy, Averroës became rapidly identified as a kind of antireligious free-thinker, and such works as *Errores Philosophorum* of Giles of Rome devoted special sections to the refutation of his ideas. Actually the Muslim Ibn Rushd and Averroës as seen by the Latin Averroists like Siger of Brabant or the Schoolmen in general are very different. The Muslim Ibn Rushd, while an avid disciple of Aristotle, was also a firm believer in revealed religion and its necessity. The Latin Averroës became identified with 'secular learning' and around his name rallied many forces which were opposed to the official theology of Christianity but which nevertheless were instrumental in the flowering of the arts and sciences during the thirteenth century. Strangely enough, Averroës was not only 'twice revealed' but also twice misunderstood, for, during the Renaissance also, many Hellenists and humanists attacked him for not having understood Aristotle properly, although a few continued to gaze upon him as the surest guide for the understanding of the Stagirite.

After Averroës, philosophy in the Islamic West and the Arab world died except for one or two instances. Shortly after Averroës, Ibn Sab'īn developed a philosophy that is much more akin to the gnosis and illumination that was now dominating the intellectual life of Eastern Islam; and Ibn Khaldūn in the eight/fourteenth century developed in his *Muqaddimah* (*Prolegomena*) the first thorough philosophy of history, which has had a great deal of influence in the West during the past century and which must be considered as the predecessor of the type of study of history and civilisation developed by Vico, Spengler and Toynbee, although within the traditional world view.

The new direction which Islamic intellectual life took was determined most of all by the school of Illumination (*ishrāq*) of Suhrawardī and the intellectual and doctrinal Sufism of gnosis (*'irfān*) of Ibn 'Arabī. Moreover, these currents established themselves upon the basis of a newly interpreted Avicennism rather than on the 'anti-Avicennan' Peripatetic philosophy developed in the Islamic West. Suhrawardī, a Persian sage, who was born in Suhraward in 549/1153, studied primarily in Isfahan and, after travelling throughout the eastern lands of Islam, settled in Aleppo, where he was killed in 587/1191. He was able to establish during this short lifespan a new intellectual perspective which continues to live to this day in the Islamic world. This new school, which is called the School of Illumination, is based on both ratiocination and mystical illumination, on the intellectual training attained through formal schooling and on spiritual purification made possible through the practice of the spiritual life. The masterpiece of Suhrawardī, the *Ḥikmat al-ishrāq* (*Theosophy of the Orient of Light*), as it has been translated by Corbin,[6] begins with a criticism of Aristotelian logic and ends with the question of spiritual ecstasy.

Suhrawardī sought to bring together in the bosom of Islamic gnosis what he believed were the two authentic traditions of philosophy and wisdom: the tradition of Greek philosophy going back to Pythagoras and the tradition of wisdom of the ancient Persian sages. He thus had a consciousness of the presence of a universal tradition and is perhaps the first in Islam to have developed the idea of 'perennial philosophy'. For him, this integral tradition of wisdom implied the synthesis of the ways of ratiocination and intuition; strangely enough he considered Aristotle the last of the Greek philosophers, with whom this integral philosophy or rather theosophy in the original Greek sense of *theosophia* became reduced to merely discursive knowledge. Another major signpost which indicates a parting of the ways between Islamic and Western intellectual history is the fact that in the West philosophy essentially begins with Aristotle whereas for Suhrawardī and his considerable intellectual posterity it ends with him.

Suhrawardī was studied avidly in the East and his writings were translated into languages as far apart as Hebrew and Sanskrit. Through his teachings Islamic philosophy spread into India for the first time. But he was not translated into Latin and therefore was not known directly in the West. Certain Latin authors. such as Roger Bacon, however, seem to have come indirectly to know about his ideas, and mention themes and motifs which can be easily traced back to Suhrawardī.

A generation later than Suhrawardī, Ibn 'Arabī performed a pilgrimage in the other direction, coming from Andalusia to settle in Damascus. This giant of Islamic gnosis and the authority *par excellence* on Islamic esoteric doctrine was born in Murcia in 560/1165 and after spending his youth in Andalusia set out for the East as the result of a vision of the Prophet of Islam. After spending some time in Egypt and encountering difficulty from certain exoteric religious scholars, he went to Mecca to write, in this holiest of Islamic cities, the *al-Futūḥāt al-makkiyyah* (*Meccan Revelations*), which is a summa of esoteric knowledge in Islam. Later he settled in Damascus, there to write his most celebrated work, the *Fuṣūṣ al-ḥikam* (*Bezels of Wisdom*), and to die in 638/1240. Not the least remarkable aspect of his life, which was so intertwined with visions and wonders, is the enormous corpus of many hundreds of works he has left behind, works which transformed the intellectual life of the Islamic world from Morocco to Indonesia.

Sufism, which is the esoteric aspect of the Islam revelation and is completely rooted in the Holy Quran and prophetic traditions, had not, for the most part, explicitly formulated its doctrinal teachings before Ibn ʻArabī. The earliest Sufis had presented the pearls of gnosis through the silence of their spiritual presence or through allusions. Rarely had they spoken openly of all aspects of Sufism, even when occasionally someone like the two Ghazzālīs, Abū Ḥāmid and Aḥmad, or ʻAyn al-Quḍāt Hamadānī, had written on some particular aspect of Sufi doctrine. Suhrawardī also belonged to the Sufi tradition but his task was the establishment of a kind of 'isthmus' between discursive philosophy and thought and pure gnosis. It was therefore left to Ibn ʻArabī and his disciples, especially the incomparable Ṣadr al-Dīn al-Qunyawī, to formulate explicitly the teachings of Sufism in vast doctrinal treatises dealing with metaphysics, cosmology, psychology, anthropology and, of course, with the spiritual significance and symbolism of various traditional sciences. These works were henceforth studied in various official centres of Islamic learning in addition to the special centres where Sufi teachings were imparted.

Ibn ʻArabī was not directly translated into Latin, but he and the Sufis in general exercised some influence through the esoteric contact that came to be made between Islam and Christianity by way of the Order of the Temple and the *fideli d'amore*. Elements of Ibn ʻArabī are particularly discernible in Dante and also in Raymond Lull. The 'gnostics' among Christian mystics, such as Meister Eckhart, Angelus Silesius and Dante himself, in fact reveal certain similarities to Ibn ʻArabī and his school, a situation which is often due more to a similarity in spiritual types than to historical influences. In this order such influences must of necessity remain at the level of providing a means of expression or a particular language of symbolism rather than the vision itself from which flow the truths expressed by these mystics. In the same way, Sufism itself did not make any more use of neo-Platonism or Hermeticism than finding therein an appropriate means of expression for its own verities coming from the Islamic revelation and the 'Muḥammadan Poverty' which makes the Sufi life and vision possible.

After the seventh/thirteenth century, the intellectual contact between Islam and Christianity came nearly completely to an end, never to be seriously revived until today. Spain, which had been the main point of contact, ceased to play this role after its reconquest by Christians mostly because the Jews, who had acted as an intermediary, were dispersed or found themselves in a different cultural climate, and also because the Christian mozarabs, that is those who had adopted Arab ways, also disappeared. It is of interest to note that the Jews, who had written their theology and philosophy in Arabic until the sixth/twelfth century, began to write in Hebrew only after the destruction of Muslim power in Spain. The contacts made possible in Sicily and in the Holy Land also came to an end about the same time through the Crusades, and two sister civilisations which had followed a similar and parallel course for centuries began to go their own ways.

But, contrary to what most Western sources have written, the intellectual life of Islam did not by any means come to an end merely because of the termination of this contact. In the seventh/thirteenth century, the philosophy of Avicenna was revived by Khwājah Naṣīr al-Dīn al-Ṭūsī, an intellectual figure of the first magnitude who also revived the study of mathematics and astronomy. In fact, it was he and his student Quṭb al-Dīn al-Shīrāzī who proposed the first new medieval model for planetary motion, which was later employed by Copernicus and which Copernicus most likely learned through Byzantine Greek sources. It was also Ṭūsī who established the first complete astronomical observatory in history, which through the observatories of Samarqand and Istanbul became the model for the earliest modern European observatories such as those of Tycho Brahe and Kepler.

Ṭūsī answered the charges brought against Avicenna by Rāzī and other theologians and revived his teachings, and trained many outstanding philosophers himself. Henceforth Persia, which had provided most of the Islamic philosophers until now, became almost the exclusive home of Islamic philosophy. Gradually the teachings of Avicenna, Suhrawardī and Ibn ʿArabī, as well as those of the theologians, became synthesised in vast metaphysical systems which reached their peak during the eleventh/seventeenth century with Mīr Dāmād and Ṣadr al-Dīn Shīrāzī. These metaphysicians, who are the contemporaries of Descartes and Leibniz, developed a metaphysics which was no less logical and demonstrative than those of their European contemporaries and yet which included a dimension of gnosis and intuition which the European philosophy of the period completely lacked. Quite justly, Corbin has called Ṣadr al-Dīn Shīrāzī, whom many Persians consider the greatest Islamic philosopher, a combination of a St Thomas and a Jakob Böhme which the context of Islam in its Persian manifestation alone could make possible.[7] Moreover, these dominant intellectual figures of the Safavid period established a new school of philosophy which has survived to this day in Persia itself as well as in the Indo-Pakistan subcontinent and other surrounding regions where the influence of Persian culture has been felt. As for its significance for the West, this philosophical tradition presents a most interesting parallel, in fact the only one that exists, with which Western philosophy itself can be compared. Based in their discursive aspect upon the same Greek sources and inspired by two religions that are akin in many ways, Islamic and Western philosophy finally developed in two completely different directions. When one studies the *existenz* philosophy of the German existentialists or the nihilism of some of the French existentialists, one should also study the philosophy of Being of a man like Ṣadr al-Dīn Shīrāzī, who draws the mind to horizons which European philosophy has not been able to reach since it lowered its gaze at the end of the Middle Ages from the study of Being to the possibilities of human reason and the limits of rationalism.

For centuries Islamic intellectual life was influential in the West to the extent that the history of ideas in the two worlds are nearly inseparable. Now the later development of Islamic philosophy and the living tradition of philosophy and gnosis which have survived in the Islamic world to the present day can once again provide ideas to fertilise the soil of Western intellectual life. This philosophy can at least aid the few who through the dim glass of phenomenology, existentialism, structuralism, etc., are searching for a more penetrating vision of reality than that which the discursive and totally earthly and mentally bound philosophy of the West since the seventeenth century has been able to provide for them. Likewise, in the Islamic world itself, this rich intellectual heritage is the only foundation upon which any intellectual activity worthy of being called Islamic must be carried out.

Notes

1 See R. Walzer, 'Islamic Philosophy', in *The History of Philosophy East and West*, London, 1953, vol. II, p. 131; also in Walzer's *Greek into Arabic*, Oxford, 1962.
2 See E. Gilson, 'Les sources gréco-arabes de l'augustinisme avicennant', *Archives d'histoire doctrinale et littéraire du Moyen Age*, vol. IV, 1929, pp. 5–149.
3 See E. A. Moody, 'Galileo and Avempace', *Journal of the History of Ideas*, vol. XII, no. 2, 1951, pp. 163–93; no. 3, 375–422.
4 See H. Corbin, *Avicenna and the Visionary Recital*, trans. W. Trask, New York, 1960.
5 See H. Wolfson, 'The Twice-revealed Averroës', *Speculum*, vol. 36, 1961, pp. 373–92.
6 See the two prolegomena of Corbin to Suhrawardī's *Opera Metaphysica et Mystica*, vol. I, Tehran, 1976; and vol. II, Tehran, 1977. See also his *En Islam iranien*, vol. II, Paris, 1971.
7 See Ṣadr al-Dīn Shīrāzī, *Le livre des pénétrations métaphysiques*, ed. by H. Corbin, Tehran, 1964, French introduction.

The Sciences

7

The Cosmologies of Aristotle and Ibn Sīnā: a Comparative Study in the Light of Islamic Doctrines

> And with Him are the keys of the invisible. None but He knoweth them. And He knoweth what is in the land and the sea. Not a leaf falleth, but He knoweth it, not a grain amid the darkness of the earth, naught of wet or dry but (it be noted) in a clear record.
> (*Quran*, VI: 8)

> La circular natura, ch'è suggello
> Alla cera mortal, la ben sua arte,
> Ma non distingue l'un dall'altro ostello.
> (*Dante*, Paradiso, VIII; 127–9)

I

The cosmological perspective deals with the ultimate causes of the Universe, its origin, constitution, and qualitative content. In traditional doctrines, whether Greek, Christian, or Islamic, cosmology is always concerned with the application to the cosmos of universal principles which are of a metaphysical nature. Despite differences of application of these universal truths among various traditional cultures, the overall aim of traditional cosmology has remained the same. As has been clearly stated, 'L'objet central des sciences traditionnelles est l'unicité de tout ce qui existe.'[1] Needless to say, the aim of this kind of science is not the same as that of modern science. Whereas the traditional sciences are eminently qualitative and seek through the understanding of the symbols present in nature to gain knowledge of the Reality that transcends nature, modern science is quantitative and deals with phenomena of nature as pure facts without any desire to relate them to any other order of Reality.

As a first step in a study of comparative cosmology, one must try to understand ancient and medieval cosmologies from their own points of view. These cosmologies describe the whole of the Universe as an icon for contemplation; they are not childish attempts to find fantastic causes for natural occurrences. To attain an understanding of them as symbols one must first accept the legitimacy of the traditional sciences which have a different end from their modern counterparts. In fact, there are an indefinite number of sciences pertaining to the same subject but with different perspectives, each true to the extent that it can reveal the aspect of Reality corresponding to its particular point of view. One may say that ancient and medieval cosmologies, like most of the art of those periods, are not 'naturalistic' but, rather, try to understand through nature that which lies beyond it. To criticise a Chinese landscape according to the standards of naturalistic art would be to misunderstand its whole message. The same parallel may be drawn for traditional cosmology, whose true significance evades the critic who is seeking quantitative and naturalistic descriptions of the world.

Turning now to the question of Islamic cosmology in particular, it must be said at the outset that in the study of things Islamic many Western scholars often tend to attribute a Greek origin to all that has a resemblance to Greek ideas. This tendency is especially true when applied to a Muslim philosopher like Ibn Sīnā, who has sometimes been considered merely a follower of Greek philosophy in Islamic dress.[2] If, however, the above definition of cosmology as a qualitative description of the Universe is accepted, one can rest assured that there will be similarities among the views of various traditional authorities such as Ibn Sīnā on this subject, because Truth like the sun belongs to all cultures, although historical influences may also be present.

In the case of Aristotle and Ibn Sīnā, there is both borrowing and analogy. The extent of the influence of Aristotle in the Mediterranean world and the fact that he provided a common language of discourse and dialogue for the members of the Abrahamic tradition, namely Jews, Christians and Muslims, warrants a comparative study of the cosmology of this 'pagan' philosopher with that of the Muslim Ibn Sīnā, a study which reveals the similarity in the morphological structure of their respective cosmologies and the historical influence of one on the other.

Ancient and medieval people based their sciences on certain basic symbols connected intimately with the very reality of nature. One of these is space, which symbolises all the possibilities inherent in the Absolute which is also the Infinite and therefore 'Total Possibility'. Within space there are the six directions, the four cardinal points and the zenith and nadir. The upward direction always implies an 'ontological' elevation and therefore also a spiritual, social, or physical one, and the downward direction, a corresponding degradation. This natural identification remains in many expressions in various modern languages, such as 'moving up in the world'. Lightness and heaviness of materials are closely associated with this symbolism since light objects move upwards, relative to heavy ones.

Another set of symbols deals with geometric forms. The sphere is the most perfect figure and is characteristic of the lightness and mobility associated with the spirit. The cube, on the other hand, is the most stable and rigid of the forms and is naturally connected with the substantial pole of the cosmos and the stability of matter. The universality of these symbols can be seen by their presence in cultures as varied as the Christian, Muslim, Chinese and Sioux.[3] Aristotle, as well as Ibn Sīnā, made full use of these and many other symbols in his exposition of cosmology, a cosmology which always preserved its symbolic character for the ancient and medieval people in whom the 'esprit symboliste' was still very much alive.

II

Because for Aristotle cosmology is a branch of physics and physics is 'preceded' by metaphysics although 'read' after physics, an understanding of his cosmological scheme can best be achieved by a study of his 'science of Being' which forms the subject of the *Metaphysica*. Aristotelian metaphysics is essentially ontology dealing with being *qua* being. This science is superior to all other sciences since it deals with the most universal of all subjects.[4] As Aristotle himself states, 'Divine Science belongs to God.'[5] 'Physics also is a kind of wisdom, but it is not of the first kind.'[6]

Pure Being polarises into essence (form) and substance (matter). Every object in this world is composed of these two principles in various degrees. As pure essence lies above manifestation, so does pure substance lie beneath it. The modern notion of matter, going back to Descartes, was alien to the Greeks and in fact to non-Western people in general. In fact, it did not gain a real foothold in the West until the eighteenth century. Matter for Aristotle, as for St Thomas, was either *materia prima*, which is the universal substantial pole of the cosmos, or *materia secunda*, the substantial pole of a particular manifestation. In the words of Aristotle, 'Substance has two senses: (a) the ultimate substratum, which is no longer predicated on anything else, and (b) that which is a "this" and separable – and of this nature is the shape or form of each thing.'[7] Concerning essence he says, 'The essence of each thing is what it is said to be *propter se*.'[8] Much has been said of the conflict between Aristotle and Plato regarding the meaning of essence or 'idea'. Actually Aristotle's concept of essence takes into consideration its immanent aspect whereas Plato's deals with the transcendent aspect.

'Everything changes from that which is potentially to that which is actually.'[9] In this manner, all change is envisaged as a flow from potency to act. But with change comes movement, whose meaning played an ever-increasing role in the thought of Aristotle, especially in his metaphysics. There he states that 'no movement is infinite, but every movement has an end'.[10] To this idea he adds the eternity of time and motion, and as a consequence of these ideas arrives at the well-known concept of the Eternal Prime-Mover who moves all things while He remains stationary.[11] This idea can best be understood through the symbolism of the wheel. Every point on it rotates except the centre through which the axle is fastened. The latter remains motionless yet supports the whole wheel which moves about it. If by inverse analogy – or by what mathematically is called a 1/Z transformation – one transforms the centre of the wheel to the space surrounding it, one can see the image of Aristotle's cosmology and the position of the Prime-Mover with respect to the cosmos.

The cosmology of Aristotle is outlined mostly in the *De Caelo*. The treatise *De Mundo* also deals with this subject; however, the authenticity of the latter is seriously doubted. The content seems to point to neo-Platonic origins, and its attribution to Poseidonius, who lived in the first century BC, seems justified. Certain aspects of the subject are dealt with in the *Physica, De Generatione et corruptione* and *Meteorologica*, especially in the sections concerned with the elements and their properties.

The Greeks, like the Hindus and the Chinese, had five cosmological elements, four of them – fire, air, water and earth – constituting this world and the fifth, the ether, constituting the heavens. All the beings of this changing world were made up of the four sublunary elements, and their various proportions determined the specific properties of each one. 'Thus then five elements, situated in spheres in five regions, the less being in each case surrounded by the greater – namely, earth surrounded by water, water by air, air by fire, and fire by ether – make up the whole universe. All the upper portion represents the dwelling of the gods, the lower the abode of mortal creatures.'[12] 'Thus then a single harmony orders the composition of the whole heaven and earth and the whole universe by the mingling of the most contrary principles.'[13] The symbolism of this picture with the heavier elements, the more material or substantial ones, located towards the bottom and the lighter or essential ones towards the top, is clear if the natural 'value' of the upward direction of space is always kept in mind.

In the *De Caelo* Aristotle presents his picture of the world with the spherical earth at the centre surrounded by concentric spheres all rotating about a pole which runs through the Universe. Within this general scheme, distinction is made between rectilinear and circular motion and earthly and heavenly bodies. Aristotle argues that since the elements are simple, natural bodies, that is to say they contain a principle of movement within themselves, their natural movement is also simple. Now it must be noted that the only simple motions are straight (equal to up and down) and circular. Of these two types of motion, the straight motion belongs to the four elements. But since every simple motion is the motion of a simple body, there must be a simple body whose nature it is to move in a circle.[14] He proceeds to show the priority of circular motion to rectilinear motion and the superiority of bodies possessing circular motion. Having concluded that there must be a simple body having circular motion which is eternal by nature, he arrives at the existence of ether.[15]

Concerning the uniqueness of the world he states that since every element moves naturally in a certain direction and to a certain fixed goal, if it moves one way only when constrained then it may be taken that its natural motion is in the opposite direction to that. If there are several worlds, they must all be composed of the same elements; therefore the elements of all alike must have the same natural motions. This means that 'all the earth must move naturally towards the same centre and all the fire towards the same circumference. But this is impossible if there are several worlds, each with its own centre and circumference. There can be only one centre and circumference, or, in other words, only one world.'[16] He adds other forms of reasoning drawn from the doctrine of form and matter and the concept of the natural place of things to supplement the above arguments for the uniqueness of the world.

As to the indestructibility of the world, he states that the view that the world is alternately generated and destroyed means no more than that the elements are combined in one formation or another. But in reality, there is nothing involved that can be called generation and destruction, but only change of shape or arrangement.[17] He envisages, therefore, an eternal world ever changing but without a beginning. This change is naturally confined to the corruptible part of the cosmos.

The motion of the outer heavens is everlasting and all-embracing, perfect and eternal. Since the earth is surrounded by the spheres which have eternal motion, it no longer has need of any other support. In this way, Aristotle dismisses the myth of Atlas and the theory that souls move the heavens just as our souls move our bodies. The heavens are spherical and move from right to left – a point held also by the Pythagoreans – and have up and down directions which are reversed for us who live in the lower hemisphere. It is the sphericity of heaven – owing to its being a primary body – that imposes a spherical shape on all subsequent spheres including the earth.

About the stars, Aristotle states that they are made of ether and emit heat and light by ignition of air beneath them, due to friction caused by their movement.[18] The motion of stars is not self-caused but results from their being set at fixed points in the revolving heavens. The speed at which each star moves in its own circle is proportional to its distance from the outermost sphere. Aristotle completely rejects the Pythagorean theory of the harmony of the spheres and any relations between the motion of the stars and music.

After refuting the several theories of the earth which had preceded him, Aristotle describes the earth as a sphere at rest with its centre corresponding to the centre of the Universe. In fact, there must be an earth, for it is that which remains at rest in the middle.[19] This necessity implies the existence of its contrary, fire, and consequently the two intermediate elements, air and water. This in turn implies the coming-to-be and change which is characteristic of the earth.

In summary, the cosmology of Aristotle envisages the heavy element earth located at the centre of the Universe surrounded by a series of concentric spheres, each with a greater portion of lighter elements, until the realm of the heavens is reached, where only the eternal and unchanging ether is present. The whole system moves about an axis which is the *axis mundi*; the motion, retraced through intermediate causes, returns to the Prime Cause which is the Unmoved Mover, the *Causa Prima* of the Universe. The symbolic quality of this scheme can be seen when looked at in its totality, and there is little wonder that it served as the cosmological pattern for the *Divine Comedy* where each sphere corresponds to a grade of being and an inner state of the adept who is undertaking the spiritual journey.

III

With the possible exception of Ibn Rushd, no one in the cadre of Islamic civilisation deserves to be compared more with Aristotle than Ibn Sīnā. The latter occupies such a position not only because of the similarity of his thought to the ideas of the Greek philosopher but also because of his universality of interest. We have already dealt briefly with his biography and have referred to the fact that he was a child prodigy and also a master of both the religious and intellectual sciences while still in his teens. To quote his own words, 'So by the time I reached my eighteenth year I had exhausted all these sciences. My memory for learning was at that period of my life better than it is now, but today I am more mature; apart from this, my knowledge is exactly the same, nothing further having been added to my store since then.'[20] Even more remarkable is that he learned medicine by simply reading books found in libraries to which he had access. Indeed, by this self-taught method he became a leading physician of his day when he was seventeen years old.

Of particular interest is Ibn Sīnā's encounter with Aristotle's *Metaphysica*. We are told in the *Autobiography* recorded by his favourite student Abū 'Ubayd al-Juzjānī, that he read the work forty times and memorised it in its entirety, but still could not understand its content. Only after reading *Aghrāḍ mā ba'd al-ṭabī'ah* (*On the Objects of the Metaphysica*) by Abū Naṣr al-Fārābī did he understand Aristotelian metaphysics. Henceforth, Ibn Sīnā always acknowledged his debt to both Aristotle and Fārābī as his teachers and masters.

Many of the works of Ibn Sīnā are concerned with cosmology, some directly and some only indirectly. These include not only such philosophical works as *al-Shifā'* (*The Book of Healing*), the *al-Najāt* (*The Book of Salvation*) and the *Ishārāt* (*The Book of Directives and Remarks*) but also his medical works, especially the *al-Qānūn fi'l-ṭibb* (*Canon of Medicine*). Also his symbolic recitals contain a mystical cosmology of great depth and significance.

Ibn Sīnā's physics uses much of the Aristotelian terminology. Such concepts as form and matter, primary and secondary qualities, and accidents and nature of various forces are defined in a manner similar to that of Aristotle. Thus, change is explained as the passage from potency to act and time as a factor intrinsically connected with motion. 'Time can only be imagined in connection with movement. Where one cannot feel movement one cannot feel time.'[21] Again, he writes, 'The creator of time does not precede it in time but *in principio*.'[22] Ibn Sīnā also envisages the natural position of each body according to its properties. 'The body abandoned to itself takes a certain position and a certain figure. It has in its nature something which obliges it to do so.'[23]

As to causes, Ibn Sīnā states six: matter of the composed, form of the composed, the given of the accident, form of the matter, the agent and end. But since the matter of the composed is analogous to the given of the accident, and the form of the composed with the form of the matter, the six causes are reduced to the four of Aristotle, namely the formal, material, efficient, and final. Ibn Sīnā also follows Aristotle in distinguishing between rectilinear and circular motion and considering the world to be without temporal origin.

If there are many resemblances between the physics of Ibn Sīnā and his predecessor, there is some difference in the metaphysical formulation and cosmology. Ibn Sīnā made two important divergences from Aristotle on these subjects. The first is the distinction between essence and existence which for Aristotle was only a logical distinction.[24] Ibn Sīnā made this distinction ontological. For him there is a distinction between existence and essence, in every being, except the Divine Being. The fact that every existent in whom this distinction is to be found has to come into being through an agent in whom these two are united, leads to the division of beings into the contingent and necessary.

In the *Shifā', Najāt, al-Mabdā' wa'l-ma'ād* (*The Beginning and the End*) as well as in some of the short treatises such as *al-Risālat al-'arshiyyah* (*The Treatise of the Divine Throne*), Ibn Sīnā proves first of all that there is a Necessary Being; and then, in conformity with the Islamic ideal which is dominated by the concept of Unity, proceeds to prove its uniqueness and oneness. 'Since it is thus established that the Necessary Being cannot be two, but is all Truth, then by virtue of His Essential Reality, in respect of which He is Truth, He is United and One, and no other shares with Him in that Unity; however the all-Truth attains existence, it is through Himself.'[25]

The ternary division of beings into body (*soma*), soul (*psyche*), and spirit or intelligence (*nous*) which was well known to the early Greek philosophers is also to be seen in the system of Ibn Sīnā as well as most other Muslim philosophers and cosmologists. In addition to this tripartite division, Ibn Sīnā makes a clear distinction between the multiple states of being, the hierarchical superiority of a higher state to a lower one, and the correspondence of this hierarchy with upward movement and direction in the cosmos. His whole cosmology depends upon the correspondence between the microcosm, man, and the macrocosm, the Universe, so that the constitution of the one corresponds to the constitution of the other. 'Nous avons nommé intelligence ce qui en reçoit rien que ce qui est en elle, mais qui donne; âme ce qui reçoit de l'intelligence et qui donne; corps ce qui reçoit (des deux précédents) et qui ne donne pas. Ces trois ordres englobent toutes les formes de l'existence.'[26] Rectilinear movement is associated with bodies composed of the four elements, and circular motion with intellectual substances, of which the heavens are made.

To solve the problem of the existence of multiplicity in the face of unity – a problem which lies at the heart of the mystery of creation – Ibn Sīnā resorts to the concept of 'emanation' from Pure Being through various levels and degrees of existence. 'Il ne peut que la multiplicité et la diversité procèdent d'une seule Vérité.'[27] This emanation takes place in such a way that the beings near the periphery of the Universe and close to the Primary Body which surrounds the cosmos are closer to the Necessary Being and purer than bodies near the earth. In fact, Ibn Sīnā envisages all change as the result of the desire of all beings to reach the perfection which belongs to the Necessary Being.

A summary picture of Ibn Sīnā's cosmology, at least in its Peripatetic version, is to be found in the *Najāt*.[28] There, he describes the hierarchy of the multiple states of being with Allah at the summit who brings into being the Pure Spirit which is called the Primary Cause. From this Cause come the souls, bodies of the spheres, and the intelligences. From the intelligences proceed Jupiter and so forth, down to the lowest sphere, which is the moon. With this last planet, the moon, is connected the tenth and last pure intelligence, which is the intellectual agent *(al-'aql al-fa''āl)* from which emanates the sublunary world. Ibn Sīnā assigns a number to each sphere which is related to its 'idea' and immaterial principle. The soul of the spheres acts as an intermediary between the intelligences and the heavenly bodies.

From the above outline, one can see two basic divergences between Ibn Sīnā and Aristotle. The first may be said to be related to the urgent need on the part of Ibn Sīnā to conform to the monotheistic viewpoint. This urge led to the doctrine of the Necessary Being and the ontological separation between the Necessary and contingent beings. The second comes from trying to preserve the Unity of the Necessary Being while at the same time seeking to explain multiplicity. This problem which had also faced Plato as well as the neo-Platonists led Ibn Sīnā to adopt the emanation theory which led him to a cosmology in some ways more akin to the neo-Platonic than to the Aristotelian perspective. The importance of this phase of Ibn Sīnā's thought – away from Aristotle and towards Plato and Plotinus – can be realised if we study his last works, especially *The Visionary Recitals*, in which the journey of the soul through the cosmos is described in symbolic and non-Aristotelian language. It is safe to say that conditions imposed by the Islamic tradition as well as neo-Platonic influences are sufficiently evident in the work of Ibn Sīnā to distinguish his cosmology from that of Aristotle, to whom he professed so much debt and from whom he learned so much.

IV

The place of Ibn Sīnā's cosmology, and in fact perspective, in Islamic thought must be studied in the light of the monotheistic nature of the Islamic tradition. Islam, like Judaism and Christianity, issues from the Abrahamic tradition, and, if it is said to differ in some respect from its predecessors, this is principally in its insistence on the Unity of Allah. The fundamental formula of Islam, the first *Shahādah*, is the formula *La ilāha illa'Llāh*. Although usually translated 'There is no god but God', this formula in a metaphysical sense means that there is no power, agent, or reality if it is not The Power, The Agent, The Reality.

In this manner the Absolute Unity of Reality is established. All phases of Islamic culture, whether art, science, or philosophy, reflect this predominance of the idea of Unity.

Now, philosophy may be considered as either the love of wisdom – *philo* and *sophia* – or, as it has come to mean in modern times, the reflections and reactions of an individual applying his human faculty of reason to the cosmic environment surrounding him. The distinction between the two types is fundamental in Islamic thought; wisdom, which has its origin in either revelation or pure intellectual intuition which is given to only a few individuals, is called *ḥikmah* in Arabic, while the philosophy whose authority is no higher than human reason is sometimes called *falsafah*, although this technical difference of terminology is not always preserved and sometimes *falsafah* is used interchangeably with *ḥikmah*. The first, embodied in the writings of the Sufis and certain theologians and illuminationists, like Ghazzālī and Suhrawardī (Shaykh al-ishrāq), is essential to Islamic civilisation, while rationalistic philosophy belongs to its outward aspect and is in a sense incidental to the mainstream of Islamic thought as witnessed by its disappearance in the Sunni world after the eighth/fourteenth century. In fact, one may say that the second definition of philosophy is largely peculiar to Western civilisation, since it is not found in other civilisations, such as those of China and India, and only incidentally in the Islamic and Jewish traditions.

The attitude of Islam towards knowledge can best be understood from the *sūrah* of the Quran quoted at the beginning of this chapter. According to the Islamic view, Allah is the knower of all things and the cause of all events. His Knowledge, Power and Unity overshadow the possibility of any secondary cause.[29] This is not to imply that the study of nature and natural causes is futile. On the contrary, both the Quran and *Ḥadīth* give specific instructions to man to study God's creation. However, this study should be directed towards an understanding of His Wisdom in creation rather than to the discovery of any causes which may be placed alongside Him, thereby destroying His Unity.[30]

One may then ask what the place of Ibn Sīnā's cosmology, and cosmology in general, would be within the perspective of the Islamic tradition. As is well known, Ghazzālī dealt a heavy blow to Islamic philosophy in the rationalistic sense in his *Tahāfut al-falāsifah* (*Incoherence of the Philosophers*), in which he specifically attacked Ibn Sīnā and accused him of heresy in certain aspects of his thought.[31] Generally, the greatest criticism made of the philosophers was their extension of the use of reason to realms which were beyond its legitimate sphere. Ibn Sīnā, especially towards the latter part of his life, came to place greater emphasis upon intuition, but the fact that he proposed to discover all realms of knowledge in the human language of reason made him the target of attack from the spokesmen of the theological perspective as well as from some of the Sufis. Nevertheless, it is clear that Ibn Sīnā contributed greatly to many branches of Islamic knowledge, particularly in the intellectual sciences *(al-'ulūm al-'aqliyyah)*, and he will always remain an Islamic philosopher, despite his use of Aristotelian cosmology and Platonic and neo-Platonic ideas. The effect of the conditions imposed upon his thought by the Islamic tradition can be clearly seen in many points in which he differed from his Greek predecessors, such as the differences mentioned above between his metaphysics and that of Aristotle.

The Quran contains in veiled language the germ of Islamic cosmology. But just as Islamic art, while remaining completely Islamic, made use of Persian and Byzantine influences, so did Islamic cosmology, while adhering to the Quranic ideal, make use of Greek thought as a means of expression. Both the concentric system of Aristotle and Ptolemy and occasionally the heliocentric system similar to that of the Pythagoreans were used, each to provide in its own way the background for the journey of man to God.[32] But, when cosmology came to be used as an instrument of Islamic thought, it was usually divorced from discursive reason and presented in its symbolic sense as an icon for contemplation.

The Divine Comedy of Dante makes similar use of cosmology, in this case Aristotelian, for completely Christian ends. Dante's connection with Islamic sources has been discussed by Miguel Ásin Palacios, Enrico Cerulli, and others.[33] Yet, no matter what the historical connections may be, *The Divine Comedy* offers a perfect example, in the West, of the place of cosmology in a religious tradition. Likewise, the cosmology of Ibn Sīnā and those of a similar nature which were taken from Aristotle and the neo-Platonists, and Islamicised, served a spiritual function in the hands of the *ḥakīms* and Sufis. These sages divorced these cosmological schemes from the limitations imposed on them by the language of discursive thought in which they were clothed so as to make them an object of contemplation and bring out their symbolic aspect. That Ibn Sīnā had begun to move towards this view himself is seen in some of his last works, such as *The Visionary Recitals*; there the spiritual journey through the various degrees of existence to the abode of Pure Being replaced the theoretical discussion of his earlier writings, and the cosmos became transformed into a symbol which provided the background for man's spiritual journey.

The comparative study of the cosmologies of Aristotle and Ibn Sīnā shows that, although deeply influenced by his predecessor, Ibn Sīnā moved towards an integration of Aristotelian cosmology with Islamic beliefs. Thus he created a cosmology which served an important purpose in Islamic thought. Although the rationalistic and syllogistic aspects of his thought were criticised by Ghazzālī and others, his cosmology, once divorced from its syllogistic mode of presentation, was adopted by many later *ḥakīms* and Sufis who demonstrated clearly its value for the contemplative life. Therefore, by adopting Aristotelian cosmology in its neo-Platonic version to the Islamic perspective, Ibn Sīnā was able to make a permanent contribution to the total structure of Islamic thought, even though the syllogistic and rationalistic aspect of Aristotelianism which he had adopted was finally rejected as an independent and all-embracing closed system in Islam.

Notes

1 T. Burckhardt, 'Nature de la perspective cosmologique', *Études Traditionelles*, vol. 49, 1948, p. 216.
2 T. J. De Boer, *History of Philosophy of Islam*, London, 1933, pp. 131–53.
3 René Guénon, *La Grande triade*, Paris, 1946.
4 *Metaphysica*, in the series *The Works of Aristotle*, ed. by W. D. Ross, Oxford, 1924, bk. IV, I.
5 ibid., bk. I, 2.
6 ibid., bk. IV, 3.
7 *Metaphysica*, bk. V, 8.
8 ibid., bk. IV, 5.
9 ibid., bk. IX, 2.
10 ibid., bk. III, 5.
11 ibid., bk. XII, 6, 7.
12 *De Mundo*, in *The Works of Aristotle*, ed. W. D. Ross, vol. III, ch. 3. Although probably not by Aristotle, the *De Mundo* summarises his teaching on this point and deserves to be quoted.
13 ibid., ch. 3.
14 *De Caelo*, in *The Works of Aristotle*, ed. by W. D. Ross, vol. II, bk. I, 2.
15 ibid., bk. I, 3.
16 ibid., bk. I, 8.
17 ibid., bk. III, 1–3.
18 ibid., bk. II, 7.
19 ibid., bk. II, 14.
20 A. J. Arberry, *Avicenna on Theology*, London, 1951, p. 13.
21 *Najāt*, Paris, 1900, p. 31. The cosmology of Ibn Sīnā, including the question of time, has been thoroughly investigated in S. H. Nasr's *An Introduction to Islamic Cosmological Doctrines*, London, 1978, part III. In the last chapter of this work we have dealt with the esoteric cosmology of Ibn Sīnā's visionary recitals.
22 *Najāt*, p. 31.
23 *al-Ishārāt wa'l-tanbīhāt* (*Book of Directives and Remarks*), Beirut, 1951, p. 109.
24 A. M. Goichon, *La Distinction de l'essence et de l'existence d'après Ibn Sīnā*, Paris, 1937.
25 Arberry, *Avicenna on Theology*, p. 26.
26 Ibn Sīnā, *Le Livre de science*, Paris, 1955, I. p. 177.
27 ibid., p. 177.
28 *Najāt*, p. 75.
29 The need for causality seems to differ between Muslims and modern Westerners, and the arguments regarding faith given in Muslim theology address themselves to an audience whose concept of causality differed from that of post-Renaissance Europeans.

30 W. M. Watt, *The Faith and Practice of al-Ghazali, 'Deliverance from Error . . .'*, III, London, 1953.

31 L. Gardet, 'Quelques aspects de la pensée avicennienne', *La Revue Thomiste*, 1939.

32 For the heliocentric system and its significance, see the translation of *al-Insān al-kāmil* by 'Abd al-Karīm al-Jīlī in R. A. Nicholson, *Studies in Islamic Mysticism*, Cambridge, 1921; also Cambridge, 1967.

33 See Miguel Ásin Palacios. *Islam and the Divine Comedy*, trans. by H. Sunderland, London, 1926.

8

The Meaning of Nature in Various Perspectives in Islam

Usually when 'Islamic thought' is discussed attention is limited to the schools that prevailed during the early centuries, and even then only to the theologians (*mutakallimūn*) and the Peripatetic philosophers (*mashshā'iyyūn*). In this field as in so many others, rarely has the study of Western scholars extended to include Islamic intellectual life in its totality. Therefore, often the views of the Hermeticists, Illuminationists (*ishrāqīs*), Sufis or gnostics (*'urafā'*) and of the followers of the school of Mullā Ṣadrā regarding metaphysical and philosophical questions are neglected. Our intention is to discuss the different conceptions of nature held in various schools and the question of the integration of these conceptions in the total view of Islam. We shall restrict ourselves to the views of the theologians, Peripatetic philosophers, gnostics and the school of Mullā Ṣadrā.[1]

The theologians of the Ash'arite school – who although of much importance have been overemphasised as establishing the criteria of orthodoxy in Islam – represent the 'atomistic' conception of nature. This conception is closely allied to the psychological make-up of the Arabs and is also reflected in their language.[2] In the view of these theologians as well as of many of the Mu'tazilites whom they opposed on many issues, the discontinuity between things is more real than their continuity so that they conceive of nature as a domain of separate, concrete entities between which there is no 'horizontal' nexus. They atomise matter, space and time and break the bond of causality which appears to connect things together. All events in nature become, therefore, independent of each other and there is no relationship between one moment in the life of nature and the next.

This segmented and divided reality finds its cohesion and connection in the Divine Will which creates all things at every moment and is the direct cause of things. That is why this view has been referred to as 'voluntarism'.[3] The Ash'arites in reality deny causality in a general sense only to absorb all secondary causes in the Prime Cause and dissect nature into separate and discontinuous segments in order to have the 'gaps' filled by the Divine Will, which directly orders all things. In this view, one can in fact assert that nature as usually understood melts away in the Divine Will and 'laws of nature' become reduced to 'habits of the human mind'. Yet there is a unicity in nature through the single Will which governs it and there is an interrelation between things in that they are all caused directly by the Prime Cause.

While speaking of the *mutakallimūn*, it must be remembered, however, that some of them, especially among the Mu'tazilites, were interested in the study of nature and saw the wisdom of God in nature. Al-Jāḥiẓ speaks of *kalām al-dīn* and *kalām al-falsafah*, the second encompassing natural philosophy, while al-Jāḥiẓ's teacher al-Naẓẓām was especially attracted to experimentation with and observation of natural phenomena.[4] But this tendency in *kalām* is to be seen mostly in the earlier centuries, while among the Ash'arites the 'melting' of nature into the Divine Will predominates, even if some of them, such as Fakhr al-Dīn Rāzī, were drawn to the study of the natural sciences.

With the Peripatetic philosophers – such as Fārābī, Ibn Sīnā or Khwājah Naṣīr al-Dīn al-Ṭūsī in the East, or their Western counterparts such as Ibn Bājjah and Ibn Rushd – a diametrically opposed view is entertained in that these philosophers emphasise the continuity of things and the importance of the chain of cause and effect in nature. Like the Alexandrian cosmologists and the Greek philosophers whom they follow in many questions, the Muslim Peripatetics consider nature as the principle of change, and physics as the science dealing with things that change. Moreover, for them there is a continuity in nature. Bodies are not composed of atoms but are continuous, since each body is composed of form and matter.[5] Similarly, space and time are continuous and a point in space or a moment of time is no more than an aspect of a continuous reality abstracted by the mind and having no separate objective existence.

The philosophers also uphold a rigorous doctrine of causality and consider every phenomenon in nature to be the effect of a set of causes, which once manifested must of necessity produce the effect in question. Although by no means opposed to the action of Divine Will in nature, they base their view on a chain of cause and effect which connects every event – not directly but through this chain – to the Prime Cause.

Nature in the view of the Peripatetics is a contingent domain, in the sense that it is a contingent being *(mumkin)* and depends completely upon God or the Necessary Being *(wājib al-wujūd)* in order to gain existence. As such, it has no ontological independence but relies completely upon the Necessary Being for its existence. Yet it has a relative reality of its own and one can legitimately speak of nature as separate from the Divine Will. One can consider nature as the domain of change situated ontologically below the intelligible world from which it receives its existence, as well as the manifold forms displayed in it. It is a domain characterised by continuity, since everything in it is made of form and matter, exists in the continuous matrices of time and space and is bound by a continuous chain of cause and effect. Although completely opposed to the view of the theologians on these questions, the philosophers also in turn emphasise the ontological dependence of nature upon the Necessary Being and the unicity of nature affirmed through the chain of cause and effect which relates all things in the Universe together.

In the Sufi or gnostic perspective, the Universe is neither the mere background for human actions as it is with the theologians nor an aspect of reality that must be fitted into a general philosophical system as with the philosophers. Rather, it is a reality comprised of symbols whose understanding marks a stage in the gnostic's journey towards God. In the Sufi perspective, nature is a vast panorama of symbols which must be understood and interiorised before it can be transcended. And the spiritual travail itself enables the Sufi to gain a vision of the inner meaning of nature, so that for him, natural phenomena are transformed from facts to symbols, and nature becomes metaphysically transparent.[6]

In the theoretical aspect of Sufism, or gnosis, there is an elaborate doctrine regarding nature. Moreover, in the writings of some of the Sufis, such as Ibn 'Arabī and 'Abd al-Karīm al-Jīlī, earlier Hermetical ideas concerning nature, as found in the writings of such masters of alchemy as Jābir ibn Ḥayyān, as well as in the so-called pseudo-Empedoclean cosmology of Ibn Masarrah and other traditional cosmologies, are integrated into the Sufi perspective. Ibn 'Arabī considers nature as the feminine, expansive and dynamic aspect of the Creative Act and gives it a significance transcending the formal and created order.[7] He also, like Jābir, distinguishes between two conceptions of nature which became known in the West later as *natura naturans* and *natura naturata*.

The Sufis in general, especially those of the school of Ibn 'Arabī, consider the cosmos as the theophany (*tajallī*) of the Divine Truth (*al-Ḥaqq*) which is renewed at every moment. Creation is annihilated and re-created at each instant, which is also asserted in a sense by the theologians. The whole of the Universe goes through the continuous process of expansion and contraction (*al-ratq wa'l-fatq*). In the first phase of the process, the Divine Breath or the 'Breath of the Compassionate' (*nafas al-raḥmān*), which is the ultimate substance of the cosmos, manifests all things by exteriorising and giving existence (*ex-*

sistere) to the immutable celestial archetypes (*al-a'yān al-thābitah*), while in the second phase all things return to their Divine Origin wherein they are eternally present. The cosmos thus relies absolutely upon its Divine Source without which it would be literally nothing.

The school of Ibn 'Arabī also asserts that reality is not ultimately multiple; rather, it is inwardly or essentially and not in any sense 'materially' or 'externally' unified. This doctrine of *waḥdat al-wujūd*, which can be translated as either the 'transcendent unity of Being' or 'oneness of Being' and which has unfortunately often been misconstrued as pantheism,[8] implies the essential unity of all things with each other and with their Divine Cause.

It is the cardinal doctrine which integrates multiplicity into unity and displays the interrelatedness of all domains of reality. It is through the realisation of this doctrine that the Sufi is able to see in nature a determination (*ta'ayyun*) of a higher state of being and a domain which not only veils but also reveals the Divine essences. In it he finds not only peace and refuge from the turmoil of an artificial world created by man, but also an aid in his path towards realisation. For him nature has its own spiritual methods and metaphysics. In its order and interrelatedness, it displays the principle of Unity (*tawḥīd*) and the subservience of all things to the Divine Principle.

With Mullā Ṣadrā and his school, the views of the gnostics, the illuminationists, theologians and philosophers are integrated into a new intellectual perspective which possesses an originality of its own.[9] As far as the meaning of nature is concerned, the followers of this school combine the doctrine of celestial archetypes and immanent forms in nature and emphasise the continuous 'transubstantial motion' (*al-ḥarakat al-jawhariyyah*) of all things in this world. It is well known that the Muslim Peripatetics – following the Stagirite and his Alexandrian commentators – believed that motion was possible only in the categories of accident and not in the substance of things. Although they believed in a changing nature whose forms were never the same, they did not accept the view that any being could change substantially. Only its accidents could change, or form could be taken away from matter and a new form given to it by the Tenth Intellect, for this reason called the 'Giver of Forms' (*wāhib al-ṣuwar*).

By asserting the unity and principality of existence (*wujūd*) over quiddity (*māhiyyah*), Mullā Ṣadrā makes possible a conception of the cosmos in which there is substantial change, that is to say one in which things change not only in their accidents (*a'rāḍ*) but also in their substance (*jawhar*). Everything is in a process of becoming until it reaches the plenum of its archetypal reality. There is, in fact, a 'vertical evolution' in the cosmos which, however, must not in any way be interpreted in the spirit of a Teilhard de Chardin or of similar types of exponents of evolution.[10] The substantial change and becoming of Mullā Ṣadrā are 'spatial' rather than 'temporal' in the sense that a being seeks to attain a state which is already actualised 'here' and 'now' and not something that will be actualised in some future moment. Mullā Ṣadrā's conception of nature is nevertheless a dynamic one, while at the same time he preserves the archetypal aspect of things, their interrelation and unity.

No attempt has been made here to discuss all the schools in Islam nor penetrate to the full depth the views of any one of them. We have briefly outlined the views of four schools regarding nature, four schools which being formed to suit different mental and psychological needs are of necessity of different outlooks. Yet they are all unified in their final goal, and for this very reason it was possible for Islam – whose role has never been to level out into uniformity, but to integrate – to absorb them into its perspective. This common goal is to demonstrate the Unity of the Divine Principle, the consequent unicity of nature and the interrelatedness of all things, and finally the absolute dependence of nature and the natural order upon the Divine Will. This goal was achieved in various degrees by the schools and perspectives outlined here, and it is this point which makes these perspectives – regardless of whether they originated from the Islamic revelation or elsewhere – conformable to the Islamic point of view.

Notes

1 We have dealt extensively with the conceptions of nature in Islam in our *An Introduction to Islamic Cosmological Doctrines*.

2 So much study has been devoted to Ash'arite theology in the West that there is no need to elaborate those views here. It should be added, however, that Ash'arite 'atomism' is not characteristic of all Islamic theology, and least of all of Shi'ite theology.

3 On the metaphysical and cosmological dilemmas caused by Ash'arite 'voluntarism' see F. Schuon, *Islam and the Perennial Philosophy*, trans. J. P. Hobson, London, 1976, chapter 7, 'Dilemmas within Ash'arite Theology'.

4 See R. Paret, 'An-Naẓẓām als Experimentator', *Der Islam*, vol. 25, 1939, pp. 228–33. In his study of *kalām*, van Vloten considered the term *mutakallim* to stand practically for natural scientist at least in the third/ninth century. See G. van Vloten, *Ein arabischer Naturphilosoph im 9. Jahrhundert*, Stuttgart, 1918.

On the whole question of the relation of *kalām* to the natural sciences and mathematics, see S. Heinen, 'Mutakallimun and Mathematicians', in *Der Islam*, vol. 55, no. 1, 1978, pp. 57–73.

5 Because of the attacks of theologians on the theory of hylomorphism many Muslim philosophical works such as *al-Ishārāt wa'l-tanbīhāt* of Ibn Sīnā begin with a defence of this view and an attack against atomism.

6 See our 'Contemplation and Nature in the Perspective of Sufism', chapter 19 of this volume; and F. Schuon, *Stations of Wisdom*, trans. G. E. H. Palmer, London, 1961, chapter 3, in which this question is discussed within a more universal context.

7 See T. Burckhardt, 'Nature sait surmonter nature', *Études Traditionelles*, vol. 51, 1950, pp. 10 ff. For a general discussion of traditional cosmology see T. Burckhardt, 'Cosmology and Modern Science', *Tomorrow, Summer and Fall*, 1964, vol. 12, no. 3 and 4. Also in J. Needleman (ed.), *The Sword of Gnosis*, Baltimore, 1974, pp. 122–78.

8 For a rejection of the accusation of pantheism against the Sufis see T. Burckhardt, *Introduction to Sufi Doctrine*, trans. by D. M. Matheson, Lahore, 1959, chapter 3; and S. H. Nasr, *Three Muslim Sages*, Cambridge, Harvard University Press, 1964, pp. 104–5.

9 Mullā Ṣudrā, the foremost 'theosopher' (*ḥakīm*) of recent centuries in Islam, is rather unknown in the Occident although he is considered one of the greatest Muslim sages in Persia and his school still exists today. Regarding his life and doctrines, see the introduction of H. Corbin to Mullā Ṣadrā's *Le Livre des pénétrations métaphysiques*, and 'The Life, Doctrines and Significance of Ṣadr al-Dīn Shīrāzī', chapter 14 in this volume.

10 The evolutionist philosophy of Teilhard de Chardin results from a lack of knowledge of metaphysical principles. By ignoring these principles he makes the greater come into being from the lesser and considers intelligence as the outcome of the evolution of blind and unconscious matter.

'The speculations of Teilhard de Chardin provide a striking example of theology that has succumbed to microscopes and telescopes, to machines, a "fall" that would have been unthinkable had there been here the slightest direct intellectual knowledge of the immaterial realities'. F. Schuon, *Understanding Islam*, trans. by D. M. Matheson, London, 1963, p. 32, n. 2.

9

Hermes and Hermetic Writings in the Islamic World

One of the important results of the contact between the Egyptian and Greek traditions in Alexandria was the emergence of a particular school of wisdom known as Hermeticism. This school left a profound mark upon the science and philosophy of both the Western world and Islam. During the Middle Ages, Christians, Jews and Muslims considered Hermes to be the founder of the sciences. Indeed, treatises attributed to him were studied by scholars of nearly every branch of science. During this period such Muslim figures as Jābir ibn Ḥayyān,[1] the Ikhwān al-Ṣafā', al-Jildakī, al-Majrīṭī, Ibn Sīnā and Suhrawardī, and also important Western thinkers such as Raymond Lull, Albert the Great, Roger Bacon and Robert Grosseteste were profoundly influenced by Hermeticism, the Western figures mostly through contact with Islamic sources. Also during the Renaissance in the West added interest in the Hermetic tradition was seen in the writings of such well-known scientists and philosophers as Ficino, Agrippa, Paracelsus and even Bruno.[2] It may further be added that the thinkers of the Renaissance used Hermeticism to dethrone the reigning Aristotelian world view and in certain cases even Christianity itself.[3]

Even in the seventeenth century, despite the change of perspective in the sciences of nature, interest in Hermeticism was sustained by such central figures of modern science as Newton and Boyle and persisted in England well into the eighteenth century. In Germany also, the great gnostic Jacob Böhme adopted Hermetical language. Through him the influence of this school may be discerned in the poetry of Goethe, as well as in the school of *Naturphilosophie*.[4]

Altogether, Hermeticism, with its own particular philosophy of nature and cosmology, has had a profound influence upon both Western civilisation and Islam. Research in the origin and doctrines of this school is therefore one of the means of discovering the nature of a major strand in the fabric of the intellectual life of both Islam and

Christianity. Such research is particularly pertinent to the understanding of a special form of science and philosophy which was cultivated in medieval times, and subsisted alongside the more well-known Aristotelian intellectual disciplines.

The Identity of Hermes

Before dealing with Hermetical writings, it is important to dwell on the identity of Hermes himself, with whom the wisdom of this school is identified. During the Middle Ages Hermes was considered to be the same as the Thoth of the Egyptians, the Ukhnūkh of the Hebrews, Hūshang of the ancient Persians and Idrīs of the Muslims. His followers, in whatever land they lived, considered him a prophet who had brought a Divine message to mankind and who was the founder of the sciences. However, before Egyptian and Greek traditions combined in Alexandria, no school known as Hermeticism had as yet come into being.[5] The personalities of Hermes and Thoth were quite distinct. Hermes was a Greek deity and Thoth one of the most ancient Egyptian deities playing an important role in the Egyptian pantheon.

In Greek mythology Hermes was the son of Zeus and Maia.[6] Later he became identified with the Mercury of the Romans, whose special mark was the caduceus.[7] The first reference to Hermes as the founder of the Hermetic school occurs in the letter of Manetho to Ptolemy II, written before 250 BC, in which Hermes is referred to as the son of Agathedemon.[8] However, before this time Hermes was well known as a mythological figure and his relationship and identity with Mercury were widely accepted. One might say that the belief held by certain Muslim scholars that Idrīs was the Buddha is based on this relationship between Hermes and Mercury and a certain morphological resemblance between these two spiritual figures.[9]

The Egyptian god Thoth or Tahuti was at first a solar deity identified through his particular symbol, the ibis. His main temple was located at Ounou or Khnoumou[10] in middle Egypt. The Greeks called it Hermopolis. Later he became the god of wisdom, medicine, writing and architecture. He appeared always with his feminine counterpart Nehemahut who is universal nature and also *sophia*. Thoth was also the tongue and heart of the god Re, in the sense that he was essentially the Divine Word and possessor of that holy invocation which made union with the Divine possible. Thoth was also the god of measurement and calculation of the motion of the heavens and appears in the story of Osiris as a magician.

In the process of unification of the Egyptian Thoth and the Greek Hermes and the appearance of Hermes as the founder of the school of Hermeticism, Thoth lost that aspect of his being which was purely celestial. It was primarily as a cosmic force that he became combined with the Greek deity. Hermeticism is also concerned more with cosmology and the sciences of nature than with pure metaphysics. That is why the symbol of Alexandrian Hermes was also the caduceus, which represents human alchemy and the psychic forces existing between the physical and intelligible domains.[11] Hermes himself was the link between the corporeal and spiritual worlds and the interpreter of the realities of the higher plane of existence for men living in the world of generation and corruption.[12]

From 250 BC onwards when the name of Hermes first appeared as the founder of a school many treatises and books appeared in his name. Soon he was known as the master of Asclepius and Isis and Osiris. The Hermetic school expanded rapidly and by the first century AD it was one of the most important scientific and philosophical schools in Alexandria. Important works were composed in the name of the Great Hermes[13] which contained the essential teachings of this school. For centuries, these works rivalled Christian texts and even gained religious authority.

Writings Attributed to Hermes

The surviving works attributed to Hermes are:

(a) The *Hermetic Corpus* consisting of *Poimandres* and fourteen sermons of *Asclepius.*

(b) The *Perfect Sermon* or *Asclepius* whose original Greek text is lost but of which a Latin translation survives.

(c) Twenty-seven summaries of Stobaeus, the philosopher who lived at the end of the fifth and the beginning of the sixth century AD.

(d) Twenty-five pieces found in Christian works not found in other works.

(e) Segments found in the writings of Zosimus, Fulgentius, Iamblichus, and the Emperor Julian.[14]

In addition, many treatises on astrology, alchemy, medicine and mathematics attributed to Hermes are to be found, the titles of which are indicated in *Bibliotheca Graeca*.[15] Berthelot lists the alchemical works attributed to Hermes.[16] Steinschneider also lists sixteen works under the name of Hermes translated into Arabic.[17]

After the Middle Ages, the first complete collection and publication of Hermetic writings was executed by the famous Italian philosopher Marsiglio Ficino. It was he who published the collection in Latin in 1471. This work attracted so much attention that it was reprinted twenty-two times during the Renaissance and translated into Italian in 1549. The original Greek text was published for the first time in 1554, to be followed three years later by a French translation. In 1650 the

Hermetic writings were translated from Arabic into English, while a German edition appeared in 1702. In modern times the collection has been edited and published three times, first by Mead in English, as already indicated, second by Scott, also in English,[18] and third by Nock and Festugière in French.[19] The last is the most complete and exact, based on detailed research on the Greek text. Each of these editions contained the basic Hermetic writings.

Hermes in the Islamic World

With the spread of Graeco-Alexandrian sciences and the lore of the Ḥarrānians among the Muslims, the name of Hermes became even more famous. Muslim scholars believed him to be Ukhnūkh or Enoch,[20] who was identified with the prophet Idrīs to whom reference is made in the Quran.[21] During the third Islamic century, the Sabaeans of Ḥarrān,[22] in order to gain an accepted status in Muslim society as a 'people of the book', claimed Hermes as their prophet and the writings attributed to him as their sacred scripture. It is quite likely that they were instrumental in creating the Muslim belief in three Hermes.[23]

In Islamic annals three Hermes were known, each of whom possessed distinct characteristics which might be summarised as follows:

1 The first Hermes or *Hirmis al-harāmisah* whom some considered a descendant of Gayomarth and believed he was the same as Ukhnūkh and Idrīs.[24] He was considered the first man to have gained a knowledge of the heavens and to have instructed people in medicine. He was believed to be the inventor of the alphabet and writing, and the teacher of the wearing of clothing to mankind. It was also he who built houses in which to worship God and foresaw the storm of Noah.

2 The second Hermes or the Babylonian Hermes, who lived in Babylon after the storm and was a master in medicine, philosophy and the science of property of numbers, and who revived science and philosophy after the storm. It was he who rebuilt Babylon after Nimrod and spread science there. He was also the master of Pythagoras.

3 The third or Egyptian Hermes, who was born in Manaf near Fusṭāṭ (which had been the centre of science before Alexandria) and was the student of Agathedemon. He built numerous cities, including Edessa, and made many journeys during which he established traditions for the people of each climate in accordance with their particular conditions. He wrote a book on animals and was a master in the sciences of medicine, philosophy, alchemy and the properties of poisons. The third Hermes devised feasts at moments of the first appearance of the crescent of the moon, the entrance of the sun into each sign of the

Zodiac and auspicious astrological conjunctions. He left certain proverbs on the importance of science, philosophy and justice and was the master of Asclepius.[25]

The Muslim philosophers considered Hermes or Idrīs to be the source of wisdom or *sophia* and the first of philosophers and sages (*ḥukamā'*) (hence the title of Abu'l-Ḥukamā' or 'Father of philosophers'). Moreover, Shakyh al-ishrāq Shihāb al-Dīn Suhrawardī, as well as his student Muḥammad Shahrazūrī, considered him one of the 'theosophers' (*muta'allihūn*).[26] Shahrazūrī is in fact one of the first to call Hermes the 'Father of philosophers'.[27] For Suhrawardī in his *Muṭāraḥāt*, Hermes was the origin of a wisdom or *sophia* which passed on the one hand through Asclepius, Pythagoras and Plato to the Greeks and on the other through Gayomarth, Farīdūn and Kay Khusraw to the Persians and finally became united during the Islamic period in the teachings of the Illuminationist school.[28]

Likewise, Ṣadr al-Dīn Shīrāzī, the greatest of the later Muslim sages, writes: 'Know that wisdom (*ḥikmah*) began originally with Adam and his progeny Seth and Hermes, i.e. Idrīs, and Noah because the world is never deprived of a person upon whom the science of Unity and eschatology rests. And it is the greatest Hermes who propagated it (*ḥikmah*) throughout the regions of the world and different countries and manifested it and made it emanate upon the "true worshippers". He is the "Father of philosophers (*Abu'l-ḥukamā'*) and the master of those who are the masters of the sciences".[29]'

References to Hermes in Islamic sources are numerous, and one cannot cite all of them in this study. From what has been mentioned, however, it is clear that for Muslims Hermes was the founder of philosophy and the sciences, especially astronomy and astrology, alchemy and medicine, and many important inventions were attributed to him. Also from the determination of his age as 365 years one can see that he was essentially a solar hero; this is borne out by many stories and myths connected with his name. It is of particular interest to note that, according to traditional sources, Hermes did not die but was taken from the world alive to heaven, and he is now subsisting alive in the celestial world like Christ whose solar nature is obvious from all aspects of his manifestation in this world.

Hermetic Writings in Arabic and Persian

The most important source of knowledge of Hermetic writings in Arabic is the *al-Fihrist* of Ibn al-Nadīm. In this work, twenty-two treatises of Hermes are named, thirteen on alchemy, four on theurgy (*ṭalismāt*) and five on astrology.[30] Of these works only a few remain intact; of the rest, but a name remains. According to the research of Massignon,[31] the following Arabic translations of Hermes survive:

Kitāb qarāṭīṣ al-ḥakīm, Kitāb al-ḥabīb, Kitāb tankalūsh attributed to Ibn Waḥshiyyah, which Nallino believed to have been based on a Pahlavi text,[32] and *Kitāb al-masmūmāt Shānāq*.[33]

In addition to these works, there are several other Arabic texts attributed to Hermes. Very likely these contain some Greek material. The most important of these is the *Mu'āḍilat al-nafs* or *Zajr al-nafs* (*De Castigatione animae*) which Afḍal al-Dīn Kāshānī translated into Persian as *Yanbū 'al-ḥayāt*,[34] the well-known *Sirr al-khalīqah* attributed to Bālīnūs, and *Qabas al-qābis fī tadbīr Hirmis al-Harāmis*.[35] Moreover, there are several sayings attributed to Hermes found in Ibn al-Qifṭī, Shahristānī, and several occult works such as *Kitāb al-astimākhīs*, *Kitāb al-falakiyyat al-kubrā* and the 'Commentary of Hermes' upon *Kitāb al-'ilm al-makhzūn fī asrār al-'ālam al-maktūm*.

Also in the list of Arabic works of Hermes, mention should be made of the *Ṣaḥā'if* or *Codices* of Idrīs in the *Ṣaḥīfah* (*Codex*) cited in Majlisī's *Biḥār al-anwār*.[36] According to Ibn al-Nadīm (p. 22), thirty codices were revealed to Hermes and this was the third revelation to mankind. Today, two *Books of Enoch* have survived: the *Secret Book of Enoch*, whose original was Greek and is known as the *Sicilian Book of Enoch*, and the other the *Book of Enoch*, which was originally in Aramaic or Hebrew and is known as the *Ethiopian Book of Enoch*. The *Codex* cited in *Biḥār al-anwār*, however, cannot be identified with either of these texts and is an independent work.[37]

In discussing Hermetic writings in Arabic, one cannot avoid mentioning also writers in the Muslim world whose works are wholly or partly based on Hermetic sources. One of the most significant of these works is the already cited *Sirr al-khalīqah*, which was composed during the caliphate of al-Ma'mūn.[38] It is attributed to Apollonius of Tyana and is said to be based on the *Kitāb 'ilal al-ashyā'* of Hermes. According to the author, the manuscript of this work was found in a cave beneath the statue of Hermes in Tyana. It was in the same place that an emerald tablet was found upon which the famous alchemical text, the *Tabula Smaragdina*, was inscribed.[39]

The Jābirian corpus should also be mentioned in connection with Hermetic writings. Many of its treatises such as *Kitāb al-ḥajar* and *Kitāb al-tadwīr* refer to Hermes, while others display a definite Hermetic colour.[40] Also, in the *Turba Philosophorum* Hermes is cited as one of the original founders of alchemy. This celebrated alchemical text was revealed in a recent study by Plessner to have been written by Ibn Umayl, one of the students of Jābir's school. The works of Ibn Waḥshiyyah, such as *al-Falāḥat al-nabaṭiyyah*, *al-Tankalūsh*, and *Maṭāli 'al-anwār*, which show Babylonian, Sabaean, Indian and neo-Platonic influences, are also closely connected with Hermetic writings and display many similarities to them.

One might safely say that all those Muslim authors who were inclined towards a study of alchemy, astrology and the other occult sciences were influenced to some degree by the Hermetic school. In alchemical writings, the *Ghāyat al-ḥakīm*[41] is especially pertinent from this point of view. Among astrological works, the writings of Abū Ma'shar al-Balkhī and 'Abd al-Jalīl al-Sijzī display strong Hermetic tendencies. In these fields, however, the influence of Hermeticism is to be seen everywhere, so that much written on these subjects naturally falls into the category of Hermetic works.

Hermetic Science and Philosophy and its Influence upon Muslim Thinkers

As already mentioned, Hermeticism was propagated by the Sabaeans who made known to the Islamic world the writings that were attributed to Hermes. Many groups of Shi'ite origin, such as the Nuṣayrīs and Druses, held Hermeticism in high esteem. Early Shi'ism in general was more sympathetic to its teachings than to the more prevalent Aristotelian school and even accepted some of its tenets.[42] It was after the religious edict (*fatwā*) of al-Istakhrī against the Sabaeans in 321/933 that they gradually embraced Islam. And upon the death of Ḥakīm ibn 'Īsā ibn Marwān they were left without a religious leader and guide.

Although Hermetic influence diminished officially after this period, its presence persisted through astrology, alchemy and Hippocratic medicine, all of which had preserved their close connection with the Hermetic world view. Thus many followers of Hermeticism are found among the students and propagators of these disciplines. For example, belief that there is no distinction between the Divine Qualities and Names and His Essence, a characteristic of Hermetic teachings, is seen in the pseudo-Empedoclean corpus, and, according to Ibn al-Qifṭī, it was influential in the doctrines of al-'Allāf, the famous Mu'tazilite theologian, and Ibn Masarrah, the Andalusian ascetic and sage.[43] It was through Dhu'l-Nūn al-Miṣrī, a Sufi and alchemist, that Hermetic ideas, such as the incapability of Aristotelian syllogism to reach metaphysical and gnostic truths, entered into Sufism and left their mark on such masters as Abū Sa'īd al-Kharrāz and al-Ḥallāj.

Certain Hermetic cosmological doctrines, as for example the basic doctrine of the correspondence between the microcosm and macrocosm, are seen in many Sufi cosmological works, especially those of Ibn 'Arabī, such as the ***Fuṣūṣ al-ḥikam*** and certain chapters of ***al-Futūḥāt al-makkiyyah***. The basis of this doctrine, however, is universal and is clearly found in the Quran and in certain ***ḥadīths*** as well as in the sayings of 'Alī.[44]

Altogether, the Hermetical cosmological doctrines were mainly integrated into Sufi gnosis by Ibn 'Arabī. This fact may be seen not only in his writings but also in the writings of most of the prominent representatives of this school, such as Ṣadr al-Dīn al-Qunyawī, 'Abd al-Karīm al-Jīlī, Ibn Turkah Iṣfahānī and Ibn Abī Jumhūr. Many of these masters of Islamic gnosis employed symbols derived from Hermetic sciences.[45] In philosophy too, although Hermeticism as such began to decline after the fourth/tenth century, it was integrated into the writings of many of the Ismā'īlī philosophers such as Ḥamīd al-Dīn Kirmānī and during the sixth/twelfth century into the Illuminationist school by Suhrawardī. Its influence is also evident in the writings of later *ishrāqīs* and among other sympathisers of this school such as Quṭb al-Dīn Shīrazī, Jalāl al-Dīn Dawānī and Ṣadr al-Dīn Shīrāzī.[46]

In theodicy, Hermeticism held the absolute transcendence of the Deity and the impossibility of human reason to reach knowledge of It through its own powers. The only path to the knowledge of the Divine is self-purification, which finally leads to illumination of the soul and the spiritual vision of the Truth. This view is similar to that of Sufism and for this reason Islamic gnosis was attracted to certain aspects of Hermeticism which it integrated into its world view.

Another aspect of Hermeticism, which was influential in Islamic philosophy especially in the Illuminationist school and can be seen in many theosophical works after the sixth/twelfth century, is the belief in a heavenly guide who aids man in his quest for truth and is the reality with whom man finally unites in his spiritual quest. The name of this guide, who is the same as the Ḥayy ibn Yaqẓān of Ibn Sīnā[47] and the 'celestial witness' (*al-shāhid fi'l-samā'*) of some of the Sufis of the seventh/thirteenth century, is 'Perfect Nature'. As Suhrawardī writes in his *al-Muṭāraḥāt*: 'Hermes said I met a spiritual being who conveyed to me the science of things. I asked him who art thou? He said I am thy Perfect Nature.'[48] Also in his *al-Wāridāt wa'l-taqdīsāt*, Suhrawardī addresses a beautiful prayer to 'Perfect Nature' in the name of Hermes, in which 'Perfect Nature' is called both the celestial father and the spiritual son.

Other Muslim thinkers have also written of the Hermetic 'Perfect Nature', such as the Andalusian sage Ibn Sab'īn[49] who was deeply influenced by Hermeticism. Ṣadr al-Dīn Shīrāzī, besides mentioning Hermes often in his works, speaks of 'Perfect Nature' in nearly the same terms as Suhrawardī.[50]

The repetition of this theme among Muslim sages brings up the question of its exact meaning. The most detailed discussion of 'Perfect Nature' in Muslim sources is in the *Ghāyat al-ḥakīm* (*Picatrix*), which is one of the best known alchemical works in Arabic. From an examination of this work and segments of other sources bearing on this subject, it seems that the Hermetic 'Perfect Nature' is the celestial counterpart or *alter ego* of each human soul which remains in heaven after the fall of the soul into the human body. For this reason, the soul is always in search of its other half in order to complete and unify its own being.

Belief in the existence of the human soul in the spiritual world before its entrance into the body and its separation from its celestial half after being born in this world was well known in Zoroastrianism, as was the idea that the celestial half of the soul is its guardian angel on earth. The heavenly counterpart of the human soul was called *Daena*, who in the *Mazdyasnā* appears as a beautiful young maiden.[51] The striking resemblance between the figure of *Daena* and the Hermetic 'Perfect Nature' is one more indication of a link between Hermeticism and the wisdom of ancient Persia.

In the *Ghāyat al-ḥakīm* 'Perfect Nature' is considered a secret hidden in the bosom of philosophy, revealed only to those who reach the highest stations of wisdom. It is the source of power through which man grows in his knowledge, science and philosophy.[52] In this work, Hermes also has a vision of a spiritual reality whose identity he seeks. The reply is that he is his 'Perfect Nature'. The author of *Ghāyat al-ḥakīm* writes further that it is the 'Perfect Nature' which guides man in this life and helps him overcome his difficulties; in the same way that Aristotle foretold the victory of Alexander in Persia, because of the domination of his 'Perfect Nature'.[53]

In a prayer of much beauty, Hermes calls upon 'Perfect Nature' as the luminous source of nature and considers the four physical natures (heat, cold, dryness and humidity) as four hypostases of 'Perfect Nature' which are thus also spiritual entities and sources of knowledge.[54] 'Perfect Nature' is man's spiritual reality which guides his inner life. For this reason, Hippocrates called it the 'Sun of the Philosopher' (*Shams al-ḥakīm*) and the key to science and philosophy.[55] For this reason also, 'Perfect Nature' is the real teacher of the soul in guiding it from childhood until its full realisation of knowledge and science in the age of maturity.

In the seventh chapter of *Ghāyat al-ḥakīm* on the Sabaeans, there is a prayer to Hermes in which all the characteristics of 'Perfect Nature' are bestowed upon Hermes himself, and he is addressed by various names thus: 'We call thee by all thy names in Arabic oh 'Uṭārid, in Persian oh Tīr, in Roman oh Hārūs, in Greek oh Hermes, and in Indian oh Būdd.'[56] Thus, in reality Hermes and 'Perfect Nature' are one and the same, so that Hermes could address 'Perfect Nature' as his celestial father and spiritual son. The Hermes who earlier sought his celestial half finally became the object of the spiritual quest and appeared as the master and guide for those who seek to attain knowledge.

The influence of Hermeticism was by no means limited to philosophy and the philosophy of nature. It is to be seen in many branches of the sciences of nature. In the physical sciences, the Hermetic school believed in the unity of the world and opposed the Aristotelian division of the world into the sublunar and celestial. It had a conception of nature based on analogy and correspondence between various orders of being, between elements, colours, forms, qualities, sounds, and internal and external senses. The harmony and concordance of these cosmic and natural qualities are described in the *Rasā'il* of the Ikhwān al-Ṣafā' and astrologically in such works as *al-Tafhīm* of Bīrūnī. Belief in a relation between the events of this world and the movement of the planets – again a concordance between two levels of existence – and cycles which govern cosmic phenomena is also characteristic of this school. The Hermeticists emphasised individual and concrete causes in physics and shunned the Aristotelian quest for the general one. They sought a particular cause for each particular effect and chose an 'experimental' and concrete method much closer to that of the Stoics than the Aristotelians. This difference of approach is also seen in the two grammatical schools of Kufa and Basra. The Kufans from the beginning followed the logical methods of the school of Pergamon, which was mostly Stoic, while the Basra group followed the syllogistic methods of the Alexandrian Peripatetics.

Similarly, Hermetic alchemy always preserved a close contact with the Hippocratic school of medicine, which also sought the immediate causes of illness. This bond continued into the Islamic period and led to the development of an experimental method which, once shorn of its metaphysical and mystical matrix, became the basic method of science. This tendency to develop an experimental method in the sciences of nature during the Islamic period is seen particularly in the case of Muḥammad ibn Zakariyyā' al-Rāzī, who employed this method both in medicine and in alchemy, which he tore away from its symbolic content.[57]

The Hermetic school cultivated an Illuminationist school in philosophy and considered inner purification the means of attaining the truth, in opposition to the rationalistic tendencies of the Peripatetics. In the sciences of nature, this school distrusted the syllogistic method and sought to rely on a knowledge of concrete causes which could be observed and experienced. This tendency was so strong that, although Hermeticism is more 'mystical' and less rationalistic than Aristotelianism, it contributed in the West to the rise of the experimental method during the Renaissance and the seventeenth century, once it was separated from its symbolic and metaphysical content. In fact, it was most often in its name that opponents of the medieval Christian synthesis sought to attack and destroy Aristotelianism.[58]

In the Muslim world Hermeticism must be considered one of the most important factors in the construction of the Islamic view of the

Universe. Its mark on both Islamic philosophy and science was a permanent one; it even entered into religious and metaphysical speculation as well as into Arabic and Persian poetry and prose. The figure of Hermes came to be regarded as that of the first teacher in science and philosophy, and through him it became possible for Muslims to integrate Greek science and philosophy into their world view without feeling that they were going anyway outside the Abrahamic prophetic tradition. For this as well as for its own intrinsic value, the Hermetic corpus in Islam deserves to be seriously studied. Such a study will provide some of the essential aspects of Islamic science, philosophy and cosmological doctrines and make known one of the means through which Muslims were able to create a unified world which embraced not only the Islamic principle of Unity but also the sciences inherited from antiquity.

Notes

1 Although some orientalists doubt the existence of Jābir, there is no reason to deny that such a figure existed, even though some writings of the Jābirian corpus were written later by Ismā'īlī authors. F. Sezgin has offered extensive new evidence concerning Jābir. See his *Geschichte des arabischen Schrifttums*, Band IV, Leiden, 1971, pp. 132–269.

2 Bruno, long considered a sort of 'free-thinker', has been shown to be most profoundly influenced by certain Hermetic doctrines. See F. Yates, *Giordano Bruno and the Hermetic Tradition*, Chicago, 1964.

3 See M. Eliade, 'The Quest for the "Origins of Religion" ', *History of Religions*, vol. 4, No. 1, Summer 1964, pp. 154–69. During the Middle Ages the doctrines of Hermeticism, being esoteric, were rarely divulged. However, they manifested themselves externally in architecture, city planning and literature. During the Renaissance, there was a certain desecration of these 'Lesser Mysteries' which made a knowledge of them more outwardly disseminated. The rapport of the Rosicrucians and Freemasonry with Hermeticism is well known. See O. Wirth, *Le Symbolisme hermétique dans ses rapports avec l'alchimie et la Franc-Maçonnerie*, Paris, 1910.

4 This school, which emerged in Germany as a reaction against the mechanistic universe of classical physics, shows definite traces of the Hermetic philosophy of nature. Its many followers included several well-known scientists, among them Ostwald.

5 'Il faut noter tout d'abord que ce mot "hermétisme" indique qu'il s'agit d'une tradition d'origine égyptienne, revêtue par la suite d'une forme hellénisée, sans doute à l'époque alexandrine, et transmise sous cette forme, au moyen âge, à la fois au monde islamique et au monde chrétien, et ajoutons-nous, au second en grande partie par l'intermédiaire du premier.' R. Guénon, *Aperçus sur l'initiation*, Paris, 1953, p. 259.

6 Regarding the mythological personality of Hermes, see the article on Hermes in *Hastings' Encyclopaedia of Religion and Ethics*; 'Hermes Trismegistos', by W. Kroll in *Paulys Real-Encyclopädie*; and R. Guénon, 'Hermès', *Le Voile d'Isis*, 1932, pp. 193–202, English translation in *Studies in Comparative Religion*, Spring 1967, pp. 79–83.

7 The earliest statues of Hermes display this special mark of the deity.

8 See the introduction of G. R. S. Mead to *Thrice-Greatest Hermes*, vol. I, London, 1949, p. 105.

9 Idrīs and the Buddha have been considered one because of certain remarkable resemblances. In India, Mercury was called Buddha, meaning wisdom, and the name Buddha or Shakya-Muni is derived from the same root; also according to Buddhist sources, he was illuminated by the light of Mercury. Moreover, there is a resemblance between the name of the mother of Idrīs and the Buddha, between Maia and Maya-Devi, the name of the Buddha's mother.

Buddha also corresponds to the Odin of the Scandinavians, whom Romans considered the same as Mercury. In English, the day of Mercury (Mercredi in French) is thus called Wednesday (the day of Wotan or Odin) as derived from the Germanic tradition. A similar figure is to be found in the Quetzalcoatl of the Aztecs, whose symbol, consisting of wings and snakes, resembles that of Hermes.

Altogether, one can find in various traditions figures resembling Hermes which bear profound similarities to each other. This does not mean that they are identical. For example, there are essential differences between the Buddha and Hermes in that the former died, while the latter was taken to heaven alive. See R. Guénon, 'Hermès'.

'Idris, who is mentioned in the Thora as Henokh, they call Hermes, whilst according to others Hermes is identical with Budhasaf'. Bīrūnī, *Chronology of Ancient Nations*, translated by C. E. Sachau, London, 1879, p. 188.

10 Concerning Thoth and his importance among the Egyptians, see G. Nagel, 'Le Dieu Thoth d'après les textes égyptiens,' *Eranos-Jahrbuch*, 1942, pp. 104–9; A. Rusch, 'Thoth', in *Paulys Real-Encyclopädie*; E. A. Wallis Budge, *Gods of the Egyptians*, London, 1904; and Mead, *Thrice-Greatest Hermes*.

11 Hermetic sciences, therefore, bear a close resemblance to the Hatha Yoga of the Hindus. See Guénon, 'Hermès', pp. 193 ff.

12 Many European languages still preserve this meaning in the word hermeneutic, which means precisely the interpretation of the inner meaning of a text.

13 This title was first given by Muslims and later adopted by Hebrew and Latin authors after translations were made from the Arabic.

14 See the introduction of Mead to *Thrice-Greatest Hermes*.

15 *Bibliotheca Graeca*, Leipzig, 1971, vol. I, lib. i, cap. vii.

16 M. P. E. Berthelot, *Collection des anciens alchimistes grecs*, Paris, 1888; *La Chimie au moyen-âge*, Paris, 1893.

17 M. Steinschneider, *Die arabischen Übersetzungen aus dem Griechischen*, Leipzig, 1897, Zweiter Abschnitt, Mathematik, p. 187–94.

18 W. Scott, *Hermetica*, 4 vols., Oxford, 1924–36.

19 A. J. Festugière et A. D. Nock, *La Révélation d'Hermès Trismégiste*, 4 vols, Paris, 1949–54.

20 Nöldeke derives this name from Andreas (*Zeitschrift für Assyriologie*, xvii, 84) but this seems most unlikely and has been rejected by the majority of later authorities.

21 'And make mention in the Scripture of Idrīs. Lo! he was a saint, a Prophet' (Quran xix: 56 – Pickthall translation). 'And (mention) Ishmael, and Idrīs, and Dhu'l-Kifl. All were of the steadfast' (Quran, xii; 85).

22 One should not confuse the Sabaeans of Ḥarrān with the true Sabaeans. The latter were likely disciples of John the Baptist, and emigrated from the vicinity of the Jordan River to Mesopotamia where some are still found. The Ḥarrānians had a religious and philosophical view comprised of Greek, Chaldean, Gnostic and other elements, differing greatly from the views of the real Sabaeans or Mandaeans. See S. H. Taqizadeh, 'Sābi'īn', *Yaghmā*, year 12, 1338, pp. 97–105; E. Drower, *The Mandaeans of Iran and Iraq*, Oxford, 1937; D. Chwolsohn, *Die Ssabier und der Ssabismus*, St. Petersburg, 1856; J. Pedersen, 'The Sabians', *Volume of Oriental Studies presented to E. G. Browne*, Cambridge, 1922, pp. 383–91.

23 Concerning the close relation between the Sabaeans of Ḥarrān and Hermetic writings in whose spread they played an important role, see the above-mentioned classical work of Chwolsohn: also L. Massignon, 'Inventaire de la littérature hermétique arabe', in *La Révélation d'Hermès Trismégiste*, vol. I, appendix III: A. E. Affifi, 'The Influence of Hermetic Literature on Moslem Thought', *Bull. London School of Oriental and African Studies*, 1951, vol. xiii, part 4, pp. 840–55; E. Blochet, 'Études sur le gnosticisme musulman', *Rivista degli studi orientali*, 4, 1911-12, pp. 47–79 and 267–300.

As Massignon has cited in his above-mentioned article, the Sabaeans of Ḥarrān were Hermeticists in the sense that they considered Hermes one of their prophets and in fact the originator of their rites and sought to disseminate his esoteric philosophy. Thābit ibn Qurrah, one of the most famous scientists of Ḥarrān, translated the *Kitāb al-nawāmīs* of Hermes from Syriac into Arabic. A manuscript in the British Museum (add. 7475) of Sinān ibn Thābit contains a translation from the Hermetic corpus into Arabic. Aḥmad ibn Ṭayyib al-Sarakhsī, the famous student of al-Kindī, considered Hermes the founder of the Sabaean religion, and wrote that his master, al-Kindī, was covered with joy when he read the 'Sermon of Hermes' to his son.

Shams al-Dīn al-Dimashqī in his *Nukhbat al-dahr* considers *Ṣābi'īn* to be derived from *Ṣābī*, which according to him, was the name of the son of Hermes. See Chwolsohn, op. cit., vol. II, pp. 409–10.

24 'It is he whom the Ḥarrānians mention as prophet and the Persians as one whose ancestor was Gayomarth who is Adam. The Hebrews mention that he was before the storm and was Ukhnūkh which in Arabic is Idrīs.' Ibn Abī Uṣaybi'ah, '*Uyūn al-anbā*', Cairo, 1299; p. 16.

Bīrūnī indicates indirectly that Hermes lived about 3300 BC See the *Chronology of Ancient Nations*, p. 342.

25 Concerning the three Hermes among Muslims, see '*Uyūn al-anbā*' pp. 16–17; Ḍ. Durrī, *Kanz al-ḥikmah*, the Persian translation of Shahrazūrī's *Nuzhat al-arwāḥ wa rawḍat al-afrāḥ*, Tehran, 1316, pp. 61 ff.; Ibn al-Nadīm, *Fihrist*, Leipzig, 1871–72, p. 267 and p. 312–13; *Ta'rīkh al-ya'qūbī*, Beirut, 1379, vol. I, p. 11; al-Mas'ūdī, *Murūj al-dhahab*, Cairo, 1301, p. 48; Ibn al-Athīr, *Ta'rīkh al-kāmil*, Cairo, 1301, pp. 22–3; Tha'ālibī, *Qiṣaṣ al-anbiyā'*, Leiden, 1922, p. 81; Shahristānī, *al-Milal wa'l-nihal*, Cairo, 1367, vol. II, pp. 202–6; Diyārbakrī, *Ta'rīkh al-khamīs*, Cairo, 1283, p. 66; Ibn al-Qifṭī, *Ta'rīkh al-ḥukamā'*, Cairo, 1326, pp. 3–6; *Kitāb al-bad' wa'l-ta'rīkh* attributed to Abū Zayd al-Balkhī, Paris, 1906, vol. III, pp. 115 ff.; Majlisī, *Biḥār al-anwār*, Tehran, 1315, vol. XIX, part 2, pp. 317–23; Ibn Juljul, *Tabaqāt al-aṭibbā'*, Cairo, 1955, pp. 5–10.

In these and many other sources, accounts of the three Hermes are given which are often repetitious, most of them insisting on their role in propagating the sciences and the teaching of many sedentary arts.

26 See Suhrawardī, *Opera Metaphysica et mystica*, ed. by H. Corbin, vol. II, Tehran, 1977, p. 5 f.

27 ibid., p. 10.

28 See *Opera Metaphysica et mystica*, vol. I, Tehran, 1976, pp. 502–3 and p. xlii of Corbin's introduction; also S. H. Nasr, *Three Muslim Sages*, p. 62 and S. H. Nasr, 'Suhrawardī', in *A History of Muslim Philosophy*, ed. by M. M. Sharif, vol. I, Wiesbaden, 1963, p. 376.

29 *Risālah fi'l-ḥudūth*, in *Rasā'il* of Ṣadr al-Dīn Shīrāzī, Tehran, 1302, p. 67.

30 The names of these works may be found in the *Fihrist*. Names are omitted here because their transliteration into Latin letters involves cumbersome reading and adds little of value. These works have been cited in the *Fihrist*, pp. 267, 312, 353, and the article of Massignon already mentioned. See also J. Ruska, *Tabula Smaragdina*, Heidelberg, 1926, pp. 4 ff.

In other works, such as *Ṭabaqāt al-umam* of Qāḍī Ṣā'id al-Andalūsī, *Ta'rīkh al-ḥukamā'* of Ibn al-Qifṭī, the *Muqaddimah* of Ibn Khaldūn, and *Kashf al-ẓunūn* of Ḥājjī Khalīfah, other works by Hermes are cited not found in the *Fihrist*. See Massignon, op. cit., pp. 392–3.

31 Massignon, op. cit., p. 393.

32 *Oriental Studies presented to E. G. Browne*, p. 361.

Ruska believed that Hermeticism entered into Sassanid Persia before Islam, as we can observe in astrological and pharmacological texts. (*Tabula Smaragdina*, p. 168). Massignon goes a step further in asserting that Hermeticism entered Persia after the Achaemenids conquered Egypt. There is little doubt that Hermeticism was known to the Persians before the rise of Islam. Indeed, certain schools such as the Manichaeans displayed definite interest in Hermetic cosmology and natural philosophy.

33 For what exists in Arabic translations of Hermetic writings, see Berthelot, *La Chimie au moyen-âge*, III; Ruska, *Tabula Smaragdina*; B. Strauss, *Das Giftbuch des Shanāq*, Berlin, 1934; and other references by Massignon in his above-mentioned article.

M. Plessner in 'Hermes Trismegistus and Arab Science', *Studia Islamica*, vol. 2, 1954, p. 48, considers Massignon's list incomplete and adds to it the 'Sayings of Hermes' in *Ādāb al-falāsifah* of Ḥunayn ibn Isḥāq (Apollonius of Tyana), *Kitāb sirr al-asrār* of 'Uṭārid al-Bābilī, certain parts of which are preserved in the *Ghāyat al-ḥakīm* attributed to al-Majrīṭī.

34 The Arabic text of this treatise was first published by P. Philémon, Beirut, 1903, and later by A. Badawi in *al-Aflāṭūniyyāt al-muḥdathah 'ind al-'arab*, Cairo, 1955, pp. 51—116.

For the Persian translation see Afḍal al-Dīn Kāshānī, *Muṣannafāt*, ed. by M. Minovi and Y. Mahdavi, vol. I, Tehran, 1952, pp. 331–85.

35 This treatise has been analysed and translated into German by A. Siggel, 'Das Sendschreiben das Licht über das Verfahren des Hermes der Hermesse dem, der es begehrt', *Der Islam*, vol. 24, 1937, pp. 287–306.

36 *Biḥār al-anwār*, vol. xix, part 2, pp. 317–23.

37 Also noteworthy is the recent archaeological discovery in Egypt in which five Hermetic treatises were found in Coptic, four of them new; the fifth was the well-known Asclepius, previously known only in Latin. See Plessner, op. cit., p. 50.

38 P. Kraus believed that Muḥammad ibn Zakariyyā' Rāzī knew the author.

39 This most important of Hermetical alchemical works appears at the end of *Sirr al-khalīqah*. See P. Kraus, *Jābir ibn Ḥayyān*, vol. II, Cairo, 1942, p. 272, and the already mentioned work of Ruska. The *Tabula Smaragdina* appears also at the end of certain other works such as *Kitāb inkishāf al-sirr al-maktūm min 'ilm al-kāf*.

The *Sirr al-khalīqah* is important in the Hermetical school in Islam, as it left an influence on Jābir and his followers. Its importance was discovered by Sylvestre de Sacy over a century ago. He translated it into French in *Notes et extraits des manuscrits*, tome iv, Paris, 1798. It is an independent work and not translated from the Greek, although it made use of the *Poimandres*.

40 See Kraus, op. cit., p. 44. See also the extensive study devoted to Jābir in F. Sezgin, op. cit.

41 This work, which is known in the West as *Picatrix* (from Hippocrates), is one of the essential texts of Western alchemy. See H. Ritter, *Das Ziel des Weisen*, Berlin, 1933.

For the names of other Muslim alchemists influenced by Hermeticism, see Kraus, op. cit., vol. I, pp. 188–202.

42 See Massignon, op. cit., p. 385.

43 See M. Ásin Palacios, *Abenmasarra y su escuela*, Madrid, 1914.

44 This idea has been beautifully expressed in many Arabic and Persian poems, such as

the *Gulshan-i rāz* and *Mathnawī*, as well as in the *Diwān* of Ḥaḍrat 'Alī (1310, p. 48). Rūmī writes in his *Mathnawī*: 'Thus thou art in form the microcosm but in meaning thou art the macrocosm.'

The concordance between certain Hermetic teachings and those of the Shi'ite Imāms is of great significance for the later integration of this sapiential knowledge into Islam. An early Shi'ite author like Shamalghānī al-Kūfī officially defended Hermeticism.

45 See T. Burckhardt, *La Clé de l'astrologie musulmane d'après Mohyiddin ibn Arabi*, Paris, 1950; new edition, Paris, 1976.

46 Ibn Waḥshiyyah in his *Falāḥat al-nabaṭiyyah* writes that the Illuminationists (*ishrāqīs*) were the descendants of the sister of Hermes. See his *Ancient Alphabet and Hierographic Characters*, London, 1806, p. 100 of the Arabic text; and H. Corbin, *Les Motifs zoroastriens dans la philosophie de Sohrawardi*, Tehran, 1946, p. 18.

47 There is no doubt that the three treatises of Ibn Sīnā, *Ḥayy ibn Yaqẓān*, *Salāmān wa Absāl* and *Risālat al-ṭayr*, have a Hermetic aspect and *Salāmān wa Absāl* was an alchemical treatise translated by Ḥunayn into Arabic, even though S. Pines has recently proposed a Buddhist origin for it. *Ḥayy ibn Yaqẓān* bears much resemblance to the first chapter of *Poimandres*. The guide of this treatise is like Hermes, the soul which has been freed from the prison of the corporeal world is like Thoth, and the 'eternal king' is like the 'Pure good' of Hermeticism.

See A. E. Affifi, 'The Influence of Hermetic Literature . . .'. Concerning the three treatises of Ibn Sīnā, see H. Corbin, *Avicenna and the Visionary Recital*, translated by W. Trask; and S. H. Nasr, *An Introduction to Islamic Cosmological Doctrines*, chapter 14.

48 Suhrawardī, *Opera* . . . , vol. I, p. 466; also Corbin, *Les motifs zoroastriens* . . . , pp. 56–7.

Corbin has devoted an extensive study to the Hermetic 'Perfect Nature' and its relation to Islamic philosophy. See his 'Le récit d'initiation et l'hermétisme en Iran', *Eranos-Jahrbuch*, 1959, pp. 155 ff.; also his 'L'Homme de lumière dans le soufisme iranien', in *Ombre et Lumière, Volume de l'Académie Septentrionale*, Paris, 1960; also Paris, 1971.

49 Ibn Sab'īn is one of the most important Hermetic philosophers in Islam and his writings are particularly pertinent for an understanding of Hermeticism in the Islamic world.

See A. E. Affifi, op. cit., also A. Badawi, 'Kitāb al-iḥāṭah li Abī Muḥammad 'Abd al-Isḥāq ibn Sab'īn . . .', *Ṣaḥīfah ma'had al-dirāsāt al-islāmiyyah*, vol. 6, No. 1–2, pp. 11–34: L. Massignon, 'Ibn Sab'īn et la critique psychologique dans l'histoire de la philosophie musulmane', *Memorial Henri Basset*, Paris, 1928, II, pp. 124 ff.; and E. Lator, S. I., 'Ibn Sab'īn de Murcia y su 'Budd al-'ārif', *Al-Andalus*, vol. IX, 1944, pp. 371, 417.

50 *Al-Shawāhid al-rubūbiyyah*, Tehran, p. 109.

51 Chinese Manichaean texts, as well as those in Coptic, also point to the presence of such a figure in Manichaeism known as Manuhmēd or Manvahmēd.

See Corbin, 'Le récit visionnaire . . .', p. 171; G. Widengren, *The Great Vohu Manah and the Apostle of God*, Uppsala, 1945, p. 18.

52 *Ghāyat al-ḥakīm*, p. 187.

53 ibid., p. 191.

54 ibid., pp. 189–90.

55 ibid., p. 184.

56 ibid., p. 232.

57 This question is more fully discussed in the following chapter on Rāzī and Jābir.

58 Many Renaissance scholars and philosophers such as Ficino and Agrippa used Hermeticism to attack Peripatetic philosophy. See P. O. Kristeller, *Renaissance Thought*, New York, 1961, chapter 3.

Selected Works on Hermeticism in Arabic and Persian

Abū Zayd al-Balkhī, *Kitāb al-bad' wa'l-ta'rīkh*, Paris, 1906.
Badawi, A. (ed.), *al-Aflāṭūniyyāt al-muḥdathah 'ind al-'arab*, Cairo, 1955.
Bīrūnī, *al-Āthār al-bāqiyah*, Leipzig, 1878.
Danechpazhuh, M. T., *Fihrist-i kitābkhāna-yi Mishkāt*, Tehran, 1956 on.
Pour-Davoud, I., *Adabiyyāt-i mazdyasnā*, vol. II, Bombay, 1931.
al-Dimashqī, Sh., *Nukhbat al-dahr*, St Petersburg, 1866.
al-Diyārbakrī, *Ta'rīkh al-khamīs*, Cairo, 1283.
Ḥājjī Khalīfah, *Kashf al-ẓunūn*, Istanbul, 1360 on.
Ibn 'Arabī, *al-Futūḥāt al-makkiyyah*, Cairo, 1293.
Ibn 'Arabī, *Fuṣūṣ al-ḥikam*, Cairo, 1946.
Ibn al-Athīr, *Ta'rīkh al-kāmil*, Cairo, 1301.
Ibn Juljul, *Ṭabaqāt al-aṭibbā' wa'l-ḥukamā'*, Cairo, 1955.
Ibn al-Qifṭī, *Ta'rīkh al-ḥukamā'*, Cairo, 1326.
Ibn al-Nadīm, *al-Fihrist*, Leipzig, 1871–2.
Ibn Abī Uṣaybi'ah, *'Uyūn al-anbā'*, Cairo, 1299.
Ikhwān al-Ṣafā', *Rasā'il*, Cairo, 1928.
Jābir ibn Ḥayyān, *Mukhtār rasā'il*, Cairo, 1354.
Kāshānī, Afḍal al-Dīn, *Muṣannafāt*, vol. I, Tehran, 1952.
Lāhījī, M., *Sharḥ-i gulshan-i rāz*, Tehran, 1958.
Lughat-nāma-yi Dehkhodā, articles 'Idrīs', 'Ukhnūkh', 'Hermes', Tehran 1951 on.
al-Majrīṭī, *Ghāyat al-ḥakīm*, Berlin, 1933.
al-Mas'ūdī, *Murūj al-dhahab*, Cairo, 1301.
Mo'īn, M., 'Bālinās-i ḥakīm', *Dānish*, vol. I, 1328, pp. 445–9, 532–40.
Niẓāmī Ganjawī, *Iqbāl-nāmah*, Tehran, 1936.
Ṣadr al-Dīn Shīrāzī, *Rasā'il*, Tehran, 1302.
Sā'id al-Andalūsī, *Ṭabaqāt al-umam*, Beirut, 1912.
Shahristānī, *al-Milal wa'l-nihal*, Cairo, 1367.
Shahrazūrī, M., *Kanz al-ḥikmah*, translated by Ḍ. Durrī, Tehran, 1937.
Suhrawardī, *Ḥikmat al-ishrāq* (ed. H. Corbin), Tehran, 1977.
al-Ṭabarī, *Ta'rīkh al-rusul wa'l-mulūk*, Leiden, 1879–1901.
al-Tha'ālibī, *Qiṣaṣ al-anbiyā'*, Leiden, 1922.
al-Ya'qūbī, *Ta'rīkh al-ya'qūbī*, Beirut, 1379.

Works in European Languages

Affifi, A. E., 'The Influence of Hermetic Literature on Moslem Thought', *Bull. School of Oriental and African Studies*, London, 1951, vol. XIII, part 4, pp. 840–55.
Ásin Palacios, M., *Abenmasarra y su escuela*, Madrid, 1914.
Bardenhewer, O., *Hermetis Trismegisti qui apud Arabes fertur de Castigatione Animae Liber*, Bonn, 1893.
Beausobre, *Histoire critique de Manichée et du manichéisme*, Amsterdam, 1734.
Berthelot, M. P. E., *Collection des anciens alchimistes grecs*, Paris, 1888.

Berthelot, M. P. E., *La Chimie au moyen âge*, Paris, 1893.
Blochet, E., 'Études sur le gnosticisme musulman', *Rivista degli studi orientali*, 4, 1911–12, pp. 47–79.
Burckhardt, T., *Die Alchemie*, Freiburg 1960; English trans. by W. Stoddart as *Alchemy, Science of the Cosmos, Science of the Soul*, Baltimore, 1971.
Burckhardt, T., 'Commentaire succinct de la Table d'Émeraude', *Études Traditionelles*, Nov.–Dec. 1960, pp. 332–4.
Corbin, H., *Avicenna and the Visionary Recital*, translated by W. Trask, New York, 1960.
Corbin, H., 'L'Homme de lumière dans le soufisme iranien', (in *Ombre et Lumière*) *Volume de l'Académie Septentrionale*, Paris, 1960; also Paris, 1971.
Corbin, H., *Les Motifs zoroastriens dans la philosophie de Sohrawardi*, Tehran, 1946.
Corbin, H., 'Le récit d'initiation et l'hermétisme en Iran', *Eranos Jahrbuch*, 1949, pp. 87–121.
Darmstaedter, E., *Die Alchemie des Geber*, Berlin, 1922.
Eliade, M., *Le Yoga, immortalité et liberté*, Paris, 1960.
Eranos-Jahrbuch, 1942.
Evola, J., 'Les opérations hermétiques', *Études Traditionelles*, Nos 366–7, 1961, pp. 201–10.
Evola, J., *La Tradizione Ermetica*, Bari, 1948.
Festugière, A. J., and Nock, A., *La Révélation d'Hermès Trismégiste*, 4 vols, Paris, 1949–54.
Fleischer, H. L., *Hermes Trismegistos an die menschliche Seele, Arabisch und Deutsch*, Leipzig, 1870.
Guénon, R., *Aperçus sur l'initiation*, Paris, 1953.
Guénon, R., 'Hermès', *Le Voile d'Isis*, 1932, pp. 193–202; English trans. in *Studies in Comparative Religion*, Spring 1967, pp. 79–83.
Kraus, P., *Jābir ibn Ḥayyān*, 2 vols, Cairo, 1942–3.
Kroll, W., 'Hermes Trismegistos', *Paulys Real-Encyclopädie*.
von Lippmann, E. O., *Entstehung und Ausbreitung der Alchemie*, Berlin, 1919–31.
Massignon, L., 'Inventaire de la littérature hermétique arabe', Appendix III in Festugière, A. J. and Nock, A. D., *La Révélation d'Hermès Trismégiste*.
Massignon, L., *Receuil de textes inédits concernant l'histoire de la mystique en pays d'Islam*, Paris, 1929.
Mead, G. R. S., *Thrice-Greatest Hermes*, London, 1949.
Mieli, A., *La Science arabe et son rôle dans l'évolution scientifique mondiale*, Leiden, 1939; also Paris, 1966.
Nallino, C. A., *Raccolta di scritti editi e inediti*, 6 vols, Rome, 1939–48.
Nock, A. D., see Festugière.
Nyberg, H. S., *Kleinere Schriften des Ibn al-'Arabī*, Leiden, 1919.
Pedersen, J., 'The Sabians', *Volume of Oriental Studies presented to E. G. Browne*, Cambridge, 1922, pp. 383–91.
Pietschmann, R., *Hermes Trismegistus ägyptischen und orientalischen Überlieferungen*, Leipzig, 1875.
Plessner, M., 'Hermes Trismegistus and Arab Science', *Studia Islamica*, 2, 1954, pp. 45–59.

Plessner, M., 'Neue Materialen zur Geschichte der Tabula Smaragdina', *Der Islam*, XVI, 1927, pp. 77–113.
Reitzenstein, R., *Poimandres: Studien zur griechische-ägyptischen und frühchristlichen Literatur*, Leipzig, 1904.
Rusch, A., 'Thoth', *Paulys Real-Encyclopädie*.
Ruska, J., *Arabischen Alchemisten*. I–II, Heidelberg, 1924.
Ruska, J., *Griechische Planetendarstellungen in arabischen Steinbüchern*, Heidelberg, 1919.
Ruska, J., 'Studien zur Geschichte der Chemie' (*Festschrift Edmund O. von Lippmann*), Berlin, 1927.
Ruska, J., *Tabula Smaragdina: ein Beitrag zur Geschichte der Hermetischen Literatur*, Heidelberg, 1926.
Ruska, J., *Turba Philosophorum: ein Beitrag zur Geschichte der Alchimie*, Berlin, 1931.
Sarton, G., *Introduction to the History of Science*, I., Baltimore, 1927.
Scott, W., *Hermetica*, Oxford, 1924–36.
Steinschneider, M., *Die arabischen Übersetzungen aus dem Griechischen*, Leipzig, 1897.
Stapleton, H. E., and Sherwood Taylor, F., 'The Sayings of Hermes quoted in the mā' al-waraqī of Ibn Umail', *Ambix*, vol. 3, Nos 3 and 4, 1949, pp. 69–90.
Strauss, B., *Das Giftbuch des Shānāq*, Berlin, 1934.
Suhrawardī, *Opera Metaphysica et Mystica*, vol. I, Tehran, 1976, vol. II, Tehran, 1977, Prolegomena by H. Corbin.
Wallis Budge, E. A., *Gods of the Egyptians*, London, 1904.

10

From the Alchemy of Jābir to the Chemistry of Rāzī

No two figures are better known in the annals of Islamic alchemy than Jābir ibn Ḥayyān and Muḥammad ibn Zakariyyā' Rāzī, the Latin Geber and Rhazes. Both men were celebrated masters of alchemy. Both are believed to have belonged to the same school by later generations of alchemists in the Islamic and Western worlds.[1] Yet a study made of the writings of both men clearly reveals that, although Rāzī employed the language of Jābirian alchemy, he was in reality dealing not with alchemy but with chemistry. One might even say that Rāzī transformed alchemy into chemistry, even though alchemy endured long after him and chemistry continued to be cultivated in the bosom of alchemy. Thus the chemistry of Rāzī was by no means independent of alchemy.[2]

Before discussing the philosophical and religious divergences between these two men which led also to the separation of chemistry from alchemy, it is worthwhile to note the similarities and differences in the alchemical views of the two authors. Or, rather, a comparison must be made between the Jābirian corpus, of which certainly much was written by Jābir himself, and some of the treatises added later by Ismā'īlī authors, and the writings of Rāzī. Scholars studying these writings differ as to how closely Rāzī followed Jābirian alchemy.[3] And in fact there is both similarity and difference when their alchemical and chemical ideas are compared.

Jābir believed that the elixir contained animal and plant substances as well as minerals, while Rāzī limited it to minerals and only casually mentioned animal and plant substances.[4] Rāzī divided metals into seven species, including *khārṣīnī*, just like Jābir in his *Kitāb al-khamsīn*. However, contrary to Jābir, Rāzī showed no interest in the numerical symbolism connected with this division. Jābir sought to discover the ultimate causes of things, while Rāzī, following the views of the Peripatetics among the physicians, denies openly that such a possibility existed.[5] Rāzī in his *al-Madkhal* and *al-Asrār* did not follow the Jābirian view that minerals are composed of sulphur and mercury but believed that they are constituted of body (*jasad*), spirit (*rūḥ*) and soul (*nafs*).[6] However, the Jābirian belief that there are five principles, the first substance, matter, form, time and space, certainly bears a close resemblance to the famous five eternal principles of Rāzī.[7]

Rāzī also closely followed the terminology of Jābirian alchemy. He adopted not only technical names from Jābir but also titles of books. A large number of Rāzī's writings in this field bear the same titles as those of Jābir, while some are simply modifications of names of works belonging to the Jābirian corpus.[8] This is particularly significant in the case of so independent a philosopher as Rāzī. Even in the classification of simples (*'aqāqīr*), which is among the most important scientific achievements of Rāzī in the field of chemistry, he followed the example of Jābir's *al-Ustuqus al-uss al-awwal.*

One may then ask why Rāzī's works have been called the first book of chemistry in the history of science.[9] We have several alchemical works of Rāzī extant, such as *al-Madkhal al-ta'līmī*, which served as a basis for the section on alchemy of *Mafātīḥ al-'ulūm*,[10] and, most important of all, the *Sirr al-asrār*, well-known to the Western world as *Liber Secretorum Bubacaris*.[11] Throughout these works there is a description and classification of mineral substances, chemical processes, apparatus, and so forth, so that these works could be easily translated into modern chemical language. There is no interest in the symbolic aspect of alchemy, in the discussion of metals and their transformations as symbols of the transformation of the soul. The correspondence between the natural and spiritual worlds which underlies the whole world-view of alchemy[12] has disappeared, and we are left with a science dealing with natural substances considered only in their external reality, although the language of alchemy and some of its ideas are still preserved.

The reason for Rāzī's departure from the alchemical view must be sought in the peculiar philosophical position which he held. As we know from many later sources, including Bīrūnī, who was scientifically sympathetic to him, Rāzī wrote several works against prophetic religion and even denied prophecy as such.[13] He thus rejected a central theme of Islamic philosophy, which is 'prophetic philosophy'. Moreover, Rāzī was particularly opposed to Ismā'īlism and carried out a series of highly philosophical debates with one of the leading figures of Ismā'īlism, Abū Ḥātim al-Rāzī.[14] When the religious and philosophical attitudes implied by Rāzī's position are analysed, it becomes clear why he transformed Jābirian alchemy into chemistry.

According to Shī'ism in general, and Ismā'īlism in particular, the sciences of nature are related to the science of revelation. Revelation possesses an exoteric (*ẓāhir*) and an esoteric (*bāṭin*) aspect and the process of realisation is to begin from the exoteric and reach ultimately the esoteric. This process is called *ta'wīl* or hermeneutic interpretation, which is applied by the Shi'ah, and also in Sufism, to the Holy Quran in order to discover its inner meaning. Only prophecy and revelation can enable man to make this journey from the exterior to the interior, to perform this *ta'wīl* which also means a personal transformation from the exterior man to the inner one.[15]

Applied to nature, *ta'wīl* means penetrating the phenomena of nature to discover the noumena which they veil. It means a transformation of fact into symbol and a vision of nature not as that which veils the spiritual world but as that which reveals it.

Alchemy is precisely such a science, one based on the appearances of nature, particularly the mineral kingdom, not as facts in themselves but as symbols of higher levels of existence. It is not accidental that Jābir was both a Sufi and also a Shi'ite and that in fact the Jābirian corpus later became closely associated with Ismā'īlism, which added certain treatises to the original body of Jābir's works.

Jābir, while also interested in natural occurrences, never divorced the facts of the natural world from their symbolic and spiritual content. His famous balance (*mīzān*) was not an attempt to quantify the study of nature in the modern sense but 'to measure the tendency of the World Soul'. His preoccupation with numerical and alphabetical symbolism, with the study of natural phenomena as determinations of the World Soul and with specifically alchemical symbols all indicated that Jābir was applying the process of *ta'wīl* to nature in order to understand its inner meaning.

Rāzī, by rejecting prophecy and the process of *ta'wīl* which depends upon it, also rejected the application of this method to the study of nature. In so doing, he transformed the alchemy of Jābir to chemistry. That is not to say that he stopped using alchemical terminology or ideas, but in his perspective there was no longer any balance to measure the tendency of the World Soul, nor any symbols to serve as a bridge between the phenomenal and noumenal worlds. The facts of nature were studied as before, but as facts, not symbols. Alchemy was studied not as real alchemy but as an embryonic chemistry. The religious and philosophical attitude of Rāzī was therefore directly connected to his scientific views and was responsible for this transformation. In fact his case is one of the clearest examples of how philosophical and religious questions have played a role in many significant developments of science and in the history of science in general, displaying the intimate relation between man's view towards the sciences of nature and his vision of Reality as such.

Notes

1 *Rutbat al-ḥakīm* considers Rāzī to be a disciple of the school of Jābir, while in almost all Latin alchemical texts the names of both men appear as unquestionable masters of alchemy.

2 See G. Heym, 'Al-Rāzī and alchemy', *Ambix*, vol. I, no. 3, 1938, pp. 184–91; and J. R. Partington, 'The Chemistry of Rāzī', *Ambix*, vol. I; no. 3, 1938, pp. 192–6.

3 For example, P. Kraus in his *Jābir ibn Ḥayyān*, vol. II, pp. 3 ff., does not believe that there is any direct and close relation between them, while N. E. Stapleton in 'Chemistry in Iraq and Persia in the Tenth Century AD', written with R. F. Azo and M. Hidayat Husain, in *Memoirs of the Asiatic Society of Bengal*, 1927, pp. 317–415, considers Rāzī as a direct disciple of Jābir.

4 Kraus, op. cit., p. 3.

5 Kraus, op. cit., p. 95, cites from Rāzī's *Kitāb al-khawāṣṣ* to this effect.

6 Stapleton, op. cit., pp. 320 ff.

7 Kraus, op. cit., p. 137.

Regarding the five eternal principles of Rāzī and his general philosophical views, see R. Walzer, *Greek into Arabic*, pp. 15–17.

8 Stapleton, op. cit., pp. 336–7, where he cites fifteen works of Rāzī which have either identical or modified titles of works of Jābir and seem to deal with the same subject.

9 Stapleton, op. cit., p. 320.

10 The text of this works has been translated with commentary by Stapleton in the above-mentioned articles.

11 This work, whose title may have also been *Kitāb al-sirr* as cited by Ibn al-Nadīm, is the most basic work of Rāzī on chemistry, one in which the transformation of alchemy into chemistry may be clearly discerned. It was well known during the later centuries in the Islamic world not only in its original Arabic version but also in a Persian recension, and it was also influential in the West. But everywhere it was considered an alchemical work rather than a chemical one, because in the medieval world view there was no completely secularised domain of nature to which a totally 'non-symbolic' science could apply. Therefore, although much chemistry was contained in the medieval alchemical tradition, especially in the case of Rāzī, it was never totally divorced from alchemy.

The *Sirr al-asrār* was translated and thoroughly studied by J. Ruska, *Al-Razi's Buch Geheimnis der Geheimnisse*, Berlin, 1937.

12 Concerning the real meaning of alchemy, about which so much mis-leading material has been written, see T. Burckhardt, *Alchemie, Sinn und Weltbilt*; also S. H. Nasr, *Science and Civilization in Islam*, New York, 1970. 'The Alchemical Tradition'.

13 One of Rāzī's famous works on this subject is *The Refutation of Prophecy* (*al-Radd 'ala'l-nubuwwah*). See Bīrūnī, *Epître de Beruni contenant le répertoire des ouvrages de Muhammad b. Zakariya al-Razi*, trans. and ed. P. Kraus, Paris, 1936.

14 See P. Kraus, 'Raziana', *Orientalia*, vol. 4, 1935, pp. 300–4, vol. 5, 1936, pp. 35–56, 358–78. The complete debate between the two Rāzīs which centres mostly upon the question of prophecy runs throughout the many chapters of *A'lām al-nubuwwah* (*Peaks of Prophecy*), ed. by S. al-Sawy and Gh. Aavani, Tehran, 1977. Later Ismā'īlī authors such as Ḥamīd al-Dīn Kirmānī in his *al-Aqwāl al-dhahabiyyah* and Nāṣir-i Khusraw in his *Jāmi' al-ḥikmatayn* were to continue this debate.

15 This theme has been thoroughly studied in the many writings of H. Corbin. As far as it concerns Rāzī and his rejection of the alchemical view, see Corbin (with the collaboration of S. H. Nasr and O. Yahya), *Histoire de la philosophie islamique*, Paris, 1964, pp. 194–201.

11

The Study of Natural History in the Islamic World

Inasmuch as the sciences studied in any traditional civilisation, that is to say one based upon a Divine revelation, depend upon the metaphysical and religious bases of that civilisation, the Islamic sciences, as already mentioned, have always echoed and reflected the central Islamic doctrine of unity (*tawḥīd*). Just as the Islamic religious and moral sciences have originated from Divine Unity and aim to return man to it, the natural sciences have tried to discover the interrelation of all created beings and the unity which underlies the world of multiplicity. We have already shown that it is a general feature of all medieval cosmological sciences[1] that they seek to express the 'unicity of all that exists'. This is especially true in the Islamic natural sciences, such as natural history, where this goal has been central, and the idea of the unicity of nature and the interrelatedness of all parts of the Universe has remained complementary to and a necessary consequence of the Oneness of the Creator.

The most legitimate and meaningful way of studying a science is with respect to its ultimate aim and from the point of view of those who have cultivated it. We shall therefore best understand natural history as cultivated by Muslims if we keep in mind that their primary aim, unlike that of the modern natural sciences, has been to arrive at the unity lying behind the veil of the multiplicity of natural forms by a synthetic and qualitative study of nature.[2]

As studied by the Muslims, natural history covers a large number of fields and includes not only such subjects as geology, botany, zoology and anthropology, but also cosmogony and sacred history.[3] Natural history means essentially the history of nature in the vastest sense of the word. Because Muslims have never separated the spiritual and the secular, they have usually written natural history within the context of sacred history. Ṭabarī and Mas'ūdī illustrate this clearly in their universal histories. The many allusions in the Holy Quran to natural phenomena and the fact that the verses of the sacred book as well as the phenomena of nature are called *āyāt* (signs) signify that in the Islamic perspective there is a fundamental affinity between the Divine and natural orders. This unitary vision indicates, therefore, the legitimacy of connecting sacred history with natural history.

The question of the 'signs' of nature leads to another basic feature of Islamic natural history. Most Muslim scientists have sought to study nature in order to observe 'signs' of the Creator, to witness directly the 'vestiges' of God in His handiwork.[4] This is a feature which seems most irritating to some modern scientists who aim to discover only the immediate and material causes of things. But from the point of view of Islam no science can be considered legitimate which does not ultimately consider things in reference to their Divine Origin and which does not take into account the Transcendent Cause of all finite beings. The marvels and wonders of nature and the moral and spiritual lessons drawn from plant and animal life mentioned by the Muslim natural historians, which many modern historians have ridiculed, have been, from the point of view of Islam itself, the most beneficial and basic elements of natural history. They have led the reader to a recognition of the Divine Agent present in nature.

The Islamic perspective is, from a certain point of view, very practical. The sciences which this perspective has nourished and matured are all in a sense 'useful', that is to say they correspond to a basic need of man as envisaged in Islam. They may, like agriculture, medicine, and the sciences of history and society, be useful in the limited sense and fulfil man's physical and social needs. Or, like logic and theology, they may be useful in preventing people from being misled by false reasoning and therefore serve man's religious needs. Or, finally, like the esoteric doctrines, which include a symbolic science of the natural order, they may be useful in fulfilling the need for spiritual realisation of the few who seek God here and now. But Islam has never considered simple curiosity or intellectual passion either a virtue or a basic need of man and for this reason has never legitimised a science based only on curiosity.[5] The desire of natural historians to draw moral and spiritual lessons from the phenomena of nature is, therefore, legitimate from the point of view of Islam because it is spiritually meaningful and fulfils a need. To find the weight of a certain leaf of a tree to be so many grams is, from this point of view, a secondary and unimportant inquiry unless it leads to higher knowledge. The modern criticism of Muslim natural historians on this point is, therefore, unwarranted and based on a misapprehension of their point of view.

There is yet another aspect of Islamic natural history which modern scientists find difficult to understand: the description of strange animals and plants and magical properties of nature so credulously recorded by medieval authors. One finds similar accounts in ancient books like Pliny's *Historia Naturalia*. The creatures described in these texts, which appear strange today, are of several types. One type is of strange animals, especially sea animals, which could certainly have existed and later become very rare or extinct. Now that they can no longer be observed their description seems fantastic. Another type is of animals and plants like the dragon, unicorn, and mandrake, which originally had symbolic meaning only, but the symbolism in certain cases was so forgotten that they came to be erroneously described as ordinary living creatures although usually their 'trans-physical' significance was not neglected.[6]

As for the apparent frequency of 'strange' phenomena within nature and the innocence with which medieval authors recorded them, it must be noted that the minds of those people were not as 'hardened' as those of the moderns, and that nature in its turn was not taken to be so 'dense' and 'coagulated' and as far separated and removed from the psychical world as now.[7] Therefore, while reading ancient and medieval texts, it should be kept in mind that, just as the people of those ages, like the people of certain parts of Asia, Africa, and America today, regarded nature from a point of view different from that of modern science, nature also revealed to them an aspect of itself different from that which it reveals to those moderns whose mental constitution is no longer capable of perceiving nature's more subtle elements. There is, of course, much misinformation due to the narrative and exaggerated style characteristic of the poetic mind of many Muslims. But on the whole most of the content of Islamic natural history can be understood in terms of either direct observation of physical realities or symbolism, that is, the description of the subtle aspects of nature the reality of which is not in any way affected by the modern quantitative sciences which, from their own quantitative point of view, refuse to consider them.

Types of Islamic writings containing material on natural history, particularly on plants and animals, which form the centre of our interest in this chapter, are quite diverse. Muslim authors have rarely had a taste for over-specialisation so that one finds a discussion of the plant and the animal kingdoms not only in scientific texts but also in literary, historical, philosophical and theological works. More specially, the sources for natural history include the writings of historians, geographers and travellers, physicians, alchemists, philosophers, encyclopedists, cosmographers, moralists, theologians, Sufis, and, of course, authors writing specifically on the subject of natural history.

The *Ta'rīkh al-rusul wa'l-mulūk*, the universal history of Ṭabarī, the *Kitāb al-buldān*, the book of countries of Ya'qūbī, the *Kitāb al-bad' wa'l-ta'rīkh* of Maqdisī, the *Murūj al-dhahab* and *Kitāb al-tanbīh wa'l-ishrāf* of Mas'ūdī, the *Ta'rīkh-i jahān-gushā* of Juwaynī, and the geography of Abū 'Abdallāh ibn al-Idrīsī, all dealing with history and geography, contain valuable sections on natural history. Moreover, they provide, on the one hand, the perspective of time in the light of which Muslims have viewed the life of all creatures, a time stretching between the creation and the final annihilation of the Universe on the Last Day; and, on the other, they mention the geographical setting, the seven climates, and other terrestrial conditions which form the matrix of natural history.[8] They demonstrate, further, how closely the study of plants and animals is bound up with that of the other parts of the Universe, both terrestrial and celestial,[9] and how the history of nature is intrinsically interwoven with the history of man as well as with sacred history.

Another source for the knowledge of natural history comes from the many books of travel which survive from that period of Islamic history when the Muslim world was still more or less united and travelling from one place to another was easy. The accounts of the travels of Abu'l-Ḥasan al-Maghribī, Ibn Jubayr, Bīrūnī, Nāṣir-i Khusraw, and Ibn Baṭṭūṭah, to mention just a few names, provide a wealth of information on the plants and animals which these men observed themselves, while other sources are the accounts which they heard from others. The interpretation which they gave to their observations varied greatly, depending on their knowledge and experience as travellers. One often finds simple description, as in the case of Maghribī, or detailed physical observation and inference based upon it, as in the case of Bīrūnī, or philosophical and metaphysical reflection upon natural forms, as is found in the writings of Nāṣir-i Khusraw.

Besides these land travellers, there were several sea travellers like Sulayman the Merchant, who in the third/ninth century journeyed by sea to the coast of China and described many of the wonders of the Indian Ocean and the Chinese coast, and Shihāb al-Dīn Mājid, Sulayman ibn Mahrī, and Pīri Ra'īs, who in the ninth/fifteenth and tenth/sixteenth centuries travelled extensively through the Mediterranean Sea and Indian Ocean and gave a detailed description of these areas. The accounts of sea animals found in books of natural history and the fables of the sea encountered so often in *Arabian Nights, Sindbad-nāmah* and other collections of stories, both Arabic and Persian, were originally taken from the accounts of the sea travels of merchants, adventurers and occasionally military men who roamed the then known extremities of the world.

Another source of natural history, considered from quite another aspect of our subject, is medicine. Islamic medicine, the heir both to the Greek and to the Indian sciences of medicine, has always had a general theory of living beings; nearly all medical treatises have included in their introduction a general treatment of the constitution (*mizāj*) of animals, which provides a major source of information for the internal structure of animals and the functioning of their organs.[10] Moreover, since much of the treatment of diseases in Muslim medicine is based on plants, medical books have usually contained sections on pharmacology treating of the medical properties of plants. In fact, one may say that, apart from the metaphysical and philosophical study of plants and animals, most Muslim research in botany and zoology has been in the service of pharmacology, agriculture, medicine and animal husbandry. The important medical treatises such as 'Alī al-Ṭabarī's *Firdaws al-ḥikmah* (*The Paradise of Wisdom*), Muḥammad ibn Zakariyyā' Rāzī's *al-Ḥāwī* (*Continens*), and Ibn Sīnā's *Canon* contain important chapters on zoology and botany.

Alchemy, a subject closely allied to medicine and botany in ancient times and later identified more with the study of the mineral kingdom, has also much to contribute to natural history. In Chinese alchemy we find a close link between the elixir and plant life; certain modern scholars have even suggested that the Arabic word *kimiyā'* itself, from which the English word alchemy is derived, comes from the Chinese *Chin-Ia*, meaning the gold-making juice of a plant.[11] Whatever the validity of this theory may be, there is no doubt that plant and animal symbolism has a major role to play in alchemy. The writings of so many alchemists like Jābir ibn Ḥayyān or in the Western world Flamel and Basil Valentine demonstrate the importance of this symbolism. In Islamic alchemy, certain authors like Jābir have written specific treatises on plants and animals dealing with their hidden and 'occult' qualities.[12] Authors writing on the occult sciences (*al-'ulūm al-gharībah*), such as Jābir, Shams al-Dīn al-Būnī, and Jildakī, have all written treatises dealing with the psychic and symbolic aspects of both plants and animals and their influence on man's physical, psychic and spiritual life.

The philosophers have also treated plants and animals in their general consideration of the world of 'generation and corruption', to use the terminology of Aristotle. It must be kept in mind that medieval philosophy is based upon the idea of hierarchy and the chain of being which begins from the One and through the angelic and intellectual orders descends to material manifestation to rise once again through the mineral, plant and animal kingdoms to the origin of all things. The philosophers, especially the systematic Peripatetics (*mashshāiyyūn*), therefore, have always entered into a discussion of plants and animals from the point of view of their place in the great chain of being. We find examples of this type of discussion not only in the Peripatetics like Fārābī, Ibn Sīnā, and Ibn Rushd but also in the philosophers of the Illuminationist (*ishrāqī*) school like Suhrawardī and Mullā Ṣadrā, and in Sunni and Shi'ite theologians like Ghazzālī and Khwājah Naṣīr al-Dīn Ṭūsī. The most detailed and profound scientific account of plants and animals in these philosophical treatises appears in Ibn Sīnā's *Shifā'*. Here, Ibn Sīnā deals not only with the place of plants and animals in the cosmic hierarchy but also with their morphology, genesis, and growth. Sections seven and eight of the *Shifā'* on natural philosophy (*Ṭabī'iyyāt*) are among the most important pages of medieval natural history.

It is also of interest to note that Mullā Ṣadrā deals even more extensively than Ibn Sīnā with the cosmological significance of the vegetative kingdom and in fact speaks in some of his works such as the *Risālah fi'l-ḥashr*, about the resurrection of plants on the 'Day of Resurrection'.

Writings similar to the *Shifā'* in the universality of their subject-matter, but not so strictly systematised, are a number of encyclopedias which have been popular from the very early centuries of Islam. We find an early example of these in the *Book of Treasures* of Job of Edessa, written at the end of the second Islamic century.[13] A more important work of this kind is the *Rasā'il* of the Ikhwān al-Ṣafā', containing a wealth of information on plants and also on animals drawn from Indian, Persian, and Greek sources and integrated into a vast metaphysical and philosophical panorama.[14] Also of great importance for natural history is the encyclopedia of Mustawfī Qazwīnī entitled *Nuzhat al-qulūb* (*Delights of the Hearts*), written in Persian in the eighth/fourteenth century, which includes sections on plants and animals.[15] Other works of this kind include the *Kitāb al-awā'il* (*Book of Primordial Knowledge*) and *al-Nuqāyat al-usud al-muhimmah li 'ulūm jammah* (*Selection of Important Foundations for Manifold Sciences*) of 'Abd al-Raḥmān al-Suyūṭī, the ninth/fifteenth-century historian, and the *Kashf al-ẓunūn* (*The Clearing of Doubts*) of Ḥājjī, Khalīfah dealing mostly with scholars of all types, including scientists of the medieval period. All these encyclopedias contain some sections on plants and animals while some like the *Nuzhat al-qulūb* and the *Rasā'il* have large chapters devoted specifically to natural history.

Works on cosmography are in a way similar to encyclopedias, but usually they do not cover as many subjects. Moreover, they are concerned more directly with the creation of the world and its subsequent development as well as with the wonders of nature. This *genre* of writing became popular especially during the later centuries, the most famous examples being the *'Ajā'ib al-makhlūqāt* (*The Wonders of Creation*) of Abū Yaḥyā Zakariyyā' Qazwīnī and the *Nukhbat al-dahr* (*Choice of the Times*) of Shams al-Dīn al-Dimashqī, both written in the seventh/thirteenth century. These works represent a combination of natural history and mythology and provide an excellent example of the attitude of the Muslim mind, which considers that nature displays at every turn the power and wisdom of the Creator.

To mention all the sources for natural history one should include the moral, theological, and Sufi texts in which the life and qualities of plants and animals are studied with the aim of learning a moral and spiritual lesson from them. Such use of natural history, particularly of the life of animals, is very frequent in Oriental literature, as for example in the *Kalīlah wa Dimnah* (*The Tales of Bidpai*),[16] the *Shāh-nāmah* (*The Book of Kings*) of Firdawsī, the *Thousand and One Nights*, and the *Gulistān* (*The Rose Garden*) of Sa'dī. Likewise, in certain theological texts animals are discussed in the light of their moral virtues. The famous *Kitāb al-ḥayawān* (*Book of Animals*) of al-Jāḥiẓ is above all a theological and moral discussion about animals.[17] In Sufi writings also, plants and animals are discussed in the light of their cosmic qualities and in relation to the initiate's (*sālik's*) journey through the cosmos. In these works, plants and animals appear primarily in the light of their symbolic aspects, which represent realities of a universal order. The *Mathnawī* of Mawlānā Jalāl al-Dīn Rūmī is particularly rich in this respect. There is also the *Manṭiq al-ṭayr* (*Conference of the Birds*) of Farīd al-Dīn 'Aṭṭār, in which the whole spiritual quest of the Sufi disciple for the Divine Presence is presented in the language of thirty birds, each symbolising a particular spiritual type.

Finally, among writings dealing with natural history, there are works devoted almost exclusively to plants and animals,[18] constituting perhaps the most important sources of our knowledge of natural history. We mention here a few of these texts. These works concern agriculture, pharmacology and botany, all dealing with plants and zoology and animal husbandry.

In agriculture, the *al-Filāḥat al-nabaṭiyyah* (*Nabataean Agriculture*) of Ibn Waḥshiyyah is the most influential of all Muslim works on the subject. Written in the third/ninth century and drawn mostly from Chaldean and Babylonian sources, the book deals not only with agriculture but also with the esoteric sciences, especially magic and sorcery, and has always been considered to be one of the most important books in Arabic on the occult sciences.[19] The agricultural section of the work was systematised and elaborated by Ibn 'Awwām in the sixth/twelfth century in his *Kitāb al-filāḥah* (*The Book of Agriculture*), which is perhaps the most important Muslim work on the subject. Ibn 'Awwām describes over five hundred plants and fruit trees – mostly those with properties useful for agriculture. These two works contain the experience of centuries of agriculture by the people of the Middle East and offer a great deal of descriptive material on the life of plants and animals.

In botany itself, early Arabic poetry has much descriptive material to offer. There were also many early works of a systematic nature, most of which have now been lost. One of the most important of these early books was the *Kitāb al-nabāt* (*The Books of Plants*) of Abū Ḥanīfah al-Dīnawarī (the celebrated third/ninth-century historian and scholar) of which only fragments have survived.[20] Among later writings in which pharmacology and botany proper are combined, the most famous works are the *Kitāb al-adwiyat al-mufradah* (*The Book of Simple Drugs*) of Abū Ja'far al-Ghāfiqī,[21] the writings of the seventh/thirteenth-century Andalusian author Ibn al-Bayṭār, perhaps the most outstanding of all Muslim botanists,[22] and the *Ḥadīqat al-azhār fī sharḥ maziyyat al-ushb wa'l-'aqqār* (*Garden of Flowers in the Explanation of the Character of Herbs and Drugs*) of the tenth/sixteenth-century Moroccan author, Qāsim-al-Ghassānī.

In zoology, the *Manāfi' al-ḥayawān* (*The Benefits of Animals*), by Abū Sa'īd Bukhtīshū' and the treatises on various wild and domestic animals by Aṣma'ī are among the earliest works on animals. To this early period belongs also the *Kitāb al-ḥayawān* (*The Book of Animals*) of al-Jāḥiẓ, the celebrated Mu'tazilite theologian and philologist. Being one of the most famous works of Arabic literature, this book, written in the third/ninth century, combines the account of the life of animals with tales, anecdotes, theological discussions and frequent quotations from Arabic poetry. The sources of this book include the Quran, the *Ḥadīth* and Arabic poetry, especially pre-Islamic poetry, which last contains many descriptions of animals that al-Jāḥiẓ often quotes to refute Greek authors, personal observations of Aristotle and information collected from various travellers.

The *Ḥayāt al-ḥayawān* (*The Life of Animals*) of Kamāl al-Dīn al-Damīrī, written five centuries after al-Jāḥiẓ, came to be acknowledged as the most important Muslim work on zoology, especially on animal psychology. It was based to a large extent upon the book of al-Jāḥiẓ as well as on the writings of the intervening encyclopedists and cosmographers already mentioned. Al-Damīrī's is the most comprehensive work of its kind in Arabic literature and has, therefore, been taught and studied extensively since the date of its composition.

The great majority of the above-mentioned authors have studied plants and animals from a very similar philosophical point of view. This derives mostly from the Greeks and, in particular, from Aristotle's exposition in the *Physica* and *De Caelo*. As mentioned earlier in this work, according to this view the Universe is divided into two parts: the heavens and the world of change or generation and corruption; the latter occupies the sublunary region. This region is made of four elements; fire, air, water, and earth,[23] arranged in concentric spheres with fire at the highest and earth at the lowest sphere. These elements combine in various ratios and, when a correct proportion is reached, one of the faculties of the World Soul or nature, as some authors have called it, forms a nexus with this combination[24] and by this wedding minerals, plants and animals come into being, each having been brought about by the coming into play of a new faculty of the World Soul or, as some have called it, a new soul.[25] All the kingdoms of nature are, therefore, united in having been made of the same four elements and given life by souls or faculties which belong to the same single power – the World Soul or nature – running through all the arteries and veins of the Universe.

As minerals, plants and animals lie in the hierarchical order of Being, they also come into existence by means of causes which are dependent upon other orders of creation, although these causes may appear to be hidden.[26] The causes are the four already mentioned by Aristotle, namely the material, the formal, the efficient and the final. The material cause for plants consist of the four elements; the formal cause, the set of planetary influences symbolising various cosmic intelligences and forces which are instrumental in sublunary changes; the efficient cause, nature or the World Soul; and the final cause for plants is their use by animals as food.[27] The causes for animals are the same except that their final cause is their use by man.[28]

The plants have the powers of the mineral soul (*al-rūḥ ʿaqdiyyah*) as well as those of the vegetative soul (*al-nafs al-nabātiyyah*) which is possessed of the three faculties of feeding (*ghādhiyah*), growth (*nāmiyah* or *munmiyah*) and reproduction (*muwallidah*).[29] The animals in turn possess all the faculties of the mineral and vegetative souls as well as the powers of motion (*muḥarrikah*) and comprehension (*mudrikah*). The animal faculties may be summarised as follows:[30]

- Animal soul
  - power of motion (*muḥarrikah*)
    - power of desire (*shawqiyyah*)
      - power of lust (*shahwatiyyah*)
      - power of anger (*ghadhabiyyah*)
    - power of motion of body (*fāʿilah*)
  - power of comprehension (*mudrikah*)

Subscribing to the view that all things are alive and that plants and animals have souls of their own, Muslim natural historians have tried to understand the behaviour of these creatures in terms of the faculties stated above and have thus averted many of the difficulties of the post-Cartesian view which regards plants and animals as ʻmachinesʼ.

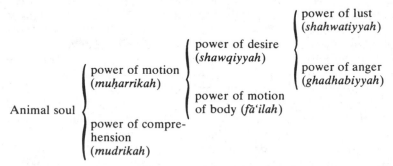

The classification of plants and animals is closely allied to the study of their faculties and is based in certain cases upon the hierarchy of the powers of the soul mentioned above. Muslim authors have followed several principles of classification, some drawn from Aristotle, especially in the case of animals, and some independently devised by them.[31]

The plants have been divided usually into trees, shrubs, grass and those intermediate between trees and shrubs and shrubs and grass. A most extensive discussion of this division is found in the seventh section of the *ṭabīʿiyyāt* of the *Shifāʾ*, where each type is clearly defined; for example, the tree is defined as a plant which stands on its stem or trunk, the shrub a plant the stem of which spreads over the earth, and the grass or herb that which has no stem. Ibn Sīnā divides plants also according to the climates of regional territories in which they grow – desert, semi-tropical regions, etc.

In Mustawfī Qazwīnī's *Nuzhat al-qulūb* a distinction is made between trees of which only the leaves and fruit are renewed yearly and the seed-bearing plants of which everything changes every year except the roots. The trees are divided into those that bear fruit and those that do not.[32] Furthermore, the seed-bearing plants are divided into the four classes of aliments (*aghdhiyah*): (i) those which are daily used for food and create one of the four humours (*akhlāṭ*) – blood, yellow bile, phlegm and black bile – which soon becomes a part of the body; (ii) medicines and spices only a little of which can be eaten for medicinal purposes and which are mostly cold and wet; (iii) perfumes (*mashmūmāt*) which have a good odour and are derived mostly from flowers; and (iv) miscellaneous plants in which the qualities of aliments and medicines are present but in a lesser degree.

Most authors dealing with the classification of plants also treat of their morphology. We find an extensive treatment of this kind in the *Shifāʾ*, where Ibn Sīnā divides the parts of plants into primary and secondary organs. The primary or essential organs are root, trunk, branches, bark, wood and pith or core, and the secondary organs are fruit, leaves and blossoms. In a somewhat different manner, the Ikhwān al-Ṣafāʾ divide the plant into nine parts – root, vessel, branch, bough, leaves, colour, fruit, shell and germ – and hold that only perfect plants possess all nine of them.

Both Ibn Sīnā and the Ikhwān make continuous comparison of plants with the animal world; in the case of the Ikhwān, as well as in the case of many later authors, comparison is also made with the celestial bodies so as to draw attention to the symbolic correspondence existing between various cosmic orders.[33] In their comparisons of plants with animals, Muslim authors were quite aware of the presence of male and female parts of plants which in most cases are united in the same plant but which in higher plants like the palm become differentiated. Ibn

Sīnā draws an analogy between seeds of plants and eggs of birds, each of which has a centre that is the source of life and a periphery that provides food for the new generation. Likewise, he compares the growth of the branch of a tree from the trunk with the birth of a new generation in the animal world.

In the classification and description of plants, one can hardly fail to mention Ibn al-Bayṭār, the greatest of the Muslim botanists. Basing himself on al-Ghāfiqī and other previous authors such as Dioscorides and Galen and making many observations of his own, he described extremely carefully over 1,400 plants from Andalusia, his homeland, as well as from the rest of the Islamic world. Furthermore, in the *Kitāb al-mughnī*, following the example of Ibn Sīnā's *Qānūn*, he gave the medicinal uses of these plants. The influence of Ibn al-Bayṭār was felt everywhere within the Islamic world from Morocco to India. Three centuries later, the Moroccan botanist al-Ghassānī was to give the best classification of plants found anywhere in Islamic literature, drawing mostly upon the information accumulated by Ibn al-Bayṭār.

In the study of animals, like that of plants, interest evolved around the constitution of plants and their classification and description. The temperament (*mizāj*) of animals including man was studied in the light of the qualities and nature of which the other kingdoms are possessed. Their relation with the bodily humours may diagrammatically be represented as follows.[34]

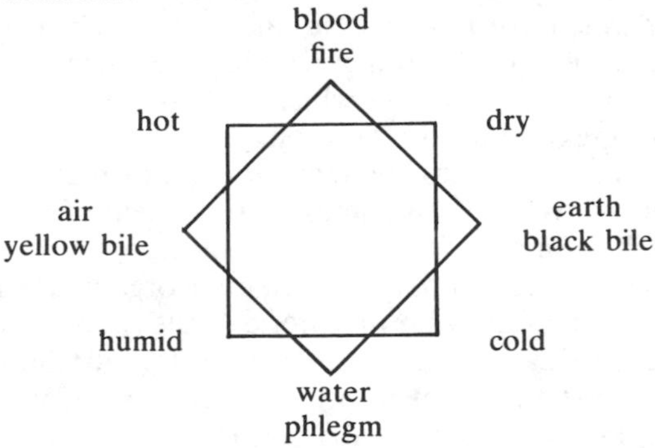

The animal constitution has been understood in terms of the equilibrium of the four humours each of which is connected with a particular internal organ. The organs in turn have been studied in the light of their function of preserving internal equilibrium. Likewise, the effect of plants both as food and as medicine upon animals has been considered with respect to their nature, that is, coldness, moisture, etc., which the two kingdoms share in common. This is one example of the underlying unity in terms of which the diversities of nature have been understood.

In the classification of animals, as in that of plants, several principles have been followed, some of them based upon Aristotle's works on animals. Al-Jāḥiẓ in his *Kitāb al-ḥayawān* divides animals according to how they move. There are, according to him, four classes of animals: those that walk, including men, quadrupeds, beasts of prey and insects; those that fly, including wild birds, hunting birds and gnats; those that swim; and those that crawl. The Ikhwān al-Ṣafā' give several types of classification. One type is similar to that of al-Jāḥiẓ and divides animals into those living in the air, such as birds and insects; those living in the sea, such as fish, crabs, frogs and snails; those living on land, such as the quadrupeds; and those dwelling in the earth, such as worms.[35] Another classification is according to the perfection of the senses, that is, the lowest animals having only the sense of touch; grubs and others having the sense of touch and taste; marine animals and certain land creatures occupying dark places having the senses of touch, taste, and smell; insects having all the senses except sight; and finally perfect animals having all the five senses.

Many Muslim authors have followed Aristotle in classifying animals according to the manner of their reproduction. We find a simplified version of it in the *Rasā'il* of the Ikhwān, where animals are divided into three classes: those which are most complete, conceive their young, suckle them and foster them; those which do not perform such functions but leap at the female and lay eggs and hatch them; and those which do none of the above things and come into being in putrefaction. More elaborate classifications of the same type are found in the writings of Ibn Sīnā, Ibn Rushd and many later commentators of the *Shifā'*, whose commentaries contain a detailed discussion of animals.

A rather general definition of animals, including the *jinn*[36] and men, is given by Qazwīnī in his *'Ajā'ib al-makhlūqāt*. He divides animals into seven classes. First, there is man who possesses a rational soul (*al-nafs al-nāṭiqah*) and whose body is a miniature model of the Universe, a microcosm, each part of which has a spiritual meaning and purpose. For example, he stands erect because of his spiritual aspiration to transcend physical existence, and his head is round because of the perfection of the spherical figure. The second type is of the *jinn*, who are composed of fire and appear in many forms. As Qazwīnī writes, God created angels from the light of fire, *jinn* from its blaze and devils from its smoke. The *jinn* occupied the earth before the coming of man, that is, the fall of Adam, and had their own religion and prophets; but because of corruption God sent angels to purify the earth, and they were dispersed to remote islands. Satan or Iblīs is himself from this species of animal.[37]

After the *jinn* come the beasts of burden like the horse, then cattle like cows, then wild beasts, then birds and finally insects and reptiles.

Qazwīnī has further a section on 'strange' animals, which are primarily mythological and symbolical, and finally a chapter on angels, their forms, function and colours.[38]

In the description of animals, there is no book in Muslim writings which is as complete as Damīrī's *Ḥayāt al-ḥayawān*, in which he is concerned with the traits, instincts, and psychology of animals and their use, medical and spiritual, for man. Following Ibn al-Bayṭār, by whom he was influenced, he classifies animals alphabetically and then gives their description, drawing on Aristotle, the natural historians, theologians, esoteric writers like Shams al-Dīn al-Būnī, Arabic poetry and the Quran and the *Ḥadīth*. In his description he often refers to the symbolic character of animals, such as the royal quality of the lion, and, as is characteristic of similar descriptive works of natural history, he intertwines the spiritual with the physical study of nature.[39]

In discussing the classification and morphology of plants and animals, a comparison may be made between the traditional concept of gradation and the modern notion of evolution. There is no doubt that many Muslim authors like Bīrūnī and the Ikhwān were quite aware of the meaning of fossils and of the fact that during other periods of the history of the earth flora and fauna of a different kind existed on the surface of the earth. Moreover, the idea of the gradation of being or the passage of the One Spirit through all the realms of nature has been expressed by many philosophers and Sufis.[40]

All schools of Islamic thought are based on the fundamental concept of the hierarchy of being but envisage it in different ways. The Peripatetics speak of the levels of the Ptolemaic cosmos as symbols of the levels of being, and the Illuminationists of the longitudinal angelic order. The Sufis of the school of Ibn 'Arabī expound their teachings in the language of the Divine Presences and the followers of Mullā Ṣadrā base their teachings upon the doctrine of transubstantial motion (*al-ḥarakat al-jawhariyyah*). The sapiential schools of Islamic thought all believed in the vertical 'movement' towards perfection in a Universe in which all the possibilities of the higher states of being are present here and now and not in some imagined time in the future. They, therefore, stand totally opposed to evolution in its modern sense, whatever may be the appearances. They reject completely the views of those modernised Muslims who themselves have been affected by the psychosis of evolution and progress.[41]

The tradition of Islamic natural history, upon which we have touched briefly, has a past going back to the first Islamic century. During this long history it absorbed much of the Greek and certain parts of the Indian and Persian sciences and created a science which was in every way more comprehensive than that which had preceded it, except the biological studies by Aristotle. This tradition was to develop as a properly Islamic science, that is to say one based upon the particular genius of the Islamic perspective which is centred upon unity. This principle is manifest in Islamic natural history in many ways, for example in the vision of the unity of nature and interrelation of all things. Muslim natural historians asserted this version so often when they affirmed the presence of the signs of God in nature and studied plants and animals for the purpose of seeing Divine Wisdom therein.

This tradition, especially that part of it which preceded the seventh/thirteenth century, was to have a profound influence on Latin Christianity and on the formation of the science of natural history in medieval times. It is well known how much seventh/thirteenth-century authors such as Albertus Magnus and Roger Bacon were indebted to it and how even during the Renaissance men like Paracelsus and Agrippa were constrained to draw largely on Islamic sources. In the Orient, this tradition has continued until the present century although in a much weakened form after the ninth/fifteenth century. Scholars in India and Persia as well as those in the Maghrib have continued to study nature as the unified handiwork of God in order to discover His Wisdom, to see 'His sign upon the horizon' as the Quran states, and to learn spiritual lessons from it. Only in following this spirit has this tradition of natural history been able to be an integral aspect of Islamic learning and remain in harmony and conformity with the spiritual and intellectual perspective of Islam.

Notes

1 We have already had occasion to discuss the meaning of the traditional cosmological sciences, including the natural sciences. The traditional sciences should properly speaking be divided into the metaphysical, dealing with God and supracosmic realities, and the cosmological, dealing with beings in the cosmos. See the already cited article of T. Burckhardt, 'Nature de la perspective cosmologique', *Études Traditionelles*, vol. XLIX, 1948, pp. 216–19.

2 See the introduction to S. H. Nasr, *Science and Civilization in Islam*; also the introduction and chapter 1 of S. H. Nasr, *Islamic Science – An Illustrated Study*, London, 1976.

In his famous *'Ajā'ib al-makhlūqāt* (*The Wonders of Creation*), Abū Yaḥyā Zakariyyā' Qazwīnī writes that presence of Divine Wisdom in every atom of the Universe and in all forms of multiplicity is itself a proof of Divine Unity, and quotes the famous verse '*wa fī kull-i shay'in lahu āyatun tadullu 'alā annahu wāḥidun*' (In everything there is a sign demonstrating that He is One).

3 But in this study we are concerned only with botany and zoology. We have also dealt with the various branches of natural history in the two works already cited in the previous note.

4 The medieval Christian scientists had a similar aim in view when they sought to observe the *vestigia Dei* in nature.

5 Our argument does not seek to make knowledge subservient to action. That knowledge is always superior to action in the Islamic perspective is indicated by such sayings of the Prophet as 'One hour of meditation is better than a thousand works of

charity' or 'The ink of the scholar is more valuable than the blood of the one who fights the Holy War'. What we wish to show is that in Islam a mental activity for its own sake, divorced from the spiritual and religious needs of man on the one hand and from his social needs on the other, has never been encouraged.

6 Most medieval authors, especially certain alchemists, were of course quite aware of animal and plant symbolism and completely conscious of what they were writing about.

7 It is difficult for many to conceive of the possibility that nature and its laws may not have always been the same, but there is no logical or scientific reason to prove that they have been uniform. In fact, this uniformity is one of the assumptions upon which the historical aspects of modern science are based. On the other hand, sacred texts and metaphysical doctrines point to the 'cyclic' change both in nature and in psychic and mental structure. R. Guénon, *The Reign of Quantity and the Signs of the Times*, trans. Lord Northbourne, Baltimore, 1978, and F. Schuon, *Les Stations de la sagesse*, Paris, 1958, pp. 119 ff. (English translation as *Stations of Wisdom*), trans. G. E. H. Palmer, London, 1961, pp. 76 ff).

8 For general information regarding these and other authors whose names are to follow, see G. Sarton, *Introduction to the History of Science*, vols I–III; A. Mieli, *La science arabe et son rôle dans l'évolution scientifique mondiale*; and B. Carra de Vaux, *Les penseurs de l'Islam*, Paris, 1921–7, vols. II and IV. Among the texts mentioned above, the *Murūj al-dhahab* (*Prairies of Gold*), translated into English by Sprenger, London, 1841, offers especially useful material on the historical and geographical framework of natural history.

9 Islamic natural historians not only divided the earth into several climates, each with its own flora and fauna in conformity with its particular terrestrial condition, but further assigned each climate to a particular planet which acted as the archetype and 'guardian angel' for that particular climate. For an example of this astrological theory, see the *Rasā'il* of the Ikhwān al-Ṣafā', Cairo, 1928, I, pp. 116 ff. and P. Duhem, *Le système du monde*, vol. II, Paris, 1914, pp. 267 ff.

10 Regarding the internal constitution of animals, perhaps no book is so masterly and complete as Ibn Sīnā's *Qānūn*. See the introduction to Ibn Sīnā, *A Treatise on the Canon of Medicine, Incorporating a Translation of the First Book*, by O. C. Gruner, London, 1930; also Ibn Sīnā, *Poème de la médicine – Urǧuza fi'ṭ-ṭibb*, Paris, 1956.

11 See S. Mahdihassan, 'Chemistry, a Product of Chinese Culture', *Pakistan Journal of Science*, 1957, vol. IX, no. 1; also his 'Alchemy, in Its Proper Setting, with Jinn, Sufi and Suffa, as Loan-words from the Chinese', *Iqbal*, 1959, vol. VII, no. 3.

12 See P. Kraus, *Jābir ibn Ḥayyān*.

13 A. Mingana, *Encyclopaedia of Philosophical Sciences as Taught in Baghdad in* c. *817 AD or Book of Treasures of Job of Edessa*, Cambridge, 1935.

14 An interesting section of the *Rasā'il* dealing with the discussion between man and animals has been translated into English as *Dispute between Man and the Animals*, by J. Platts, London, 1869.

15 See J. Stephenson, 'The Zoological Section of the *Nuzhat al-Qulūb*', *Isis*, 1928, vol. XI, pp. 285–316.

16 This famous book of tales about the animals is the Sanskrit *Panchatantra* translated into Pahlavi and later into Arabic by Ibn Muqaffa'. Various versions of it in Arabic and Persian, such as *Anwār-i suhaylī* of Ḥusayn Wā'iẓ Kāshifī, have remained very popular throughout the centuries.

17 This *genre* of writing has continued to recent times. A work called *Insān wa ḥayawān* (*Men and Animals*) by Hājjī Mullā Ismā'īl Sabziwārī, written during the last century, treating of the moral and spiritual qualities of animals, is still widely used by Persian preachers in their sermons.

18 By 'exclusively' we do not mean so strict a limitation of the subject as is found in a modern textbook on botany or zoology. Muslim sciences have been too closely

united to permit a complete separation of one subject from another so that in nearly every book dealing with plants and animals there are references to other sciences as well as to philosophy and theology.

19 Ibn Khaldūn in referring to this book writes that 'people learned the sciences of sorcery from the work and developed its manifold branches' (*Muqaddimah*, tr. F. Rosenthal, New York, 1958, vol. III, p. 156). Many Western historians have refused to believe that Ibn Waḥshiyyah could know anything about the Babylonian civilisation and therefore consider his claim to be a forgery. On this work in its relation to the general art of divination among pre-Islamic Arabs and early Muslims see T. Fahd, *La divination arabe*, Leiden, 1966.

20 M. Hamidullah, 'Dīnawarī's Encyclopaedia Botanica (*Kitāb al-Nabāt*) in the Light of Fragments in Turkish Libraries', *Mélanges F. Koprülü*, pp. 195–206. See also B. Lewin, *The Book of Plants of Abū Hanīfah al-Dīnawarī*, Uppsala, 1953, introduction, in which is discussed the influence of this early work on the later Muslim botanists.

21 This sixth/twelfth-century Maghribī botanist has given some of the most detailed descriptions of plants found anywhere in Muslim botanical literature.

22 His two most important books are the *Kitāb al-jāmi' fi'l-adwiyat al-mufradah* (*The Complete Book of Simple Drugs*), dealing with the classification of plants, and *Kitāb al-mughnī fi'l-adwiyat al-mufradah* (*The Sufficient Book of Simple Drugs*), dealing with the medical properties of plants.

23 These are not elements in the modern sense but rather the principles of elements. They are to the sensible substances of nature what the geometric points and lines are to points and lines actually drawn on a piece of paper.

24 The union of the soul, which in Muslim cosmology derives from above the cosmic spheres, with a certain combination of the elements in the sublunary region is also considered to be *ad extra* and not as in a compound. As the combination of elements attains more harmony and greater equilibrium, it becomes purer so that the combination naturally attracts the soul to itself. In the minerals, the elements are not as perfectly balanced as in animals so that they attract a lower soul unto themselves.

25 Although minerals have been considered by many Muslim authors to be transmutable into one another, plants and animals have been considered to be unchangeable. Each plant, according to the Ikhwān al-Ṣafā', for example, has a chyme (*kaymūs*) formed from a particular combination of elements which always reproduces the same plant as each animal has a sperm which propagates the same species.

26 'Although plants are obvious and visible creations, the causes of their existence are hidden and veiled from the perception of man. It is what the philosophers call "natural forces", what the *Sharī'ah* calls "the angels and troops of Allah appointed for the nurturing of plants, the generation of animals and the composition of minerals", and what we call "partial spirits".' (Ikhwān al-Ṣafā', *Rasā'il*, II, p. 130; also R. Levy, *The Social Structure of Islam,* Cambridge, 1957, p. 490.)

27 We are following here the teaching of the Ikhwān, but these views are shared by most Muslim authors writing on this subject.

28 The Ikhwān have a most interesting section in their *Rasā'il* in which the animals dispute with man over his right to use them for his own ends. They refute all of man's claims of superiority by demonstrating their own spiritual and bodily qualities and virtues. It is only by realising that there are among men a few sages and saints who in their spiritual realisation fulfil the purpose of the whole creation that animals finally agree to submit to man. See the *Dispute between Man and the Animals*. See also Nasr, *An Introduction to Islamic Cosmological Doctrines*, chapter 2.

29 The most thorough discussion of the vegetative and animal souls appear in the sixth part of the *ṭabī'iyyāt* of the *Shifā'* of Ibn Sīnā where he deals in detail with all the faculties of plants and animals and their function. See J. Bakoš, *La psychologie d'Avicenne*, Prague, 1956. See also F. Rahman, *Avicenna's Psychology*, London,

1952. Ibn Sīnā and also most other authors writings on the faculties of the vegetative and animal souls derived many of their ideas from the *De Anima* of Aristotle. The Ikhwān, however, enumerate the faculties somewhat differently, as attraction, fixation, digestion, repulsion, nutrition, formation and growth.

30 For a summary of Ibn Sīnā's views on the souls and their faculties, see E. Gilson, 'Les sources gréco-arabes de l'augustinisme avicennant', *Archives d'Histoire Doctrinale et Littéraire du Moyen Age*, vol. IV, 1929, pp. 5–149.

31 In general, the Muslims depended more upon the Greeks in the study of animals than that of plants. Whereas Aristotle's works on animals were studied extensively, the botany of Theophrastus was nearly ignored. Muslim authors had already created a science of plants drawing their terminology mostly from the Quran and Arabic poetry before the first important Greek text on plants, the famous work of Dioscorides, was translated into Arabic.

32 See the botanical section of the *Nuzhat al-qulūb*, Bombay, 1311, pp. 87 ff., where sixty-nine fruit-bearing trees and sixty-six fruitless ones are described in alphabetical order. Qazwīnī, like many other Muslim natural historians, gives not only the description of a tree, the quality of its fruit and its wood and the location where it is found, but also its medical uses, its nature – that is, whether hot or cold, dry or moist – and its appearance in literature and sacred books. As for seed-bearing plants, Qazwīnī follows a similar procedure, describing altogether 280 kinds, each class arranged alphabetically.

33 The famous scientist and compiler Bīrūnī gives a good example of this astrological correspondence. He writes, 'The various organs of a plant are distributed to different planets. Thus the stem of a tree is appropriated to the Sun; the roots to Saturn, the thorns, twigs and barks to Mars; the flowers to Venus; the fruit to Jupiter; the leaves to the Moon; and the seed to Mercury'. (*Elements of Astrology*, tr. R. Ramsay Wright, London, 1934, p. 236.)

The correspondence between plants or animals and the planets is not to show astral 'influences' as is done in contemporary astrology, which is only a residue of the real subject known by the same name in medieval times. It is to show rather that the physical world is a symbol of the intelligible world, that there is an analogy between the archetypes symbolised by the planets and their earthly shadows which are the physical forms.

34 This is a schematisation of ideas presented in Ibn Sīnā's medical poem as well as in the *Qānūn*, to which we have already referred. Pathology, based on the doctrine of humours, is a heritage from the Hippocratic tradition of medicine as systematised by Galen. See also S. H. Nasr, *Islamic Science – An Illustrated Study*, p. 160 and also chapter IV, where natural history is discussed.

35 Mustawfī Qazwīnī in the *Nuzhat al-qulūb* follows a somewhat similar procedure, dividing animals into those living on land, in the sea and in air, and subdividing each of the classes according to its more specific features.

36 They may be said to symbolise psychic forces.

37 A similar account is to be found in the *Rasā'il* of the Ikhwān. It needs to be mentioned that many traditional Islamic theological and religious sources consider Iblīs as a fallen angel rather than a *jinn*, although some such as Zamakhsharī in his *Kashshāf* have considered him to be a *jinn*.

38 We see in Qazwīnī's writings a good example of the blending of the natural and supernatural orders to which we have already referred. His description of the colours and forms of animals and angels served as an inspiration for later Persian miniaturists.

39 Damīrī also interrupts his discussion of animals at several places in order to write about Islamic history, prayers based on the Divine Names, the science of *jafr* (symbolism of letters) and other subjects.

40 A beautiful expression of this doctrine appears in the *Mathnawī* of Mawlānā Jalāl

al-Dīn Rūmī. See Book IV, verses 3637–47 of the text of *Mathnawī*, ed. R. A. Nicholson, Leiden, 1929.

41 Many Western scientists themselves have refuted Darwinian evolution on strictly scientific terms, although the theory – absurd as it is – continues to be believed in as dogma for those whose whole world view would crumble without it. See, for example, D. Dewar, *Difficulties of the Evolutionary Theory*, London, 1931; and his more extensive *The Transformist Illusion*, Mulfreesboro, 1957; also J. Servier, *L'homme et l'invisible*, Paris, 1964; and A. E. Wilber Smith, *Man's Origin, Man's Destiny*, Wheaton, Ill., 1968.

Philosophy

12

The Pertinence of Studying Islamic Philosophy Today

Philosophical ideas which have originated and developed in the West are studied avidly nearly everywhere in the Islamic world today, especially in university and academic circles. They are taught regularly in the classroom so that many of those Muslims who are the products of the modern educational system often know a great deal more about a second-rate European philosopher than about the most famous of the Muslim sages. However, this widespread influence of European philosophy in academic circles in the Islamic world is far from uniform. The discord, diversity and contrast that are so characteristic of modern European civilisation, especially in the domain of philosophy, are reflected in the modern East as well. And here historical accidents seem to be the criteria for the type of philosophical ideas which have become dominant in each Muslim country.

It is well known that in Europe, despite a general anti-traditional and rationalistic tendency that is manifested nearly everywhere, the French, English, German and other national units have preserved a certain colour of their own. The French philosophers since Descartes have been renowned for their 'geometric' and clear manner of thinking, which is already reflected in their language. The British have on their side usually tended towards empiricism and a disdain for the strict methodology found among the continental philosophers. As for the Germans, while in general they have been the most methodological and systematic of the Europeans, they have preserved a tendency towards the transcendent in their world-view which is clearly seen not only in their language but also in their music, literature and philosophy.

Now, this and other diverse elements have been instrumental in determining the study of modern philosophy in the Muslim world. Where French political influence has been dominant, it is French philosophy that has become most prevalent. For example, in Persia where, during the past century, French culture has been the most dominant European influence, the *Discourse on Method* of Descartes was the first modern philosophical work to be translated into Persian. And in university circles the ideas of the French philosophers and their methodology are the mainstay of the curriculum and have become the most important of the present modernising influences. Similarly, in sociology it is still the positivism of Comte – long forgotten as a living influence in Europe itself – that is taught practically as a revealed dogma by some, while the younger sociologists turn to the more recent French schools of Durkheim and Lévi-Strauss.

In India and Pakistan, where British influence has had the upper hand, it is naturally Anglo-Saxon philosophy that has been the formative influence in academic circles, and more particularly late nineteenth-century British philosophy. For one who first comes in contact with philosophical studies in the Indo-Pakistan subcontinent, this point is particularly startling. Here, such thinkers as Spencer are still powerful forces in academic circles, while the same figures might be completely unknown in a neighbouring country and vice versa. And even when attention is turned towards contemporary philosophy, it is logical positivism, whose influence is mostly confined to the English-speaking world, which becomes the source of attraction for certain philosophers. At the same time, this school is nearly unknown in those Muslim countries where knowledge of English is not so widespread.

The same situation exists with modifications in Arab countries and other Muslim lands. Where a group of students have been sent to Germany, they have become propagators of German philosophy. Others have become exponents of the English or French or in other cases the American and more recently even Russian schools. Moreover, the philosophical influence from the West is often limited temporally as well as spatially. As already mentioned, Comte and Spencer still reign as great authorities long after they have ceased to exercise any influence in the very *milieu* in which they were born and where they once prospered. And the new schools of philosophy – or rather 'misosophy', for they are usually the real haters rather than lovers of wisdom – spread much like dress fashion, rapidly but quite unequally and unevenly in various Muslim countries. The spread, moreover, is always accompanied by the inevitable time-lag whereby what comes into vogue in the countries which are in the process of copying has already become more or less defunct in its homeland.[1] In fact, often the more enthusiastic supporters of certain Western philosophers who are no longer fashionable in the Occident are to be found among the Westernised Easterners.[2]

It is against this heterogeneous background that European philosophy is studied in the universities of the Islamic world. Added to this fact is the almost total neglect, in modern educational circles, of the Islamic intellectual tradition which has moulded the Muslim mind for the past fourteen centuries. No wonder then that there is nearly a complete rupture between Islamic society and the newly-formed educated class, especially in matters philosophical. There is no organic bond between the two and the intellectual and philosophical activity of this class, instead of being like a flower that has grown from the soil, is more like a plant that has been artificially placed in the ground, without roots and without means of nourishing and supporting itself, so that it withers away and dies with the first wind.

Not only is there not an organic nexus between the new philosophical ideas and the ideals of Muslim society, but there is even violent opposition. This is substantiated in the often disruptive and dissolving influence that these modes of thought have on the general social and intellectual life of Islam. These ideas, imported from abroad, tend to misguide and cause deviation as well as to destroy spontaneity and creativity. They substitute instead such an artificial life that even the most avid supporters of these modern schools of thought have come to lament the sad state of affairs. But few have bothered to inquire deeply into the cause of this passivity and apathy. It stems from the fact that there is no connection between much that is studied and taught in the academic circles of the Islamic world and the inner sources of life of Islam. Few realise that all activity is not necessarily a sign of real life, that a true death is better than a false life, that the Muslims sleep on treasures of wisdom whose neglect in no way makes them non-existent.

Because the Western-educated classes in the Islamic world are on the receiving end of general influences from the West, they tend to learn even about Islamic philosophy and their own intellectual heritage from orientalists and other Occidental sources. Even now in the case of the least prejudiced and most sympathetic orientalists – with some honourable exceptions – there is a tendency to substitute that period of Islamic intellectual history which influenced the West for the whole intellectual history of the Muslim world. Thus nearly every branch of the sciences and philosophy terminates, according to most of these sources, around the seventh/thirteenth century, the very period when intellectual contact between the East and West ceased. As a result, most Western-educated Oriental students of Islamic philosophy, who rely upon standard Western sources,[3] think that for the past six or seven centuries there has been no intellectual life in Islam, and they tend to treat their own intellectual tradition as a passing phase in the history of Western civilisation.

There has been a great revival of interest in medieval civilisation on the part of Western scholars during this century and in respectable academic circles one no longer follows the prejudice of the

Renaissance and the seventeenth and eighteenth centuries in calling the medieval period or its early phase the Dark Ages.[4] Historians and philosophers in general have come to realise that the 'darkness' lay more in the ignorance of succeeding centuries than in the Middle Ages itself. Consequently, not only has there been a strong revival of interest in Thomistic philosophy, but also monumental works of research by such men as Gilson, Bréhier, Duhem, Wolfson, de Wulf and other outstanding scholars have brought to light the rich intellectual life of the medieval West. And here the early period of Islamic philosophy from al-Kindī to Ibn Rushd plays a major role as a dominant influence in the formation of Scholasticism and other intellectual perspectives in the Latin world.

The serious Western scholars who limit themselves to the early centuries in their treatment of Islamic philosophy are right in a way in that they are interested in the Western intellectual tradition in which Islamic elements play a passing role. But to regard the intellectual life of Islam from their point of view is doubly wrong for a Muslim: first because his aim is usually to study Islamic civilisation itself and not another civilisation upon which Islam exercised some influence; secondly because one cannot look at oneself through the eyes of another and hope to gain an immediate and inner knowledge of oneself. The fruit of the research of the orientalists, therefore, however valuable it may be in certain respects, cannot under normal circumstances have the same meaning for Muslims as it has for Westerners. One can hardly overemphasise the harm that the current view of Islamic intellectual history causes those who are affected by it. The Muslim student who comes to learn about his own civilisation from the standard Western sources[5] feels an immediate estrangement from his tradition. He begins to believe that his co-religionists and compatriots have not 'thought' for seven hundred years and that suddenly he is coming upon an intellectual stage in which he and those like him are the sole actors. What false feelings of arrogance, what displacement and estrangement from the rest of society have been brought about as a result of this 'learned ignorance'!

One must add to this dislocation the unsuitable categories with which most Western scholars study Islam. The words 'orthodox' and 'heterodox' are used in a way which disfigures the whole intellectual structure of Islamic civilisation. The early Western students of Islam, who were mostly missionaries with a Christian theological training, looked for the same divisions in Islam as they knew in modern Christianity. As a result Ash'arite theology came to mean orthodoxy and the doctrines of Sufism or gnosis became almost by definition heterodox. The whole meaning and role of the various schools of philosophy and theosophy have been misunderstood as a result of the application of categories alien to the structure of Islam. These and many other factors which have risen from the false view of Islamic intellectual history have made the correct interpretation of the Islamic heritage difficult, although the genuine sources, both written and oral, still exist for all who care to explore and study them.

The remedy for the ills brought about by the incomplete and partial study of Islamic philosophy is a thorough and complete investigation of the vast panorama of the intellectual life of Islam, undertaken sympathetically by the Muslims themselves.[6] A sympathetic and inward study of the subject will reveal many riches which remain hidden from the so-called 'objective' method, a method that is nevertheless restricted by the mental horizons of modern thought. As already mentioned, it will, moreover, dispel the illusion that Islamic philosophy ceased with Ibn Rushd. It will make plain the fact that in a sense Islamic philosophy – or theosophy, properly speaking – begins and not ends in the sixth/twelfth century. For at the very moment when Peripatetic philosophy, as developed by al-Kindī, Fārābī and Ibn Sīnā, had come under the severe attack of the theologians and had travelled to Andalusia where with Ibn Ṭufayl, Ibn Bājjah and Ibn Rushd it was passing through its Indian summer, a new school was rising in the East, founded by the master of Illumination, Shaykh al-ishrāq Shihāb al-Dīn Suhrawardī.

A close study of the later phase of the history of Islamic philosophy, as outlined in chapter 6, will reveal the revival of Peripatetic philosophy with Khwājah Naṣīr al-Dīn Ṭūsī, the gradual penetration of the gnostic doctrines of Ibn 'Arabī in the East and its mixture with the tenets of Peripatetic philosophy and Illuminationist theosophy, and finally a grand synthesis of the various intellectual perspectives in Islam by Mīr Dāmād and Mullā Ṣadrā.[7] This eleventh/seventeenth-century sage, in whose writings the detailed and exact arguments of an acute logician are combined with the spiritual vision and metaphysical penetration of a gnostic and seer, opened a new chapter in Islamic philosophy which has permitted this intellectual heritage to endure, despite the vicissitudes of time, to the present day. Although centred primarily in Persia and in those regions of India where Persian culture has been dominant, the school of Mullā Ṣadrā and his followers such as the thirteenth/nineteenth-century Ḥājjī Mullā Hādī Sabziwārī belong to the whole of the Islamic world and in fact to the world at large. And they must serve as the intellectual background from which any new philosophical ventures which are to have any organic link with the world view of Islam must be undertaken.

The complete study of the intellectual history of Islam will also reveal the Islamic gnostic tradition (*'irfān* or *ma'rifah*), which possesses the deepest metaphysical insights and which has survived as a living tradition to the present day from one end of the Islamic world to the other. How can a modern Muslim thinker speak of religious philosophy without tapping the inexhaustible spiritual treasures hidden in the writings of such masters of Islamic gnosis as Ibn 'Arabī, Rūmī, Jīlī, Ṣadr al-Dīn Qunyawī and others?

Also, such a study will reveal the important theologians of the later period,[8] the way they faced the particular problems of other fields of knowledge and the manner in which they defended the tenets of the faith in the face of various types of doubt. Here also, there are important figures of later centuries such as Shāh Waliallāh of Delhi or 'Abd al-Razzāq Lāhījī, who, although famous in their homeland, are not sufficiently known to the entire Islamic world.

Although it is not our intention to discuss here the various principles of Islamic philosophy, a few of its cardinal features which are of inestimable value and which should be taken into consideration by contemporary thinkers bear mentioning. First of all, Islam is a tradition based wholly upon a distinct revelation; consequently, the sense of the transcendent and the revealed is a potent force in Islamic society. No philosophy which ignores both revelation and intellectual intuition, and thus divorces itself from the twin sources of transcendent knowledge, can hope to be anything but a disrupting and dissolving influence in Islamic society. Indeed, Islamic philosophy *is* precisely 'prophetic philosophy', that is to say a world view in which the role of revelation, in both the macrocosmic and the microcosmic sense, looms large on the horizon. And it is in Islam that 'prophetic philosophy' finds its most complete and perfect expression.

Secondly, and closely connected to this point, there is the question of the relation between reason and revelation, which occupied the Muslim philosophers from the very beginning and which found its most harmonious solution in the hands of Mullā Ṣadrā, who like the sages before him expounded that Divine Wisdom or *sapientia*, that gnosis in which faith and reason find their common ground. One need hardly mention that, once the function of the intellect is reduced to reason and also revelation is limited to its most exoteric and outward level of meaning, then faith and reason can never become truly harmonised. Every attempt which is then made to bring about a harmony will meet with the lack of success that the history of modern times so amply illustrates.

Islamic philosophy also possesses a unified vision of things – that is, a view of the interrelation between all realms of knowledge. However dangerous the separative tendency (or sclerosis as some call it) of the modern sciences may be for the West, it is doubly fatal for Islam, whose sole *raison d'être* is to assert the doctrine of unity (*al-tawḥīd*) and to apply it to every aspect of life. To be able to create and maintain an interrelation between various fields of knowledge is therefore of vital importance for all who are interested in the welfare of Islamic society. And here, as in other instances, the Islamic intellectual heritage offers ample guidance.

There are numerous other traits of the philosophical and metaphysical schools in Islam which are worth discussing. Here it is sufficient to mention that there has been a continuity of intellectual tradition in Islam from the beginning to the present day, and that if this tradition is forgotten it is not because it does not exist but rather because we are sleeping over treasures. If the modern philosophies that are now being propagated in the Islamic world by Muslims themselves are to be anything more than a disintegrating factor, then the principles of Islamic wisdom (*ḥikmah*)[9] must be rediscovered and the new problems solved by appealing to these immutable principles. If this chasm which separates the world view of the newly educated minority from the vast majority of the Islamic community, and which will finally result in the dangerous situation of a house divided against itself, is to be bridged, then the principles have to be rediscovered and the roots that sink deep into the very nature of Reality re-explored.

> Everyone who is left far from his Sources
> Wishes to return to the time when he was united with It.[10]

The pertinence of studying the Islamic intellectual tradition is that it can aid us to regain those principles which alone can render our existence and activity meaningful. It can help to convert dissipative mental play which today goes under the name of philosophy into a real love of *sophia* or wisdom and a contemplative vision of the truth.

Notes

1 We have dealt extensively with this question and the trend in philosophical studies in the Islamic world during the past few decades in our 'The Development of Philosophy in the Islamic World since the Second World War', in *Handbook of Developments in World Philosophy*, ed. by J. Burr, Westport (Conn.) 1980, pp. 421–433.

2 Who can deny that in university and intellectual circles the most enthusiastic supporters of 'progress' are to be found among Westernised Orientals rather than Westerners themselves?

See S. H. Nasr, *Islam and the Plight of Modern Man*, London, 1976.

3 The most widely read works of this kind such as those of T. J. de Boer, De Lacy O'Leary, Munk, Quadri and Walzer make Islamic philosophy synonymous with the early Peripatetic school and its opponents and terminate with Ibn Rushd in the sixth/twelfth century. It has now become fashionable to add Ibn Khaldūn to the list; here again only because of his importance in the philosophy of history and sociology as they are judged by modern criteria, and not in the light of his significance according to proper Islamic systems of evaluation.

The only Western scholars who have dealt at all seriously with the later phase of Islamic philosophy are M. Horten . . . and especially H. Corbin, the only really important Western student of this aspect of intellectual history in Islam. In such works as *Terre céleste et corps de résurrection: de l'Iran mazdéen à l'Iran shī'ite*, Paris, 1978, many articles in *Eranos-Jahrbuch*, his two prolegomena to Suhrawardī's *Opera Metaphysica et Mystica, Histoire de la philosophie islamique* (with the collaboration of S. H. Nasr and O. Yahya), and *En Islam iranien*, 4 vols, Paris, 1971–2, he has introduced some of the vast riches of Islamic wisdom to the Occidental audience. For his bibliography see S. H. Nasr (ed.), *Mélanges offerts à Henry Corbin*, pp. iii-xxxii.

In this connection see also S. H. Nasr, 'Suhrawardī', 'The School of Ispahan', 'Ṣadr al-Dīn Shīrāzī' and 'Sabziwārī', in *A History of Muslim Philosophy*, edited by M. M. Sharif, 2 vols, Wiesbaden, 1963–6; and S. H. Nasr, *Three Muslim Sages*. See also T. Izutsu, *The Concept and Reality of Existence*, Tokyo, 1971; Izutsu is the second major non-Muslim scholar, who has devoted major works to the later schools of Islamic philosophy. His writings, along with those of H. Corbin, have helped to turn the attention of many young scholars to later Islamic philosophy. It is hoped, therefore, that this situation will change before long.

4 Although – alas! – this is still followed by many Western oriented Muslims, who thus become more opposed to the medieval period – both Eastern and Western – than most modern philosophers themselves, in whose example this feeling of systematic opposition to the Middle Ages was first cultivated in the East.

5 This also holds true in the case of the large number of works in Arabic and English mostly by Near-Eastern and Indo-Pakistani authors who, although Muslim, reflect essentially the orientalists' view in their writings.

6 The monumental *History of Muslim Philosophy* is an important step in this direction. In this connection, the brief study of Iqbal, *The Development of Metaphysics in Persia*, is of some interest.

7 Concerning Mullā Sadrā see the later chapters in this book; also S. H. Nasr, *Ṣadr al-Dīn Shīrāzī and his Transcendent Theosophy*, London, 1978.

8 In the field of Islamic theology, several such studies, like those of Shiblī Nu'mānī, have already been made, although there is still much to be done to complete his task and those begun by a few other Muslim scholars.

9 Needless to say, the various intellectual schools in Islam contain many elements from other civilisations but these were all Muslimised and made to harmonise with the principles of the Islamic revelation through the synthesising and integrating power of Islam.

10 هر کسی کو دور ماند از اصل خویش باز جوید روزگار وصل خویش

From Rūmī's *Mathnawī*, translated by R. A. Nicholson, vol. II, London, 1926, p. 5.

13

Islamic Philosophy – Reorientation or Re-understanding

One of the features which characterise modern man is that he always seeks to reform everything from social and economic institutions to philosophical and religious traditions, but rarely is he willing to reform himself. Without putting his inner house in order, he tries to order and shape the world around him. This persistent attitude, which manifests itself in nearly every area of life today, is based ultimately on the assumption – made either consciously or unconsciously – that man as he is today is not imperfect in a basic sense; rather, the institutions and traditions which have perennially guided and nurtured man in his earthly life are imperfect because they no longer conform to the nature of modern man. Thus, time and space and the material world which is determined by them become the criteria of the truth, so that whatever does not conform to what is called the 'times' is rejected as being out of date, as we have already mentioned in our earlier study on the *Sharī'ah*.

This whole attitude, according to which man becomes the reformer of all things but never of himself, and temporal conditions become the criteria for the judgement of the truth itself, is a heritage of the European Renaissance, in which man – in his 'earthly nature' or what in Islamic terms is called *bashar* and not in his universal nature or *insān* – becomes the 'measure of all things'. According to this humanism, which underlies so much of modern European thought, it is earthly man and his nature which determine the value and validity of things. Consequently there is no transcendent and immutable model according to which man and society are judged.

It is in this mental climate that the question of the reorientation of Islamic philosophy is usually approached.[1] There is, however, an apparent contradiction in terms when this question is approached in such a manner. To reorient means already to possess a knowledge of the goal to be pursued and then to turn one's efforts and to orient oneself towards that goal. But to know the goal to be pursued must in itself be the fruit of a philosophy and a world-view. According to what philosophy are we going to reorient Islamic philosophy except those subjective limitations and inclinations which in their totality make up our immediate environment according to which we seek to reform all things? And this attitude is precisely the result of that humanism and relativism which characterise so much of modern thought. We want to determine a goal through our own human understanding and then reorient religious thought towards it, thereby admitting, whether consciously or unconsciously, to the primacy of the human over the Divine. Considered in this manner, the possibility of simply reorienting Islamic philosophy becomes a compromise in the principles of that philosophy itself, and the question arises as to whether we should reorient or re-understand Islamic philosophy.

The word 'orient' brings to mind the whole *ishrāqī* or Illuminationist doctrine of Suhrawardī regarding the symbolism of space.[2] We know that in European languages 'orient' contains the double meaning of the East as well as turning to the correct direction. In reality, this East is not so much a geographic direction as the 'Orient of Light' which is the spiritual world transcending the world of material forms. It is also the abode of that spiritual light which illuminates us and through which we receive veritable knowledge. To orient oneself, in the real sense, means therefore to turn to that Centre and Origin from which things really issue forth, that East which is also the inner and spiritual dimension of things. It means also a penetration within ourselves and a reintegration. Applied to Islamic philosophy, this manner of thinking means then a re-penetration into its spiritual and inner contents and an absorption of its essential truths, or in other words a re-understanding in the profoundest sense of this word.

When we turn to Islamic philosophy, we find it to be full of vast stores of wisdom which today remain relatively unknown to the majority of contemporary Muslims.[3] We come to realise that so much of the knowledge which we seek elsewhere exists in its pure and unadulterated form already in our midst, although we have been practically unaware of its existence.[4]

Islamic philosophy, although rich in many fields, is based most of all on metaphysics and nearly every treatise on traditional philosophy deals with the transcendent origin and end of things.[5] The Islamic philosophers were the first to make the discussion of being the cornerstone of philosophy and sought to relate every existing thing to Pure Being which is the origin of all existence. Moreover, in metaphysics they developed a philosophy of nature within a general world view in order to create a close relationship between various forms and branches of the sciences and to relate multiplicity to unity.[6]

The Islamic philosophers developed an ethical system based not only on 'rational ethics' but on the specific teachings of the Quran. In Islamic ethics the Divine Will appears not in an abstract manner but in concrete injunctions contained in the Sacred Law or *Sharī'ah*. This Law helps human intelligence to overcome the limitations imposed on it by the passions and to see the good and evil nature of things in their true perspective. Metaphysics is, moreover, never divorced from ethics and from the practical aspect of religion in that, as the *Ḥaqīqah*, it is the inner dimension of this very *Sharī'ah* which determines man's life and conduct on earth.

Similarly, the Islamic philosophers developed an aesthetics highly refined and closely connected to metaphysics. Because the spirit of Islam is based on intelligence and discernment, every true manifestation of it possesses an aspect of beauty and harmony. The Islamic philosophers – if of course we understand by philosophers as we do throughout this essay *ḥukamā'* or 'sages' – based their conception of beauty on the notion of harmony and sobriety and conceived of beauty not as the luxury it is considered today but as a necessary condition of a truly human existence. The nature of the truth, according to them, is such that it is beautiful. And for this reason the expression of Islamic philosophy – especially metaphysics – is combined with the beauty of language and with highly artistic forms of expression.

These and many other aspects of Islamic philosophy we must thoroughly re-explore and re-understand before we take any further steps. Of course there are those who would say that despite all this richness this philosophy does not answer today's problems. To this objection, we would answer that either the problems of today are real ones, in that they concern the nature of things and man's situation in the general scheme of existence, in which case they are not really new problems but perennial ones that have been amply treated in the traditional Islamic sources; or these are problems which – like so many that modern man faces – are created by incorrectly posed questions or the stubborn attempt of man 'to live by bread alone'. In this case, even if the traditional sources do not provide an answer, their study will reveal that in reality there is no problem to start with. Finally, even if one chooses to reject Islamic philosophy, one must first of all understand it. One can scarcely reject what one does not know. The re-understanding of Islamic philosophy is therefore incumbent upon us, no matter what direction we wish to pursue in the future. No matter where one wants to go, one must start from where one is.

When all is said and done, the fact remains that the Islamic traditional teachings are couched in a language which is not easily understood by many contemporary men, especially those with a modern education. The old treatises were usually written in a syllogistic language which is no longer prevalent today. What must be done is to disengage the content of Islamic philosphy from the language which is now not well received and to present it in terms more comformable to the intellectual horizon of our contemporaries. What is needed essentially is a re-presentation of the whole body of Islamic wisdom in a contemporary language. Thus those who seek for various problems the solution offered by this form of wisdom will find it without the barrier of unfamiliar language or thought structure. The tenets of Islamic philosophy must be made well known both for the solutions they offer to perennial questions and as the basis and line of approach for the questions that specifically beset modern man as a result of the peculiar and one might say anomalous conditions of the modern world.[7]

A thorough re-understanding and re-presentation of Islamic philosophy will itself 'orient' our thought by clarifying the ultimate end of human existence and the final goal of man's terrestrial journey. Man is a theomorphic being and cannot escape the profound demands of his inner nature. Only that civilisation and form of thought can survive which conform to man's entelechy and the ultimate nature of things. The re-understanding of Islamic philosophy will once again reveal to us that end towards which man and the cosmos are ultimately oriented and towards which all things move. It thus permits us to discover the goal of life and thought itself. By revealing to us the truth, it enables us to reorient ourselves and our thoughts in its direction, on that high road whose end is union with the Truth. The question of the reorientation of Islamic philosophy reduces then to a re-understanding of it and to the discovery of the goal towards which our thoughts and efforts should be directed. Man comes to know the truth not by reorienting it but by reorienting himself so that he can become worthy of being its recipient.

Notes

1 Some people use Muslim philosophy rather than Islamic philosophy and distinguish between 'Muslim' and 'Islamic'. Such a distinction in English is acceptable on a certain level in that it distinguishes between what has flourished among people who are Muslims and what has been derived directly from the Quranic revelation. But in a more universal sense, all that became integrated into Muslim civilisation was in a sense Islamic in that its essence conformed to the spirit of Islam. Especially in the realm of philosophy, understood in its most universal sense as wisdom (*ḥikmah*), what survived after the early centuries was not only Muslim but also Islamic, in that it possessed a profound relation with the doctrines of Islam and its particular intellectual genius.

See the Introduction to S. H. Nasr, *Three Muslim Sages*.

2 See *Three Muslim Sages*, pp. 65–6; also S. H. Nasr, 'Suhrawardī' in *A History of Muslim Philosophy*, vol. I., pp. 381 ff.

3 We have dealt with this matter in the previous chapter.

4 'All civilisations have decayed; only they have decayed in different ways: the decay of the East is passive and that of the West is active. The fault of the East in decay is that it no longer thinks; the West in decay thinks too much and thinks wrongly. The East is sleeping over truths; the West lives in errors.' (F. Schuon, *Spiritual Perspectives and Human Facts*, translated by D. M. Matheson, London, 1954, p. 22.)

5 That is why so many of these treatises are called *al-Mabda' wa'l-ma'ād* in Arabic or *Āghāz wa anjām* in Persian.

6 This question and its pertinence for the Muslims of the present day is dwelt on in S. H. Nasr, *Introduction to Islamic Cosmological Doctrines*, especially the Prologue.

7 'There are no doubt contemporary philosophical problems, but there are no intellectual needs so particularly to our time as to render incomprehensible those of our fathers. Even with the best – or the worst – will in the world the foundations of the human spirit are not so quickly altered as that'. Schuon, op. cit., pp. 14–15.

14

The Life, Doctrines and Significance of Ṣadr al-Dīn Shīrāzī (Mullā Ṣadrā)

I

The medieval Christian view of Islam not only influenced the attitude of the later centuries in Europe towards Islam and Islamic civilisation but also through the spread of European culture after the Renaissance it moulded the views of the other civilisations towards Islam and even modern Muslims towards themselves. This influence holds for the various facets of Islamic civilisation as well as for the religion of Islam. As a result, what has been studied in the Western world until now has been mostly that aspect and phase of the Islamic arts and sciences which contributed to the formation of the culture of the High Middle Ages in the Latin world. Until recently, the rest has been nearly neglected.

Nowhere is this point of view more evident than in the study of Islamic philosophical and metaphysical doctrines. As mentioned in previous chapters, many outside the Islamic world have heard of Fārābī, Ibn Sīnā, Ghazzālī or Ibn Rushd. Indeed, one can find numerous studies in European languages devoted to these figures because they influenced the formation of Latin Scholasticism. But few people know the exact identity of Shaykh Shihāb al-Dīn Suhrawardī. He is usually associated vaguely with the famous Sufi family of that name. Comparably few know anything of Ṣadr al-Dīn Shīrāzī, except that he was a Persian philosopher of the Safavid period. This lack of knowledge is due principally to the fact that the writings of these and other sages of similar stature were not translated into Latin. Thus they were overlooked by the majority of Western scholars whose study of Islam was limited to the extent that it influenced the Occidental world.[1]

Yet, contrary to what appears in European languages and in the writings of those Muslims who have based their studies exclusively on such sources, the intellectual life of Islam did not end with the Spanish philosophers nor even with the onslaught of the Mongol invasion. Aristotelian philosophy found its purest disciple in Ibn Rushd and turned westward to become the dominant element in the Western world from the seventh/thirteenth century to the end of the Middle Ages. At the same time in Islam, rationalism, inherent in Peripatetic philosophy, was losing ground under the attacks of both theologians and Sufis like Ghazzālī and Fakhr al-Dīn Rāzī.[2]

In its place, the gnostic doctrines of Muḥyī al-Dīn ibn 'Arabī, the famous Andalusian sage whom Ibn Rushd was to meet at Cordova,[3] and the Illuminationist theosophy[4] (*ḥikmat al-ishrāq*) of Suhrawardī[5] came to occupy the centre of the stage. Thus Islamic intellectual life turned from rationalism to a form of knowledge based on intuition and illumination. It subsequently produced many sages who have preserved this tradition of wisdom, although to this day it remains almost completely unknown to the outside world. Moreover, while the purely gnostic teachings of Ibn 'Arabī spread throughout the entire Islamic world, the *ishrāqī* theosophy and the later schools, which combined it with the teachings of Ibn 'Arabī and also the Peripatetics, developed almost wholly in the Shi'ite world. This latter tradition of wisdom, of which Mullā Ṣadrā is perhaps the greatest representative, has since remained mostly within the boundaries of Persia. The Persian world has served as its home, even though it has journeyed occasionally westward to the Arab countries and especially eastward to India.[6]

Ṣadr al-Dīn Shīrāzī or Mullā Ṣadrā[7] is one of the greatest intellectual figures of Islam. This is true in spite of the fact that his doctrines have long remained in obscurity outside the few disciples who have to this day kept his teachings alive in Persia and in India. He was born in 979 or 980 AH in Shiraz to the famous and powerful Qawam family, his father having served as a vizier to the king.[8] Because he was the only son in the family, his father took great care to give him the best education possible. From his early days, the youth showed a remarkable aptitude and eagerness for learning, along with a deep sense of devotion and love for Islam.

After his preliminary studies in Shiraz, he set out for Isfahan, which was then the capital and intellectual centre of Persia. There he met the greatest teachers of his day, learning the transmitted (*naqlī*) sciences from Shaykh Bahā' al-Dīn 'Āmilī and the intellectual (*'aqlī*) sciences from Mīr Dāmād. He is also said to have studied with the well known Sufi and scholar, Mīr Findiriskī.[9] He soon mastered all of these subjects, especially *ḥikmah* or traditional theosophy in which he surpassed all his teachers.

Mullā Ṣadrā's open defence and propagation of gnostic doctrines (*'irfān*), however, soon brought him into difficulty with some of the exoteric authorities of the Law. Were it not for his father's influence at court, he might have come to the same end as Suhrawardī who lost his life as the result of a too carefree exposition of esoteric doctrines. As a consequence of these attacks, he withdrew from public life and retired to the village of Kahak near Qum, where he spent seven – or, according to some, eleven – years in meditation and ascetic practices.[10]

At the end of this period, Allāhwirdī Khān, governor of Fars, built a large school in Shiraz and invited Mullā Sadrā to serve as a professor. Ākhūnd, as he is called by his disciples, accepted and once again returned to his birthplace, where he spent the rest of his days teaching and writing.[11] Under his direction the school became the leading centre of learning in Persia, attracting students from many Muslim countries. It remained in this prosperous state until 1050 AH, when Mullā Ṣadrā, while making his seventh pilgrimage to Mecca on foot, died in Basra and was buried there.

As seen in this brief biographical sketch, Mullā Ṣadrā's life may be divided into three distinct phases: the period of formal study and education, the years of retirement spent in asceticism and contemplation, and his return to teaching and writing. This threefold division is important insofar as his works and doctrines are concerned, since Mullā Ṣadrā believed that neither rational demonstration and formal learning nor asceticism alone could lead one to the total vision of the truth. Rather, the two approaches must be combined in order to achieve the ultimate goal of knowledge. In fact, his own writings almost all belong to the third period of his life, in which he perfected formal learning and succeeded in purifying his soul through asceticism and by means of various spiritual exercises.

The writings of Mullā Ṣadrā may be divided into those which deal primarily with intellectual sciences and those which concern themselves with religious questions. However, in his view these two paths towards the truth are never completely divorced from each other. Of the first category, the work which stands as one of the greatest monuments of metaphysics in Islam is *al-Ḥikmat al-muta'āliyah fi'l-asfār al-arba'ah* (*The Transcendent Theosophy* [*or High Wisdom*] *Concerning the Four Journeys of the Soul*) usually known as *Asfār*, which in four books or four stages of a journey (*safar*, *asfār* being its broken plural) deals with the origin and end of all cosmic manifestation and the human soul in particular.[12] Other famous works of this genre include *al-Mabda' wa'l-ma'ād* (*The Book of Origin and Return*) *al-Shawāhid al-rubūbiyyah* (*Divine Witnesses*), *al-Ḥikmat al-'arshiyyah* (*The Book of Theosophy descending from the Divine Throne*), commentaries and glosses upon the *Shifā'* of Ibn Sīnā, *al-Hidāyah* (*Book of Guidance*) of Athīr al-Dīn Abharī and the *Ḥikmat al-ishrāq* of Suhrawardī, and many shorter treatises dealing with specific metaphysical and philosophical questions.[13] The predominantly religious works include the Quranic commentaries *Mafātīḥ al-ghayb* (*Keys to the Invisible World*), *Asrār al-āyāt* (*Secrets of the Verses of the Quran*) and the famous commentary on the *Uṣūl al-kāfī* of Kulaynī.[14] Altogether he is survived by nearly forty authentic works. In addition, there are some dozen treatises attributed to him whose authorship remains doubtful.

II

The genius of Mullā Ṣadrā lay in his ability to harmonise philosophy, based upon rational demonstration, with gnosis on the one hand and revelation on the other. Thus he brought to a successful conclusion the attempts begun by Kindī, Fārābī and Ibn Sīnā (especially in his Quranic commentaries) and continued by Ghazzālī, Suhrawardī and Naṣī al-Dīn Ṭūsī, to coordinate faith and reason or religion and science. Mullā Ṣadrā's final triumph in this coordination and harmonisation was based especially on the effort of a series of gnostics and philosophers between the sixth/twelfth and tenth/sixteenth centuries, such as Quṭb al-Dīn Shīrāzī, Mīr Sayyid Sharīf Jurjānī, Sayyid Ḥaydar Āmulī, Rajab Bursī, the Dashtakī family, Ibn Turkah Iṣfahānī, Ibn Abī Jumhūr and especially his own teacher, Mīr Damād, who harmonised Peripatetic philosophy with *ishrāqī* theosophy and gnosis and sought to integrate the whole into the religious perspective of Shi'ism.[15] They prepared the way for the final synthesis which was to take place with Mullā Ṣadrā.

The threads which were woven together to form the texture of this vast synthesis can be more or less distinguished and traced to their origin. Needless to say, Mullā Ṣadrā drew from nearly all the schools to be found in Islam, from the theologians to the philosophers and gnostics and even the Hermeticists and neo-Pythagoreans. In a general sense the main sources of his doctrines can be enumerated as follows:

(1) Islamic Peripatetic philosophy, especially that of Ibn Sīnā and, through it, the philosophy of Aristotle and the neo-Platonists, many of whose doctrines became part of Peripatetic philosophy in Islam.

(2) The *ishrāqī* theosophy of Suhrawardī and all his commentators, such as Quṭb al-Dīn Shīrāzī and Jalāl al-Dīn Dawānī.

(3) The gnostic doctrines of Ibn 'Arabī and other expositors of the teachings of his school such as Ṣadr al-Dīn Qunyawī as well as the works of other Sufi masters, such as 'Ayn al-Quḍāt Hamadānī and Maḥmūd Shabistarī.

(4) Islamic revelation, including certain sayings of the Blessed Prophet and the Shīʿite Imāms, particularly the *Nahj al-balāghah* (*The Path of Eloquence*), which all serve as the inspired basis of Islamic wisdom.[16]

By combining the rigour of Peripatetic demonstration with the ecstasy of illumination, and crowning it with evidence drawn from the Quran and *Ḥadīth*, Mullā Ṣadrā assembled diverse elements which had never before been united in the same manner.

Here space does not permit a detailed account of the doctrines of Ṣadr al-Dīn. Suffice it to mention those outstanding principles which compose the intellectual edifice he constructed and are the distinguishing features of his particular perspective and school.[17]

The whole doctrinal formulation of Mullā Ṣadrā is based on the unity (*waḥdah*), principiality (*aṣālah*) and gradation (*tashkīk*) of existence, that is to say that existence is a single reality which is also the ultimate reality of the Universe, the *māhiyyāt* or quiddities comprising its limitations, and yet it partakes of grades which differ from each other only in strength and weakness, like light which is the same reality whether it be that of the sun or of a candle but is stronger in one case and weaker in another. Mullā Ṣadrā upholds this view in opposition to the theologians (*mutakallimūn*) who believe that only the *māhiyyāt* have principiality, that is are real, and existence is no more than an abstraction, even God 'being' a *māhiyyah*. He also stands against both the Peripatetics (*mashshā'iyyūn*) and Illuminationists (*ishrāqiyyūn*), the first of whom consider existence to be principial but believe that the existence of each *māhiyyah* differs from that of others, and the second of whom believe that principiality belongs to the *māhiyyah*. Mullā Ṣadrā goes beyond those views in considering all existing things to be grades and stages of one being, which extends from Pure Being or God to the *hylé* or prime matters whose only share in being is the capability of accepting forms.[18]

Another essential doctrine of Mullā Ṣadrā is motion in the category of substance or transubstantial motion (*ḥarakat-i jawhariyyah*). He believes the latter to be hidden in the words of the pre-Socratic philosophers. As is known, the Muslim Peripatetics believed that motion could take place only in the four categories of quantity, quality, place and position, all of which are accidents. They expressly denied the possibility of change in the substance of things because they argued that such a motion would destroy the identity of that thing.[19] Mullā Ṣadrā, on the contrary, believes that all creatures in the Universe, except the separate intelligences (*mujarradāt*), which are free from all forms of potentiality and matter, partake of substantial motion, and all change occurs through this process rather than the generation and corruption of the Aristotelians. For example, the human sperm becomes a child not by casting away the form of the sperm and accepting the new human form but by a change in substance in such a way that the form of the sperm is also preserved, and in fact the new form is cast upon a 'matter' which itself consists of the form of the sperm and its matter. Or, according to the metaphor of the *ḥakīms*, each being takes on new forms as it goes through the process of transubstantial motion rather like wearing one dress over another, without casting away the previous one.

Mullā Ṣadrā even argues that at the beginning the human soul is the same as the body and only through gradual transubstantial motion does it separate from the body until it achieves complete catharsis (*tajrīd*). One may therefore say that everything in the world in the domain of corporeal and psychic manifestation is in a state of continuous substantial change and flux.

Ṣadr al-Dīn makes many uses of this principle. For example, he uses it to show the relation between the created and the eternal and to prove the created nature of the world in the sense that there was a moment when each thing in the world had no existence and so the whole world was not in existence as it is now. He also employs this principle in discussing the journey of the soul towards perfection and also the question of resurrection (*ma'ād*). In dealing with this problem, he discusses in detail how the soul 'creates' a body and an environment for itself in the other world in conformity with its inner state of being and gives detailed arguments in favour of bodily resurrection understood in the sense that the body is the 'outward projection' of the soul.

Another important doctrine connected with Mullā Ṣadrā's name and according to him revived by him for the first time in the Islamic period is the union of the intellect (*'aql*), the intelligent (*'āqil*) and the intelligible (*ma'qūl*).[20] According to this view, all knowledge implies ultimately the union of the knower and the known. In fact, our knowledge of something does not mean the presence of the form or idea of that thing in our mind, the two being separate, like the container and what is contained in it. Rather, at the moment when we are conscious of the knowledge of something our mind *is* the idea of that thing and the two are united as one reality. This principle has great bearing on the meaning of knowledge, because it implies ultimately that man is what he knows, that is to say that his being is determined by his knowledge; just as, conversely, what he knows depends upon his being, upon 'who' he is and 'what' he is.

Many other distinctive features of Mullā Ṣadrā's doctrines bear mention, among them his belief in the catharsis and immortality of the faculty of imagination (*mutakhayyilah*), independent of the body in addition to the rational faculty, belief in an intermediate world of 'suspended forms' (*al-ṣuwar al-mu'allaqah*) between the world of

Platonic ideas or archetypes and the corporeal domain, belief in the creative power of the faculty of imagination, and the interpretation of all love, even that of matter for form as a shadow of Divine Love. These are but a sampling which would take too long to explain in detail.

Altogether, much that is distinctive in Mullā Ṣadrā is to be found in a nascent or incomplete form among various philosophers and sages before him. However, the manner in which they are developed, harmonised, presented with demonstrative proof and correlated with revealed truths is unmistakably his own. One may therefore safely say that not only did Mullā Ṣadrā revive the study of metaphysics in the Safavid period, but he also established a new intellectual perspective and founded the last original traditional school of wisdom in Islam.

III

Before completing this chapter, a word may be said about the influence of Mullā Ṣadrā and also his significance in the contemporary world. As far as his influence is concerned, although he has not been well known in the Western world[21] or even in many Muslim countries outside Persia until now, in the Shī'ite world he has been the most dominant intellectual figure of the past four centuries, casting his influence upon the spiritual and intellectual life of Persia to the present day. In India also his writings, especially the *Sharḥ al-hidāyah*, have been studied and taught in Muslim schools up the present day, and many glosses have been written by well-known Indian philosophers and scholars on this work. Indeed, it came to be known simply by the author's own name as *Ṣadrā*. His disciples also left a profound effect upon many eminent Indian Muslim thinkers of the past few centuries, one of them even being influential in the life of Dārā Shukūh.

Most of the famous Persian *ḥakīms* of the past few centuries, such as Ḥājjī Mullā Hādī Sabziwārī, Mullā 'Alī Nūrī and Mullā 'Alī Mudarris Zunūzī, have been followers of his school,[22] and numerous commentaries and glosses have been written on his works.[23] His *Asfār* has remained the most exalted book on *ḥikmah* and is still taught as a textbook to the most advanced students of the subject. It remains today the most basic text in the advanced programmes of philosophy in Persian universities. Nearly all of the authorities of traditional *ḥikmah* in Persia in recent times and today, such as Sayyid Abu'l-Ḥasan Qazwīnī, Sayyid Muḥammad Kāẓim 'Aṣṣār and Sayyid Muḥammad Ḥusayn Ṭabāṭabā'ī, follow and have followed his school and keep alive his tradition through oral and written transmission. And also it is around his name and doctrines propagated by him that a revival of interest in traditional *ḥikmah* is taking place in Persia today.

As for the world at large and especially the rest of the Muslim countries, Mullā Ṣadrā offers antidotes to many present-day ills. For a world that has grown tired of rationalism and as a reaction is throwing itself into the abysmal terrors of the irrational and the subconscious, Mullā Ṣadrā offers a world view in which reason preserves its proper role while remaining subservient to the intellect which is at once its origin and source of inspiration. To remedy the danger of dry and sterile rationalism he offers illumination and intuition derived not from the chaos of the infra-human but from the world of Divine and luminous essences in which all things manifest themselves as they really are. Also, at a time when the harmony between religion and science or faith and reason is destroyed and gnosis, which is the meeting place of the two, forgotten,[24] Ṣadr al-Dīn is the guide to a universe of harmony in which the lion and the lamb lie down together.

Finally, it can be said that for those who have had some foretaste of *'irfān* or have a disciplined mind and a sound intellect not paralysed by the passions, Mullā Ṣadrā can become the light which either through demonstration or intuition will lead them from doubt to certainty and from a blurred to a clear vision of Reality. As for the Muslims in particular, he is one of the best reminders that Islam has a living intellectual tradition within it which, while being completely rational but not rationalistic, is also profoundly Islamic, and that the intellectual life of the Muslims did not stop seven centuries ago. For these and many other reasons it is worthwhile for all lovers of wisdom to study the writings and doctrines of this great sage; for he is an expositor of that perennial philosophy which remains fresh and new in every age and which, being derived from the unique source of all wisdom, is universal, conveying a message for all who have ears to hear and eyes to see the Truth no matter in what form and dress it manifests itself.

Notes

1 As already mentioned, there have been a few scholars who have made a study of Islamic intellectuality in this later phase of history, such as E. G. Browne in his *A Year among the Persians*, London, 1950; *A Literary History of Persia*, vols II–IV, Cambridge, 1906–24; Comte de Gobineau in his *Les Religions et les philosophies dans l'Asie centrale*, Paris, 1923; M. Horten in *Die Philosophie des Islam*, Munich, 1924; and *Das philosophische System von Schirazi (1640 †)*, Strasbourg, 1913; and H. Corbin, whose importance in this field has been already mentioned. See especially Corbin's long introduction to Mullā Ṣadrā's *Kitāb al-mashā'ir* (*Le Livre des pénétrations métaphysiques*), Tehran, 1963, containing an exhaustive study of his life and works as well as a discussion of his doctrines; also Corbin, 'La place de Ṣadr al-Dīn Shīrāzī dans la philosophie iranienne', *Studia Islamica*, 1963, vol. XVIII, pp. 81–113; also see Corbin's *En Islam iranien*, vol. IV. Muhammad Iqbal also, in his short work entitled *The Development of Metaphysics in Persia*, London, 1908, has devoted many pages to the study of the later Persian sages, as has T. Izutsu in his recent studies on Sabziwārī, Mīrzā Mahdī Āshtiyānī and others.

2 See our chapter on Suhrawardī in the *History of Muslim Philosophy.*

3 See Corbin, *Creative Imagination in the Sufism of Ibn 'Arabī*, trans. R. Manheim, Princeton, 1969, 'Between Andalusia and Iran'. Also S. H. Nasr, *Three Muslim Sages*, ch. III.

Ibn 'Arabī is perhaps the most influential figure in the intellectual life of Islam, casting his influence upon all schools of Sufism as well as on the various schools of theosophy based on intellectual intuition which came after him. His most famous works are the *al-Futūḥāt al-makkiyyah* (*Meccan Revelations*) and the *Fuṣūṣ al-ḥikam* (*Bezels of Wisdom*) which has been rendered in a masterly fashion into French by T. Burckhardt as *La Sagesse des prophètes*, Paris, 1953. English trans. from the French as *Wisdom of the Prophets*, trans. A. Culme-Seymour, London, 1975. For a summary and at the same time introduction to these works see Burckhardt, *An Introduction to Sufi Doctrine*, trans. by D. M. Matheson, London, 1976.

4 By theosophy we mean that wisdom which is neither theology nor philosophy but a form of *sapientia* whose attainment depends upon intuition and illumination and as it is understood in the original Greek sense, not as it is employed currently for various pseudo-spiritual movements.

5 For an account of the life, works and doctrines of Suhrawardī, see the two prolegomena of H. Corbin to Suhrawardī, *Opera Metaphysica et Mystica*, vol. I, and vol. II, and our above-mentioned articles; also S. H. Nasr, *Three Muslim Sages*, ch. II.

6 See S. H. Nasr, 'The School of Isfahan', in the *History of Muslim Philosophy*.

7 His full name is Muḥammad ibn Ibrāhīm entitled Ṣadr al-Dīn or Mullā Ṣadrā and also Ṣadr al-muta'allihīn (i.e. foremost among the theosophers). Among his circle of disciples in Persia he is often referred to simply as Ākhūnd.

8 For a full account of the life of Mullā Ṣadrā, the list of traditional sources concerning him and how the date of his birth was recently discovered see our introduction to his *Sih aṣl*, Tehran, 1380; and our article 'Ṣadr al-Dīn Shīrāzi, in the *History of Muslim Philosophy.* See also our *Ṣadr al-Dīn Shīrāzī and His Transcendent Theosophy*, Tehran-London, 1978, chapter 2.

9 For an account of these men and the spiritual and intellectual life of Isfahan at that time see H. Corbin, 'Confessions extatiques de Mîr Dâmâd', in *Mélanges Louis Massignon*, Damascus, 1956, pp. 331–49. We have dealt with these figures and the background of Mullā Ṣadrā's thought in our *Ṣadr al-Dīn Shīrāzī*, chapter 1. See also our chapter 'The School of Isfahan' in the *History of Muslim Philosophy*; and Corbin, *En Islam iranien*, vol. IV.

10 There is a large cave near the village which some believe to have been the place of retreat of Mullā Ṣadrā.

11 The Khān school still stands in Shiraz. The room in which Mullā Ṣadrā taught was rebuilt some twenty years ago and named after him.

12 This voluminous work is all but unknown to the outside world, to the extent that Gobineau (*Les Religions et les philosophies*, p. 80) thought that it was an account of his travels, and E. G. Browne (*Literary History of Persia*, vol. IV, p. 430) wrote that *Asfār* meant 'the four books' from *safar* derived from the Hebrew *sepher*, despite the fact that Mullā Ṣadrā mentions specifically in the introduction that he means by *asfār* the four stages of the journey of the soul towards its Origin.

The *Asfār*, besides being the greatest intellectual testament of its author, is also an encyclopedia of the philosophic and gnostic doctrines of previous Muslim sages such as Ibn Sīnā, Suhrawardī and Ibn 'Arabī. Mullā Ṣadrā, in addition to being a master in *ḥikmah* or theosophy, was also well versed in the history of the lives and views of philosophers, scholars and scientists (*'ilm al-rijāl*) and displays a knowledge of the views of older writers that is rarely to be found in a theosopher or *ḥakīm*. Concerning the *Asfār*, see our *Ṣadr al-Dīn Shīrāzī*, chapter 5.

13 See our article 'Ṣadr al-Dīn Shīrāzī' and our introduction to Mullā Ṣadrā's *Sih aṣl*,

pp. 9–12; for the most thorough list of his works prepared thus far see the bibliographical essay of M. T. Danechepazhuh, *Mullā Ṣadrā Commemoration Volume* (ed. S. H. Nasr), Tehran, 1380, pp. 107–20; Corbin, *Le Livre des pénétrations métaphysiques*, ch. II; and Nasr, *Ṣadr al-Dīn Shīrāzī*, ch. 2.

14 All of these works are in Arabic, written in a very graceful and clear style. The only Persian works of Mullā Ṣadrā which have survived are the *Sih aṣl*, an autobiographical study also concerned with Sufi ethics, and some poems of which all that we have been able to discover have been published with our edition of the *Sih aṣl*. There are also a few letters and short fragments in Persian which we have mentioned in our bibliographical study cited above.

15 See our introduction to the *Sih aṣl*, pp. 14–18.

16 One must make a close study of the writings of Mullā Ṣadrā to discover to what extent he was inspired by the Quran and *Ḥadīth*. The Islamic revelation has played a much greater role in the formation of Islamic intellectual sciences, especially metaphysics (*ḥikmat-i ilāhī*), than is usually supposed. This is especially true among the later *ḥakīms* for whom *ḥikmah* is nothing but the inner meaning of the revealed book.

17 See our introduction to the *Sih aṣl*, pp. 20–8, and also Sayyid Jalāl al-Dīn Āshtiyānī, 'Ṣadr al-Dīn Shīrāzī, *Indo-Iranica*, Nov. 1962; 'Ṣadr al-Dīn Shīrāzī' by Sayyid Muḥammad Ḥusayn Ṭabāṭabā'ī, *Mullā Ṣadrā Commemoration Volume*, pp. 16–25, and the article of Jawād Muṣliḥ in the same volume.

A list of other works dealing with this subject is given in our works already mentioned.

18 One might say that the view of the gnostic goes still a step further in realising that not only all existents are grades of One Being but that there is only One Being, all other things consisting in no more than its theophanies (*tajalliyyāt*) and having no existence of their own whatsoever. This is the only basic distinction between the *waḥdat al-wujūd* of the *'urafā'* and the *ḥukamā'*. For a summary of the gnostic view of unity see the admirable short treatise *al-Risālat al-aḥadiyyah*, attributed to Ibn 'Arabī, translated by 'Abdul Hadi, in *Le Voile d'Isis*, 1939, pp. 15–17, 55–72; also *Le Traité de l'Unité dit d'Ibn 'Arabī*, Paris, 1977.

19 See for example Ibn Sīnā, *al-Shifā'*; *Ṭabī'iyyāt*, Tehran, 1303, pp. 43–4.

20 This principle is traditionally attributed to Porphyry but is already alluded to by Aristotle in the *Metaphysica* (XII 9, 1075-a, 3–4) and held by the neo-Platonic philosophers. In the Islamic world also adherence to this principle is seen before Mullā Ṣadrā in the writings of Abu'l-Ḥasan al-'Āmirī (fourth century AH) and Afḍal al-Dīn Kāshānī (eighth century), although most of the Peripatetics like Ibn Sīnā (Faṣl 6, *Maqālah* 5, of the *Psychology of the Shifā'*, the Bakoš edition, pp. 23–6) attacked this view. For a discussion of this question see the article of Sayyid Abu'l-Ḥasan Qazwīnī, *Indo-Iranica*, Nov. 1961.

21 We have discussed the extent to which the European world has been acquainted with him; see S. H. Nasr, 'Acquaintance with Mullā Ṣadrā in the Occident', in the *Mullā Ṣadrā Commemoration Volume*, pp. 51–62.

22 See S. H. Nasr, 'Sabziwārī', in the *History of Muslim Philosophy*. Mullā Ṣadrā's own students, Mullā Muḥsin Fayḍ Kāshānī, 'Abd al-Razzāq Lāhījī and, of a generation later, Qāḍī Sa'īd Qummī, must also be named among his most important spiritual progenies. On Mullā Ṣadrā and these later figures, see S. J. Āshtiyānī and H. Corbin, *Anthologie des philosophes iraniens*, Tehran-Paris, vol. I, 1975, vol. II, 1976.

It is also said that one of his students, Mīrzā Muḥammad Ṣādiq Kāshānī, while studying with Mullā Ṣadrā, suddenly fell into a state of spiritual ecstasy, tore off his clothes and set out for India, where he became himself a famous master and attracted many disciples to his side.

Among Mullā Ṣadrā's spiritual and intellectual offspring in India one must include also all those like Niẓām al-Dīn al-Suhālawī, Ḥasan ibn Qāḍī al-Luknahawī,

Muḥammad Amjad al-Siddīqī and others who have written glosses and commentaries upon his works and especially on the *Sharḥ al-hidāyah*. Numerous copies of these glosses are to be found in the various libraries of India such as the Razā Library at Rampur and the Khudā-bakhsh Library in Patna (Bankipore). They merit close study as a means of determining the extent of penetration and influence of Mullā Ṣadrā's teachings in India. His influence on Shaykh Aḥmad Sirhindī is also quite obvious.

23 Even Shaykh Aḥmad Aḥsā'ī, the founder of the Shaykhī movement, who wrote a commentary upon *al-Ḥikmat al-'arshiyyah* to criticise Mullā Ṣadrā, was influenced in certain questions by him, although he was for the most part opposed to his views.

24 For the relation of gnosis to faith and reason or religion and science see F. Schuon, *Gnosis – Divine Wisdom*, translated by G. E. H. Palmer, London, 1978.

15

Mullā Ṣadrā as a Source for the History of Islamic Philosophy

Ṣadr al-Dīn Shīrāzī has been much neglected not only as a philosopher and theosopher, but also as a historian of Islamic thought. Having already dealt briefly with his life and doctrines,[1] here we shall draw attention to only one significant aspect of Mullā Ṣadrā and one which has rarely been seriously considered, namely his importance as a source for knowledge of the earlier schools of Islamic philosophy and the history of Islamic philosophy in general.

The very existence of a figure of the dimension of Mullā Ṣadrā in the eleventh/seventeenth century testifies to several centuries of intellectual activity after the period which is usually considered the termination of Islamic philosophy, namely the seventh/thirteenth century. To study the writings of Ṣadr al-Dīn is to learn of that process, whose details are still undetermined, by which Peripatetic philosophy, the Illuminationist (*ishrāqī*) doctrines of Suhrawardī, gnosis (*'irfān*) of the school of Ibn 'Arabī, and certain elements of Islamic theology (*kalām*) became gradually unified in the background of Shi'ism, leading finally to the grand synthesis of Mullā Ṣadrā.

His writings are a testimony to the presence of a living intellectual tradition before him. Through reading them one realises that he did not suddenly blossom from nothing but rather was the crowning achievement of a tendency which for several centuries had been in the making. For example, on the subject of the harmony between philosophy and religion, his solution is the final stage of a process which goes back to al-Kindī himself. The writings of Mullā Ṣadrā are, therefore, in the ideas they express as well as in the references they make to the authorities immediately preceding him, a major source of knowledge of the most obscure period of Islamic philosophy – that which extends from Khwājah Naṣīr al-Dīn Ṭūsī to Mīr Dāmād – from the seventh/thirteenth to the eleventh/seventeenth century.

Mullā Ṣadrā was not only an outstanding metaphysician and sage (*ḥakīm*), but also a great scholar who possessed a remarkable knowledge of earlier works on all the religious and intellectual sciences. It would appear that he had access to an unusually rich library, for his writings frequently refer to earlier works which are either lost for ever or are now buried in obscurity beyond the reach of present-day scholars. These include references to earlier texts and early histories of Islamic philosophy, some of which, like *al-Amad 'ala'l-abad* of Abu'l-Ḥasan al-'Amirī and *Nuzhat al-arwāḥ wa rawḍat al-afrāḥ* of Shahrazūrī, although still extant, have not yet been published and are not well known today. There are also numerous references to Shi'ite sources of *Ḥadīth* and theology which bear witness to Mullā Ṣadrā's intimate knowledge of religious as well as intellectual sciences. Finally, there are references to Greek and Alexandrian philosophers which are often quite accurate. It is, in fact, possible that Mullā Ṣadrā knew certain works on pre-Islamic philosophers in Arabic which have now been lost. His writings should, in any case, be added to those Muslim sources which help to clarify certain aspects of the history of Greek and Hellenistic philosophy.

Although references to the views of other philosophers and sages abound in most of Ṣadr al-Dīn's works, such as his commentary upon the *Uṣūl al-kāfī* of Kulaynī and the glosses upon the *Ḥikmat al-ishrāq* of Suhrawardī, it is especially in his monumental masterpiece the *Asfār* that one must seek the doctrines and ideas of other philosophers and sages.[2] The *Asfār* is, in fact, not only the most advanced and thorough work on *ḥikmah* in Islam, but also a veritable compendium on the history of Islamic philosophy. Nearly every question before being analysed and solved is treated from the point of view of the leading authorities of the various schools. Frequently the views of Fārābī, Ibn Sīnā, or Suhrawardī and Ibn 'Arabī as well as Greek philosophers are expressed with a definitive clarity.

Mullā Ṣadrā, through intellectual penetration and with astonishing lucidity, was often able to arrive at the meaning of certain ideas held by Muslim or Greek philosophers, in the latter case – of the Greeks – at ideas which were sometimes difficult to understand through sheer historical analysis alone. For example, in the first journey of the *Asfār*, he discussed the view of pre-Socratics concerning the basic substance of which objects are formed. Concerning Thales' belief that all things are ultimately made of water, he writes that the water of Thales is symbolic (*ramz*) and should not be mistaken for physical water. Rather, it is that ultimately Divine Substance which in Islam is called the 'Breath of the Compassionate' (*nafas al-raḥmān*). One is astounded by this conclusion which, although opposed to the rationalistic interpretations of nineteenth-century historians of philosophy, affirms the view of the most profound contemporary students of Greek philosophy such as Francis Cornford. In fact, had Cornford known the Islamic term 'Breath of the Compassionate', he would surely have seen its affinity and, in fact, near identity with his own understanding of the meaning of water in the doctrine of Thales.[3] This is another aspect of Mullā Ṣadrā's genius which enabled him to penetrate the meaning of some of the doctrines of the ancient sages and philosophers.

To illustrate more specifically how the *Asfār* serves as a source for the history of philosophy – especially Islamic philosophy – we shall turn to a few specific examples. On the question of what is the reality of being,[4] Mullā Ṣadrā first discusses in detail the view of the Sufis, especially of Ibn 'Arabī and his school, clarifying what they mean by the transcendent unity of Being (*waḥdat al-wujūd*), and why they believe that ultimately being belongs to God alone. He then turns to a view which, in Islamic philosophy, is called *dhawq al-ta'alluh*, and is associated most of all with the name of Jalāl al-Dīn al-Dawānī. Afterwards, he considers the views of the *ishrāqīs* and Peripatetics, clarifying with remarkable thoroughness the meaning of 'being' in the writings of Ibn Sīnā and Suhrawardī with which he was so intimately acquainted.

On the question of how existence and essence are united to each other, he first quotes extensively from Dā'ūd al-Qayṣarī's commentary upon the *Fuṣūṣ al-ḥikam* of Ibn 'Arabī and states that authorities have differed on this question.[5] He then goes on to discuss five different points of view before stating his own. These include what he calls the view of some of 'the well-known figures among nobles', which refers to some of the philosophers immediately preceding him, then Abu'l-Ḥasan al-Ash'arī, the majority of the theologians (of the later period), the Peripatetics and the *ishrāqīs*. In this question as in so many other instances, it would be difficult to find the views of these different schools on this question so clearly summarised as in the *Asfār*.

One of the problems which Mullā Ṣadrā discusses in detail for the first time is what he calls 'mental existence' (*al-wujūd al-dhihnī*), that is to say the question of the existence of things on the mental plane with which the problem of epistemology and many other basic philosophical questions are connected. Mullā Ṣadrā first quotes extensively from the *Fuṣūṣ* of Ibn 'Arabī in order to prove the existence of such a state.[6] Then, answering all the difficulties of the theologians and philosophers regarding this question, he discusses it from the point of view of theologians like Qūshjī as well as from that of the Sufis and especially of Ibn 'Arabī. Finally he proposes his own masterly solution to this basic problem whose discussion, as an independent problem, is essentially absent from early Islamic philosophy.

As a final example, we cite Mullā Ṣadrā's discussion of Platonic ideas,[7] which possesses such a long history in both East and West. Ṣadr al-Dīn begins with Plato's own view and then proceeds to that of Ibn Sīnā according to whom the 'Platonic ideas' are simply the qualities from which all dependencies have been abstracted. He criticises this view before passing to the opinion of Fārābī as expressed in his *al-Jam' bayn ra'yay-al-ḥakīmayn Aflāṭūn al-ilāhī wa Arisṭū*, according to which the 'ideas' are permanent forms in the knowledge of God which do not change or become transformed.[8] This view, too, he criticises and shows its shortcomings. Then he outlines and criticises the views of his own teacher, Mīr Dāmād, according to whom the 'ideas' are the essence of things considered in the world of 'boundless time', or *dahr*, which stands between the world of time and eternity. Following this discussion, he proceeds to analyse the views of Suhrawardī and the Illuminationists and their belief in archetypes (*rabb al-naw'*), and mentions many Mazdanean angels and their terrestrial icons (*ṣanam*) to illustrate this view.[9] Finally, he outlines the view of Plotinus in the *Kitāb al-mayāmir* (*Enneads*) and tries to interpret the words of Aristotle in his *Metaphysica* in such a way as to harmonise it with the view of Plotinus, the summary of whose *Enneads* was considered by the Muslims as the *Theology of Aristotle* (*Uthūlūjiyā*).

After this long historical discussion, in each part of which Mullā Ṣadrā outlines the views of a particular school or philosopher in clear terms and then explains or criticises them, he sets himself the task of synthesising these various views into a unified vision of things. He presents a doctrine which preserves the archetypal reality of objects without committing the errors which permitted the Peripatetics to criticise the very notion of 'Platonic ideas'. The chapter on 'Platonic ideas', in fact, demonstrates clearly Mullā Ṣadrā's method in the *Asfār*, which is one of first discussing the views of various schools and then synthesising the different doctrines into a unity which seeks to encompass them.

Altogether, Mullā Ṣadrā, besides being one of the leading intellectual figures in Islam, was also one of the most learned among the Muslim sages. We know of no other first-rate metaphysician in Islam with so much knowledge of philosophical, religious and Sufi texts. Ṣadr al-Dīn's acquaintance with the writings of such figures as Ibn Sīnā, Suhrawardī, Ghazzālī and Ibn 'Arabī, along with his important commentators, is really amazing. He is for that reason an excellent guide for an understanding of these as well as many less known figures. The writings of Mullā Ṣadrā and especially his *Asfār*, therefore, deserve to be studied not only for their own sake as one of the summits of Islamic intellectual life, but also as a valuable source of knowledge of the history of Islamic philosophy, one whose examination promises to elucidate many a dark page in Islamic intellectual history. Mullā Ṣadrā, much more than has as yet been realised, can serve as a means to gain an insight into that long and continuous intellectual activity in Islam of which he himself was one of the major products.

Notes

1 See the previous chapter and the works cited there.

2 Considering its importance as a source for both the doctrines of Mullā Ṣadrā and the history of Islamic philosophy and other intellectual sciences, it is unfortunate that this work is so little known outside Persia that such authorities as Browne and the Comte de Gobineau should even mistranslate its title.

The *Asfār* was once lithographed in Tehran in 1282/1865, in four volumes which are now rather rare. It has been republished with some of the traditional commentaries under the editorship of ʿAllāmah Sayyid Muḥammad Ḥusayn Ṭabāṭabāʾī, Tehran, 1387/1966 on. This edition in nine volumes does not include the book on substance and accidents which includes natural philosophy. There is still scope for a critical edition which could have a more international nature.

3 See especially Cornford's *Principium Sapientiae*, New York, 1957; and his *From Religion to Philosophy*, New York, 1958.

4 *Asfār*, vol. I, Qum, 1378 AH, pp. 70 ff.

5 «اختلف كلمة ارباب الانظار واصحاب الافكار فى انّ موجوديّة الاشياء بماذا»

ibid., pp. 247 ff.

6 «بالوهم يخلق كلّ انسان فى قوّة خياله مالا وجود له الاّ فيها وهذا الامر العام لكلّ انسان، والعارف يخلق للهمّة مايكون له وجود من خارج محلّ الهمّة»

ibid., pp. 266–7.

7 «فى تحقيق الصور والمثل الافلاطونيّة»

8 «صورا فى علم الله تعالى باقية لاتبدّل ولاتغيّر»

ibid.

9 See S. H. Nasr, *Three Muslim Sages*, pp. 70–4.

16

Mullā Ṣadrā and the Doctrine of the Unity of Being

It is in the nature of rational thought and the whole process of reasoning to depend on a principle or source other than itself. For modern European philosophy this source has been for the most part the sense experience of everyday life or the sentiments and emotions related to the life of the senses. These elements the modern philosopher has sought to analyse and systematise with the aid of his rational faculties. The situation in traditional philosophy in general and Islamic philosophy in particular is far different because here the source outside reason upon which reason relies and whose content it seeks to analyse is either revelation or an experience of a spiritual order situated beyond the limited experiences of common everyday life. This spiritual experience, like revelation, stands above and 'comprehends' reason (in the original Latin sense of the verb *comprehendere*, which means to embrace or encompass) rather than being 'comprehended' by it. Revelation and realisation of a spiritual and intellectual character are in fact the principles of reason, while at the same time they provide reason with the 'material' which is then analysed and systematised in order to be discursively known.

Late Islamic philosophy, which reached its summit with Ṣadr al-Dīn Shīrāzī, is a type of traditional philosophy in which the wedding between rigorous logical analysis and rational thought on the one hand and the profoundest mystical experience on the other can be clearly seen. And nowhere is this wedding more evident than in the discussion of the doctrine of the transcendent unity of Being (*waḥdat al-wujūd*), which lies at the heart both of the theosophical school of Mullā Ṣadrā, or his 'transcendent theosophy' (*al-ḥikmat al-muta'āliyah*), and of Sufism or Islamic gnosis (*'irfān*) in general.[1] The attempt of Mullā Ṣadrā to couch the basic doctrine of the transcendent unity of Being in rational terms does not hide the fact that the source of this doctrine is an *experience* of the Unity of Being, an experience made possible through the discipline provided by Islamic esotericism, which can enable man to transcend the world of multiplicity and to reach the stations of annihilation (*fanā'*) and subsistence (*baqā'*) wherein he gains a vision of the ultimate oneness of all things in their transcendent Origin.[2] If the path to the realisation of such an experience had not existed in Islam, the experience itself would have been impossible and no theoretical discussion of it would have taken place. A situation would have resulted similar at least in this respect to modern European philosophy, whose mainstream has remained unconcerned since the Renaissance with authentic spiritual realisation and those types of spiritual experiences which culminate in gnosis and illumination, precisely because since that time and until very recently the possibility of such an experience had nearly disappeared for men living in the climate of Western civilisation in Europe and in its offshoots on other continents. But in the Islamic world in which Mullā Ṣadrā was born and lived his whole life, the experience of the Unity of Being has been and continues to be an ever living possibility to which theosophers and philosophers cannot but turn their attention, for here is to be found the supreme experience of human life. In the case of Mulla Ṣadrā, as already mentioned, this experience was also achieved personally, for this remarkable Safavid sage, who was a contemporary of Leibniz, was both a rigorous logician and a gnostic and mystic of a high order.

To understand Mullā Ṣadrā's treatment of the doctrine of the transcendent unity of Being, therefore, it is necessary to review the general background of the discussion of this question before him.[3] Many different views on the transcendent unity of Being have been expounded by various philosophers and Sufis over the ages with different degrees of profundity, some revealing the Unity of the Godhead in its full splendour and others veiling this Unity by emphasising the Divine immanence and the theophany of the One in the mirror of the many. Muslim theologians and Sufis from the early period were concerned with the meaning of Unity (*al-tawḥīd*), since it stands at the heart of the Islamic revelation.[4] They distinguished between the Unity of the Divine Essence (*tawḥīd al-dhāt*), the Unity of the Divine Names and Qualities (*tawḥīd al-asmā' wa'l-ṣifāt*) and the Unity of Divine Acts (*tawḥīd al-af'āl*) which is related to the unicity of the whole created order. The philosophers also, both Peripatetic and Ismā'īlī, and also later the Illuminationists, dealt extensively with this subject, especially since Islamic ontology from its earliest stages became based upon the fundamental distinction between existence (*wujūd*) and quiddity (*māhiyyah*) and philosophers began to meditate upon the relation between the two. Of the numerous views expressed on the meaning of the transcendent unity of Being[5] the following are of particular importance for an understanding of Mullā Ṣadrā's teachings:

1 The view of certain Ismā'īlī metaphysicians espoused also by an outstanding follower of Mullā Ṣadrā's school, Qāḍī Sa'īd Qummī. According to this view, the source of reality is not Pure Being but the giver of Being or Unity (*muwaḥḥid*), which itself resides above all concepts, even that of being. It is the *Deus Absconditus*, the Supra-Being whose first Act is *kun*, *esto*, the giving of existence to all things. According to this group, unity resides in the source of universal existence itself.[6]

2 The view of the followers of the *ishrāqī* philosophers, who accept the doctrine of gradation (*tashkīk*) applied by Suhrawardī to light, but apply it to being (as was done by Mullā Ṣadrā himself) and believe in the Unity and gradation of being. The main contention of the view, which received its final systematisation at the hands of Mullā Ṣadrā, is that being is an extensive reality possessing a state of complete perfection and purity belonging to God or the Necessary Being alone as well as grades and states embracing the whole of existence and distinguished from each other through their degrees of intensity and weakness. In such a perspective, the unity of being is preserved in relation to multiplicity, which issues forth from Pure Being like the rays of the Sun, united with and yet separate from their Source.

3 The view of the foremost among the gnostics, especially of the school of Ibn 'Arabī, who have expressed the most profound metaphysical formulation of *waḥdat al-wujūd* possible, based upon their ineffable inner experience of the One.[7] According to this view, there is only one Being, that of God, besides which there is no other. In reality nothing else can even be said to exist (*lā mawjūd illa'Llāh*, as Ibn 'Arabī has stated), and things that *appear* to exist are nothing but theophanies (*tajalliyyāt*) of the One Being which alone Is. This view of the Unity of Being is called hypostatic unity (*waḥdah shakhṣiyyah*) and expresses the highest experience of the One without denying the many which is willed by the One.

Mullā Ṣadrā, while being fully aware of the implications of the first view, which places the Principle above even Being, expresses both the second and the third views in various parts of his writing and then tries in the discussion on cause and effect (*al-'illah wa'l-ma'lūl*) in his major work, the *Asfār*, to harmonise these two views and in fact also to incorporate the first by stating that that which is called Being is in its supreme state not only absolute but also free even from the condition of absoluteness. It is the *hyperousion* for which even the term Pure or Absolute Being is used only symbolically and as an aid for the mind to be able to refer to it.[8]

In seeking to harmonise the various views on the transcendent unity of Being, Mullā Ṣadrā makes use of a terminology current among later

Islamic philosophers which goes back originally to Naṣīr al-Dīn Ṭūsī, who in his *Tajrīd* used it to describe the various ways of considering quiddity.[9] Ṭūsī distinguishes between quiddity as 'non-conditioned' (*lā bi-sharṭ*), 'negatively conditioned' (*bi-sharṭ-i lā*) and 'conditioned by something' (*bi sharṭ-i shay'*). To this must be added the states of 'with no conditions' (*bi-lā sharṭ*) and absolutely non-conditioned' (*lā-bi-sharṭ-i maqsamī*), a term which came into use later when this way of considering the various aspects of quiddity began to be used for the discussion of being. In discussing Mullā Ṣadrā's doctrine of the transcendent unity of Being, this terminology must be kept in mind along with the various meanings given to this doctrine by earlier schools, of which the three meanings mentioned above are particularly important for our understanding of Mullā Ṣadrā's views on this cardinal issue.

In chapter 13 of the first book (*safar*) of the *Asfār*, Mullā Ṣadrā discusses the essential principles upon which the doctrine of unity must be based. These principles can be summarised in two categories:

1 Unity means the impossibility of division in the respect in which something is said to possess unity. And, conversely, whatever is said to possess unity is indivisible in the respect in which it possesses it.
2 The existence of multiplicity is undeniable and cannot simply be negated as if it were not there. Rather, it must be explained and related to unity.

Taking these principles into consideration, Mullā Ṣadrā believes that logically speaking four different interpretations of the unity and/or multiplicity of being are possible:

1 The unity of being and the existents.
2 The multiplicity of being and the existents.
3 The unity of being and the multiplicity of the existents.
4 The multiplicity of being and the unity of the existents.

Naturally Mullā Ṣadrā chooses the third possibility alone as being acceptable and he interprets it either in the light of the synthesis of the two views mentioned above or in some places as the unity and gradation of being in which Unity is manifested in multiplicity and multiplicity in Unity.[10] With this understanding he turns in the discussion of cause and effect in the *Asfār* to a synthesis of various doctrines and expresses in the pages whose translation appears below the heart of his doctrine of the transcendent unity of Being:

Know that things in their act of existence [*wujūdiyyah*] possess three degrees [*marātib*]: the first degree is Pure Being which is without limit. This the gnostics call the Hidden Ipseity [*al-huwiyyat al-ghaybiyyah*], the absolutely Hidden [*al-ghayb al-muṭlaq*] and the Essence of Unity [*al-dhāt al-aḥadiyyah*]. It is this Being which has no name and no quality and which discursive knowledge and perception cannot reach, for everything that possesses name and description is a concept among others and is found in the mind or in apprehension. And all that which can be attained by knowledge and perception possesses a relation with that which is other than itself and is attached to that which is different from itself. Whereas It [Pure Being] is not like that, for it comes before all things and It is in itself without change or transformation. It is pure Hiddenness and Mystery and the absolutely unknowable except by means of its concomitants and effects. And as far as its sacred Essence is concerned, It cannot be limited or determined by any determination, even that of absoluteness, for this would place Its Being under the conditions of restrictions and particularisations such as particular differences and individuating characteristics. The concomitants of His Essence are conditions for Its manifestation and not the causes of Its existence, for were such to be the case it would cause imperfection in His Essence. This absoluteness is therefore negative, requiring the negation of all qualities and attributes from the root of His Essence, and the negation of relativity and change with respect to quality, name, determination or anything else, and even the negation of these negations, since all these are concepts deduced by the mind.

The second degree is that of existence belonging to something other than the thing itself. It is relative existence conditioned by qualifications that are added to it and qualified by limiting conditions such as the intelligences, the souls, the heavens and the elements and the compounds of which men, the animals, etc., are comprised.

The third degree is that of the 'Absolute Existence in its deployment' [*al-wujūd al-munbasiṭ al-muṭlaq*] whose generality must not be confused with universality [of the concept in its logical sense]. Rather, it has another meaning, for existence is pure actuality while the universal concept, whether it be natural or metaphysical, is in potentiality. In order for it to become actualised and gain concrete existence, it needs something other than itself to be added to it. Furthermore, this 'Absolute Existence in its deployment' is not a unity in the arithmetical sense, a unit which is the principle of numbers. Rather, it is a reality deployed upon the 'temples' of possible existents [*mumkināt*] and the 'tablets' of the quiddities [*māhiyyāt*]. It cannot be bound by any particular description or determined by any defined limits such as contingency and eternity, priority and posteriority, perfection and imperfection, cause and effect, substantiality and accidentality, separation from matter and corporeality. Rather, according to the nature of its essence, without anything else being added to it, it possesses all the ontological determinations and objective modes of existence. In fact objective forms of reality issue forth from the grades of its essence and the different modes of its determination and its different states of being. It is, according to the common language of the Sufis, the principle of the Universe, the empyrean of life, the 'throne of the Compassionate', the truth by which things are created and the reality of realities. It multiplies, while it remains one, according to the multiplicity of existents, which are united with the quiddities. It is eternal with that which is eternal and created with the created. It is intelligible with the intelligible and sensible with the sensible. For this reason it is confused with the universal [in the logical sense], but it is not that. Words are incapable of describing the way it deploys itself upon the quiddities and embraces all existents, except by means of symbolism. In this way it is distinguished from the Being which does not enter under any form of symbolism, allegory or indication [and cannot be approached] except by means of its effects and concomitants.

For this reason it is said that in a way the relation of this being [the Absolute Existence in its deployment] to the existents of this world is like the relation of prime matter [the *hylé*] to particular bodies. Know that this Existence, as we have often stated, is other than the abstract, affirmative, general, evident concept conceived of in the mind, which is a contingent concept: and this truth is one of those that are hidden from the majority of discursive thinkers, especially those of the recent period.[11]

A careful analysis of this passage reveals the way in which Mullā Ṣadrā has sought to achieve a synthesis of the views of the philosophers and the Sufis on the doctrine of the transcendent unity of Being. The first way to consider being, that is Being as *lā bi-sharṭ* or non-conditioned, corresponds to the *hyperousion*, the Divine Ipseity in its absolutely unconditioned state transcending every determination including even the quality of transcending every determination.[12] As already mentioned, even the term 'Being' when used to describe this reality is only an aid for human comprehension and not a definition. The metaphysics based upon this conception of Absolute Reality is supra-ontological although using the language of ontology. Mullā Ṣadrā gives here a 'description' of Being in its highest sense, a description which is exactly that of Sufis like Ibn 'Arabī and in fact nearly repeats the words used by the Sufis of his school.[13]

In the second stage, Being is considered as *bi-sharṭ-i shay'*, or conditioned by something. This is perhaps the easiest stage of Mullā Ṣadrā's doctrine to understand, for it corresponds to the states of cosmic existence which, by nature, are ordered hierarchically, from the angelic to the terrestrial. In all of these states, being is conditioned by certain determinations which cause it to descend through the various links in the 'chain of existence' and to actualise all things within the fold of universal existence. The description of the hierarchy thus generated and seen in its relation to the source, which is Pure Being, is but another way of depicting the doctrine of unity and gradation (*tashkīk*) of Being which Mullā Ṣadrā himself expounds in so many of his other writings and which is identified by Islamic philosophers of Persia with the doctrine stemming from the 'Pahlavi sages' (*al-ḥukamā' al-fahlawiyyūn*).

Finally in the third stage, that of envisaging being as negatively conditioned or *bi-sharṭ-i lā*, Mullā Ṣadrā describes what would correspond in the terminology of the Sufis[14] to the state of 'Oneness' (*al-aḥadiyyah*) on the one hand and to the 'Breath of the Compassionate' (*nafas al-raḥmān*) or the 'Most Sacred Effusion' (*al-fayḍ al-aqdas*) – which causes the Divine Names and Qualities to enter the plane of distinction or Unicity (*wāḥidiyyah*) – on the other. This latter state is already in the domain of 'conditioned being', *bi-sharṭ-i shay'*, and stands in fact at the apex of cosmic manifestation.

In this way, Mullā Ṣadrā tries to synthesise the various views on this profoundest and most hidden and yet most manifest principle of metaphysics and to show how Being is One while various determinations and ways of considering It cause man to perceive the world of multiplicity which veils Its Unity. But in reality, for the man who possesses spiritual vision, the transcendent unity of Being is the most manifest and evident of truths and it is really multiplicity as separation that is hidden from him. Moreover, all intellectual and metaphysical discussions of the doctrine of unity are ultimately based upon this gnostic vision of the transcendent unity of Being or an intuitive intellectual participation in that beatific vision whose truth is already announced in the Quranic verse which states that God is the First and the Last, the Outward and the Inward (LVII, 3), or, in other words, the only Reality that Is.

Notes

1 See our *Ṣadr al-Dīn Shīrāzī*. We hope to deal in a subsequent volume in a more extensive manner with all of Mullā Ṣadrā's teachings, including his metaphysics, of which the present discussion forms the heart.

2 On the stations and states in Sufism leading to the experience of the One, see S. H. Nasr, *Sufi Essays*, London, 1972, chapter 5.

3 For a general treatment of this subject among Muslim thinkers see T. Izutsu, 'An Analysis of *Waḥdat al-wujūd* – Toward a Metaphilosophy of Oriental Philosophies', chapter 3 of his *The Concept and Reality of Existence*, pp. 35–55.

4 See F. Schuon, *Understanding Islam*, trans. by D. M. Matheson, London, 1963, and Penguin Books, Baltimore, 1972, pp. 16 ff.

5 For the views of various Muslim schools on this doctrine summarised in a masterly fashion by one of the most outstanding of the contemporary traditional

philosophers of Persia, see Sayyid Muḥammad Kāẓim ʿAṣṣār, *Waḥdat-i wujūd wa badā*', Tehran, 1350 (AH solar), part I.

6 See H. Corbin, 'De l'acte créateur comme *absolution* de l'être, ou de l'être absolu comme absout du néant', in his 'De l'épopée héroïque à l'épopée mystique', *Eranos Jahrbuch*, XXXV, 1966, pp. 195 ff.

7 For Ibn ʿArabī's view of the 'Unity of Being' see S. H. Nasr, *Three Muslim Sages*, pp. 104 ff.; T. Izutsu, *A Comprehensive Study of the Key Philosophical Concepts in Sufism and Taoism – Ibn ʿArabī and Lao-Tzu, Chuang-Tzu*, vol. I, Tokyo, 1966; and T. Burckhardt, *An Introduction to Sufi Doctrine*, pp. 57 ff.

8 'The use of the term Being for this supreme state is only to aid comprehension. Otherwise, whatever interpretation is given of the "Pure Hiddenness", the "Absolutely Unknowable" and the "Mysterious and Rare Griffin" is a form of determination, whereas that Truth is above all determination.' (S. J. Āshtiyānī, in S. M. K. ʿAṣṣār, *Waḥdat-i wujūd wa badā*, p. 35).

9 See T. Izutsu, 'Basic Problems of "Abstract Quiddity" ', in *Collected Texts and Logic and Language*, ed. M. Mohaghegh and T. Izutsu, Tehran, 1353 (AH solar), pp. 1–25.

10 The Muslim sages consider the degrees of knowledge to depend upon the extent to which man is able to comprehend Unity. They therefore place in a hierarchy the views ranging from the sheer experience of external multiplicity, to the realisation by the Peripatetics that the elements of multiplicity are somehow united through their existence, to the doctrine of the unity and gradation of being as stated by the later theosophers, to the realisation formulated by the Sufis that in reality there is only One Being which nevertheless manifests the many. In section 7 of the first chapter of the *Asfār*, in fact, Mullā Ṣadrā nearly equates Unity with Being and states that man becomes aware of Unity to the extent that he approaches Being and vice versa.

11 *Asfār*, lithographed edition, pp. 191–3. This section also appears in S. J. Āshtiyānī (ed.), *Anthologie des philosophes iraniens*, vol. I, pp. 173–6. An analysis of this passage with partial translation is given by H. Corbin in his French introduction to this work, pp. 69 ff.

12 A distinction must be made here between Being as *lā bi-sharṭ* and as *bi-lā sharṭ*. In the language of Mullā Ṣadrā's school the first corresponds to the Mystery of Mysteries, the Absolute and Ultimate Reality envisaged without considering the world of manifestation and determination. The second refers to the same Ultimate Reality but envisaged with consideration of the domain of manifestation. Finally, it must be added that later students of Mullā Ṣadrā in the thirteenth/nineteenth century, such as Mirza Hāshim Rashtī, Sayyid Raḍī Māzandarānī and Āqā Muḥammad Riḍā Qumsha'ī, adopted the term 'absolutely non-conditioned' (*lā bi-sharṭ-i maqsamī*) in place of *lā bi-sharṭ* to describe the same state of Absolute Ultimate Reality.

13 Shāh Niʿmatallāh Walī, who followed Ibn ʿArabī so closely in his purely metaphysical works, writes as follows in his *Risālah fī taḥqīq al-wujūd*: 'Know that Being in itself is other than mental or objective existence, for each of these is a kind of being whereas Being is what it is in Itself, i.e., non-conditioned [*lā bi-sharṭ*] and not determined by absoluteness or relativity. It is neither universal nor particular, neither general nor particularly determined, neither unity – if unity is taken as being added to Its Essence – nor multiplicity' (Shāh Niʿmatallāh Walī, *Rasā'il*, vol. 8, edited by J. Nourbakhsh, Tehran 1351 (AH solar), p. 236).

14 We have in mind especially the terminology used by ʿAbd al-Karīm al-Jīlī in his *al-Insān al-kāmil*. See al-Jīlī, *De l'Homme universel*, trans. by T. Burckhardt, Paris, 1975, pp. 31 ff.

17

The Polarisation of Being

The discussion of the transcendent unity of Being in the school of Mullā Ṣadrā is always carried out in the light of the meaning which is given to 'being' itself from the metaphysical point of view. It is therefore appropriate to turn to the meaning of 'the polarisation of being' in the school of Mullā Ṣadrā in order to cast further light upon the question of being which lies at the heart of the 'Transcendental Theosophy'.

To define being is the most easy or the most difficult task depending on whether intellectual[1] intuition is present or absent. For the intellect, which is the only faculty within man capable of knowing being *qua* being, no concept is clearer than being because the sense of being is inherent in the intellect. But where intellectual intuition is replaced by discursive reason, then being becomes 'the most obscure of terms'. This principle is clearly illustrated in the case of traditional and modern philosophy. Traditional philosophy, whether it be Oriental or Occidental, has always been dependent upon the intellect and has therefore found no difficulty in understanding the meaning of being. Occidental philosophy since Descartes, however, has been for the most part synonymous, until the advent of this century, with one form or another of rationalism and has therefore always had difficulty in understanding being. This incomprehension has been carried to such a point that certain contemporary schools of European philosophy have placed individual existence, rather than universal Being, as the foundation of their thought. Perhaps they have forgotten that the word 'existence' is derived etymologically from the Latin *ex-sistere*, *sistere* being a derived form of *stare*, meaning something which comes out of a being that is stable, namely Being itself.

In traditional philosophy, or what Leibniz called *philosophia perennis*, Being is defined with regard to the Unconditioned Reality of which it is the first determination as well as with respect to the attributes of the Universe of which it is the source.[2] For the purpose of this essay, however, we shall confine our attention to the second category because it is more suitable for the subject of philosophy, while remembering that, in pure metaphysics and gnosis, Reality is considered also in its purely unmanifested and undetermined state above both existence and Being.

The human mind, which may be considered as a passive reflection of the Universal Intellect, has a natural tendency to analyse the contents of its experience before attempting a synthesis. When perceiving a warm object, the mind, if left to its natural inclination, conceives of the heat and cold which have combined to form this warmth that lies in an intermediate realm between them. The same is the case of the four elements in terms of which the world of change has been understood in traditional physics, both ancient and medieval. Likewise, the ancient sages saw that every object consists of something which makes it have a reality and prevents it from being nothing and a limitation which distinguishes it from other objects. This 'something' they considered to be existence (or being), *wujūd*, and the limitation, essence or quiddity, *māhiyyah*, to use the terminology of Islamic philosophy in general, and of the school of Mullā Ṣadrā, upon which we base this discussion, in particular. Moreover, they placed Being above all existents, considering existence itself only in analogy with Being. They knew only too well that all things, by the fact that they exist, are plunged in Being. So we find in Islamic philosophy such definitions of *wujūd* as 'that by virtue of which it is possible to give knowledge about something' or 'that which affects all things' or 'the possibility by means of which knowledge is given about something'.[3]

It must be remembered that to say something 'is' means only in analogy with respect to Being. To answer Pascal's objection that to define being requires the use of the term 'it is' which already contains that which we wish to define, we must refer to this basic analogy between existence and Being. In certain languages like Arabic, the metaphysical truth that all things by the fact that they exist are plunged in Being is implied in the structure of the language. In Arabic, everything is *a priori* contained within the bosom of Being so that it is not even necessary to use 'is' to give a definition. The word 'is' does not appear as a copula in the sentence connecting the subject and the predicate.

Since Being is the source of all attributes in the world, every attribute may be expressed by means of the word 'is'. To say that the 'mountain is white' means in reality that Being has the attribute of whiteness. To say that that something 'is' implies either that it is not non-existent or that it possesses this or that attribute. The verb 'to be' implies, therefore, either existence or an aspect of existence just as Being is and possesses at the same time the attributes of Light, Knowledge, etc. To prove Being from the existence of objects which are all plunged in Being is useless. As St Thomas has said, the proof of Being is impossible 'not because of failure but because of superabundance of Light'.

This analogy between existence and Being is exemplified once again in the Arabic language where the same word *wujūd* denotes both particular existence and Pure Being. That which all things share in common is *wujūd* or existence and that by which all things are distinguished is *māhiyyah* or essence or, transposed into the principial order, the 'Platonic ideas' or archetypes. The symbolism of hylomorphism is related to the same truth. Matter is limitation and form is the bond which connects a particular existent to Being itself. *Wujūd* and *māhiyyah* are the two gates of universal existence. All contingent beings (*mumkin al-wujūd*) lie within these two gates: beyond one gate is utter nothingness or non-being (*'adam*) and, beyond the other, the Necessary Being (*wājib al-wujūd*) itself.

Various schools of traditional philosophy have used different terms to denote aspects of this same polarity, for example the *Yin-Yang* in Taoism, *Puruṣa-Prakṛti* in Hinduism, good and evil in Zoroastrianism, light and darkness in the Illuminationist (*ishrāqī*) school of Shihāb al-Dīn Suhrawardī and the Truth (*al-Ḥaqq*) and the archetypes (*al-a'yān al-thābitah*) in Sufism. But ultimately they imply the same polarity considered in different orders of reality. All contingent beings (*mumkināt*) lie in a hierarchy stretching from prime matter to Being Itself and are united to Being like so many concentric circles echoing their common centre.

Each being is united directly to the centre as all numbers are connected to unity without being derived from each other. The number 100 is 90 plus 10 but has certain attributes which neither 90 nor 10 possesses. This is its particularity or *māhiyyah*; but also like 90 and 10 it is formed by the repetition of unity which symbolises its being. All numbers are united in that they are all made up of 'one' and yet diverse in that each has particular features. Likewise all things are united by their existence which is the reflection of Being and separated by their own particularity or *māhiyyah*.

The principles of traditional philosophy concerning the question of Being are usually divided into the affirmative (*al-aḥkām al-ījābiyyah*) and the negative (*al-aḥkām al-salbiyyah*) ways. The affirmative way concerns unity and multiplicity, cause and effect, potentiality and actuality, substance and accident, the four Aristotelian causes and the ten categories. These are aspects of Being by which any manifested order must be studied. The negative way concerns such principles as that Being has no definition, that it is simple and not composed of parts, and that it is not a part of anything. These two ways when combined enable man to reach an integral knowledge of Being and existence to the extent that a theoretical knowledge *can* be gained of Being. On the one hand, Being is above the manifested order and nothing is outside it[4] and, on the other, all positive qualities return to it and are derived from it.[5]

In the Holy Quran creation is considered as the act of giving being and imprinting the principial ideas upon the 'tablet of non-being'. As Shaykh Maḥmūd Shabistarī writes in his famous *Gulshan-i rāz*:

That Almighty One who in the twinkling of an eye,
From *Kāf* and *Nūn* brought forth the two worlds;
With the *Kāf* of His power, He breathed upon the pen;
It cast thousands of forms on the tablet of non-being.

The metaphysical interpretation of the Quranic statement that God reveals Himself in the Universe through His Names is that Being manifests itself through its Qualities. In creation *ex nihilo* (*bi-'adam*), the nothingness, or *'adam*, is the principial state in which the Divine essences or archetypes (*al-a'yān al-thābitah*) are not as yet externalised as distinct realities. To create (*khalaqa*) means to conceive the possibilities of manifestation, determining them in the Divine Intellect and finally giving them existence (*ījād*). These two phases have been called by later Sufis *al-fayḍ al-muqaddas* or the sacred effusion and *al-fayḍ al-aqdas* or the most sacred effusion corresponding to the determination of the principial possibilities and bestowing existence upon them. The Universe in Sufi language is a set of mirrors in which Being is reflected in different degrees of irradiation (*tajallī*). As Ibn 'Arabī writes in his *Fuṣūṣ al-ḥikam*: 'In truth, all the possibilities (*mumkināt*) are reduced principially to non-existence (*'adam*), and there is no existence other than the Being of God, be He exalted, revealing Himself in the "forms" of states which result from possibilities such as they are in themselves, in their essential determinations.'[6] All things, therefore, participate in the one Being and are nothing if considered separately. The substance of every particle of creation is a manifestation of its existence as contained in space and time and having the two modes of form and number. The supreme mercy of Being, as the Sufis say, is that it embraces all things, even non-being which is its opposite. As Mawlānā Jalāl al-Dīn Rūmī has described it so beautifully:

We and our existences are non-existent: Thou art
the Absolute appearing in the guise of mortality.
That which moves us is Thy Gift: our whole being
is of Thy creation.
Thou didst show the beauty of Being unto not-being,
after

> Thou hadst caused non-being to fall in love with Thee.
> We were not: there was no demand on our part; yet Thy
> Grace heard one silent prayer and called us into existence.[7]

We have made this journey in our search for the definition of Being and have only discovered that all things are dependent upon it both in their existence and qualities. Being cannot, therefore, be defined outside itself because there is no 'outside'. On the one hand, Being is the Supreme Principle inasmuch as it is the Origin of all universal existence, and on the other hand it is itself the first determination of the Absolute Reality, the Divine Essence (*al-Dhāt*), which in its inner infinitude transcends even Being while it also contains Being and the possibility of all existence within Itself. We cannot know Being through mental concepts; we can only reach the gate of Its Presence through the supreme felicity of becoming 'nothing', of tasting annihilation (*fanā'*). The only way to know Being is to realise our own non-existence and to live in awareness of our nothingness before that Reality which alone *is* and which in its inner infinitude transcends even Being.

Notes

1 Throughout this book we have used the word 'intellect' in its original sense as the instrument of knowledge which knows immediately and not discursively. Or, as Aristotle has defined the intellect, it is 'that which is the object of its own knowledge'. The intellect knows actively and directly whereas reason can only know passively and indirectly.

2 'Beyond-Being – or Non-Being – is Reality absolutely unconditioned, while Being is Reality in so far as It determines Itself in the direction of its manifestation and in so doing becomes personal God' (F. Schuon, *Stations of Wisdom*, p. 24, n. 1).

3

«الوجود ما به يمكن ان يخبرعن»

«الوجود مايأثّر الكل»

«امكان الخبر عن الشيء وجوده»

These and other definitions of being are thoroughly discussed in the first volume of the *Asfār* of Ṣadr al-Dīn Shīrāzī and the *Sharḥ al-manẓūmah* of Hājjī Mullā Hādī Sabziwārī. See Izutsu, *The Concept and Reality of Existence*.

4 The fundamental doctrinal formula of Islam, *Lā ilāha illa'Llāh*, meaning there is no divinity but the Divine, is interpreted by Sufis to mean that there is no being other than Being itself. See for example 'Azīz Nasafī's *Tanzīl al-arwāḥ*.

5 'We are not dealing here with subjective appreciations, for the cosmic qualities are ordered both in relation to Being and according to a hierarchy that is more real than the individual; they are, then, independent of our tastes, or rather they determine them to the extent that we are ourselves conformable to Being; we assent to the qualities to the extent that we ourselves are "qualified"' (F. Schuon, *Gnosis, Divine Wisdom*, page 110).

6 See the translation of the *Fuṣūṣ* by T. Burckhardt, chapter on Jacob.

7 ***Math***. I, 602. Trans. by R. A. Nicholson. Also Nicholson, ***Rumi, Poet and Mystic***, London, 1950, p. 107.

ما عدمهائیم وهستیهای ما   تو وجود مطلقی فانی نما
یاد ما وبود ما ازداد تست   هستی ما جمله از ایجاد تست
لذّت هستی‌نمودی نیست‌را   عاشق‌خود کرده‌بودی‌نیست‌را
ما نبودیم و تقاضامان نبود   لطف تو ناگفتهٔ ما می‌شنود

Sufism

18

The Interior Life in Islam

'O thou soul which art at peace, return unto thy Lord, with gladness that is thine in Him and His in thee. Enter thou among My slaves. Enter thou My Paradise.'

(*Quran* – LXXXIX, 27–30 [trans. by M. Lings])

The function of religion is to bestow order upon human life and to establish an 'outward' harmony upon whose basis man can return inwardly to his Origin by means of the journey toward the 'interior' direction. This universal function is especially true of Islam, this last religion of humanity, which is a direct Divine injunction to establish order in human society and within the human soul and at the same time to make possible the interior life, to prepare the soul to return unto its Lord and enter the Paradise which is none other than the Divine Beatitude. God is at once the First (*al-awwal*) and the Last (*al-ākhir*), the Outward (*al-ẓāhir*) and the Inward (*al-bāṭin*).[1] By the function of His outwardness He creates a world of separation and otherness and through His inwardness He brings men back to their Origin. Religion is the means whereby this journey is made possible, and it recapitulates in its structure the creation itself which issues from God and returns unto Him. Religion consists of a dimension which is outward and another which, upon the basis of this outwardness, leads to the inward. These dimensions of the Islamic revelation are called the *Sharī'ah* (the Sacred Law), the *Ṭarīqah* (the Path) and the *Ḥaqīqah* (the Truth),[2] or from another point of view they correspond to *islām*, *īmān*, and *iḥsān*, or 'surrender', 'faith' and 'virtue'.[3]

Although the whole of the Quranic revelation is called '*islām*', from the perspective in question here it can be said that not all those who follow the tradition on the level of *islām* are *mu'mins*, namely those who possess *īmān*, nor do all those who are *mu'mins* possess *iḥsān*, which is at once virtue and beauty and by function of which man is able to penetrate into the inner meaning of religion. The Islamic revelation is meant for all human beings destined to follow this tradition. But not all men are meant to follow the interior path. As we have had occasion to mention in various works, it is enough for a man to have lived according to the *Sharī'ah* and in surrender (*islām*) to the Divine Will to die in grace and to enter into Paradise. But there are those who yearn for the Divine here and now and whose love for God and propensity for the contemplation of the Divine Realities (*al-ḥaqā'iq*) compel them to seek the path of inwardness. The revelation also provides a path for such men, for men who through their *īmān* and *iḥsān* 'return unto their Lord with gladness' while still walking upon the earth.

While the concrete embodiment of the Divine Will, which is the *Sharī'ah*, is called the exoteric dimension in the sense of governing all man's outward life as well as his body and psyche, the spiritual path, which leads beyond the usual understanding of the 'soul' as a separated and forgetful substance in the state which Christians call the 'fallen state', is called the esoteric dimension. In Sunni Islam, this dimension is almost completely identified with Sufism (*taṣawwuf*) while in Shī'ism, in addition to Sufism, the esoteric and the exoteric are intermingled within the general structure of the religious doctrines and practices themselves.[4] And even within Sunnism, there is an intermediate region between the exoteric and the esoteric, a world of religious practice and doctrines which, while not strictly speaking esoteric, are like the reflection of the inner teachings of Sufism within the whole community and a foretaste of its riches. In fact, many of the prayer manuals which occupy such a position in the Sunni world, such as the *Dalā'il al-khayrāt* (*Guides to Blessings*), were written by Sufi masters, while in the Shī'ite world, the prayers, almost all of which, such as the *al-Ṣaḥīfat al-sajjādiyyah* (*The Sajjādian Leaf*) of the fourth Imām, Zayn al-'Ābidīn, were written by esoteric authorities, partake of both an esoteric and an exoteric character.[5] Occasionally, there has even been the penetration of one domain by another, such as the sayings of many of the Imāms which have appeared in Sufi writings and even of some Sufi writings which have penetrated into certain Shī'ite prayers identified with some of the Imāms.[6]

Prayers, such as those of Khwājah 'Abdallāh Anṣārī, the great saint of Herat, contained in his *Supplications* (*Munājāt*), are at once the deepest yearning of the heart for the Ineffable and the Infinite and common devotional prayers chanted by many of the devout in the community and thus belonging to the intermediate level alluded to above:

> I live only to do Thy will,
> My lips move only in praise of Thee,
> O Lord, whoever becometh aware of Thee
> Casteth out all else other than Thee.

O Lord, give me a heart
That I may pour it out in Thanksgiving,
Give me life
That I may spend it
In working for the salvation of the world.
O Lord, give me understanding
That I stray not from the path
Give me light
To avoid pitfalls.
O Lord, give me eyes
Which see nothing but Thy glory.
Give me a mind
That finds delight in Thy service.
Give me a soul
Drunk in the wine of Thy wisdom.[7]

In the same way that the dimension of inwardness is inward in relation to the outward and the outward is necessary as the basis and point of departure for the journey towards the inward, so is the experience of the Divinity as immanent dependent upon the awareness of the Divinity as transcendent. No man has the right to approach the Immanent without surrendering himself to the Transcendent, and it is only in possessing faith in the Transcendent that man is able to experience the Immanent. Or, from another point of view, it is only in accepting the *Sharī'ah* that man is able to travel upon the Path (*Ṭarīqah*) and finally to reach the Truth (*Ḥaqīqah*) which lies at the heart of all things and yet is beyond all determination and limitation.

To interiorise life itself and to become aware of the inward dimension, man must have recourse to rites whose very nature it is to cast a sacred form upon the waves of the ocean of multiplicity in order to save man and bring him back to the shores of Unity. The major rites or pillars (*arkān*) of Islam, namely the daily prayers (*ṣalāt*), fasting (*ṣawm*), the pilgrimage (*ḥajj*), the religious tax (*zakāt*) and holy war (*jihād*), are all means of sanctifying man's terrestrial life and enabling him to live and to die as a central being destined for beatitude. But these rites themselves are not limited to their outer forms. Rather, they possess inward dimensions and levels of meaning which man can reach in function of the degree of his faith (*īmān*) and the intensity and quality of his virtue or inner beauty (*iḥsān*).

The daily prayers (*ṣalāt* in Arabic; *namāz* in Persian, Turkish and Urdu) are the most fundamental rites of Islam. They are, moreover, preceded by the ablutions and the call to prayers (*adhān*), both of which contain the profoundest symbolic significance. The form of these prayers is derived directly from the *sunnah* of the Holy Prophet; these daily prayers are considered the most important religious deed, for, as the Prophet has said, 'The first of his deeds for which a man will be taken into account on the day of resurrection will be his prayer. If it is sound he will be saved and successful, but if it is unsound he will be unfortunate and miserable. If any deficiency is found in his obligatory prayer the Lord who is blessed and exalted will issue instructions to consider whether His servant has said any voluntary prayers so that what is lacking in the obligatory prayer may be made up by it. Then the rest of his actions will be treated in the same fashion.'[8] The *ṣalāt* punctuates man's daily existence, determines its rhythm, provides a refuge in the storm of life and protects man from sin. Its performance is obligatory and its imprint upon Islamic society and the soul of the individual Muslim fundamental and beyond description.

Yet the meaning of the prayers is not to be understood solely through the study of their external form or their impact upon Islamic society, fundamental as those may be. By virtue of the degree of man's *iḥsān*, and also by virtue of the grace (*barakah*) contained within the sacred forms of the prayers, man is able to attain inwardness through the very external forms of the prayers. He is able to return, thanks to the words and movements which are themselves the echoes of the inner states of the Holy Prophet, back to the state of perfect servitude (*'ubūdiyyah*) and nearness to the Divine (*qurb*) which characterise the inner journey of the Holy Prophet as the Universal Man (*al-insān al-kāmil*) to the Divine Presence on that nocturnal ascent (*al-mi'rāj*) which is at once the inner reality of the prayers and the prototype[9] of spiritual realisation in Islam.[10]

Not only do the canonical prayers possess an interior dimension, they also serve as the basis for other forms of prayer which become ever more inward as man progresses upon the spiritual path leading finally to the 'prayer of the heart', the invocation (*dhikr*) in which the invoker, invocation and the invoked become united, and through which man returns to the Centre, to the Origin which is pure Inwardness.[11] The interior life of Islam is based most of all upon the power of prayer and the grace issuing from the sacred language of Arabic in which various prayers are performed. Prayer itself is the holy barque which leads man from the world of outwardness and separation to that of union and interiority, becoming ultimately unified with the centre of the heart and the rhythm which determines human life itself.

The same process of interiorisation takes place as far as the other central rites or pillars of Islam are concerned. Fasting is incumbent upon all Muslims who are capable of it during the holy month of Ramaḍān, a month full of blessings when according to the well-known *ḥadīth* 'the gates of heaven are opened'.[12] But the outward observation of its rules, while necessary, is one thing and the full realisation of its meaning is another. Fasting means not only abstention from eating, drinking and passions during daylight, but above all the realisation of the ultimate independence of man's being from the external world and his dependence upon the spiritual reality which resides within him. Fasting is, therefore, at once a means of purification and interiorisation complementing the prayers. In fact, it is itself a form of prayer.

The same truth holds true of the other rites. The pilgrimage or *ḥajj* is outwardly the journey towards the house of God in Mecca and inwardly circumambulation around the *Ka'bah* of the heart which is also the house of God. Moreover, the outward *ḥajj* is the means and support for that inner journey to the Centre which is at once nowhere and everywhere and which is the goal of every wayfaring and journeying. The *zakāt* or religious tax is likewise not only the 'purifying' of one's wealth through the act of charity which helps the poor, but also the giving of oneself and the realisation of the truth that by virtue of the Divine Origin of all things, and not because of some form of sentimental humanitarianism,[13] the other or the neighbour *is* myself. *Zakāt*, therefore, is, in addition to being a means of preserving social equilibrium, a way of self-purification and interiorisation, of creating awareness of one's inner nature shorn of artificial attachment to all that externalises and dissipates.

Finally, the holy war or *jihād* is not simply the defence or extension of the Islamic borders, which has taken place only during certain episodes of Islamic history, but the constant inner war against all that veils man from the Truth and destroys his inner equilibrium. The greater holy war (*al-jihād al-akbar*), as this inner battle has been called by the Holy Prophet, is, like the 'unseen warfare' of Orthodox spirituality, the very means of opening the royal path to the centre of the heart. It is the battle which must of necessity be carried out to open the door to the way of inwardness. Without this greater *jihād*, man's externalising and centrifugal tendencies cannot be reversed and the precious jewels contained in the treasury of the heart cannot be attained. The *jihād*, like the prayers, fasting, pilgrimage and religious tax, while a pillar of Islam and a foundation of Islamic society, is also a means towards the attainment of the inner chamber and an indispensable means for the pursuit of the inner life in its Islamic form.

An understanding of the interior life in Islam would be incomplete without reference to the imprint of the Divine Beauty upon both art and nature. Islamic art, although dealing with the world of forms, is, like all genuine sacred art, a gate towards the inner life. Islam is based primarily on intelligence and considers beauty as the necessary complement of any authentic manifestation of the Truth. In fact, beauty is the inward dimension of goodness and leads to that Reality which is the origin of both beauty *and* goodness. It is not accidental that in Arabic moral goodness or virtue and beauty are both called *ḥusn*. Islamic art, far from being an accidental aspect of Islam and its spiritual life, is essential to all authentic expressions of Islamic spirituality and the gate towards the inner world, for it is in the nature of beauty to interiorise, this being especially true of the beauty of sacred art. From the chanting of the Holy Quran, which is the most central expression of the Islamic revelation and sacred art *par excellence*, to calligraphy and architecture, which are the 'embodiments' in the worlds of form and space of the Divine Word, the sacred art of Islam has always played and continues to play a fundamental role in the interiorisation of man's life.[14] The same could of course be said of traditional music (*samā'*) and poetry which have issued from Sufism and which are like nets cast into the world of multiplicity to bring man back to the inner courtyard of the Beloved.[15]

Likewise, nature and its grand phenomena such as the shining of the sun and the moon, the seasonal cycles, the mountains and the streams, are, in the Islamic perspective, means for the contemplation of the spiritual realities. They are signs (*āyāt*) of God and, although themselves forms in the external world, mirrors of a reality which is at once inward and transcendent. Nature is not separated from grace but is a participant in the Quranic revelation. In fact, in Islamic sources it is called the 'macrocosmic revelation'. Virgin nature is the testament of God and gives the lie to all forms of pretentious naturalism, rationalism, scepticism and agnosticism, these maladies from which the modern world suffers so grievously. It is only in the artificial ugliness of the modern urban setting, created by modern man to forget God, that such ailments of the mind and the soul appear real and the Divine Truth unreal. Modern sceptical philosophies are the products of those living in urban centres and not of men who have been born and who have lived in the bosom of nature and in awareness of His macrocosmic revelation.[16] In Islamic spirituality, nature acts as an important and in some cases indispensable means for recollection and as an aid towards the attainment of inwardness. Many Muslim saints have echoed over the ages the words of the Egyptian Sufi Dhu'l-nūn who said:

> O God, I never hearken to the voices of the beasts or the rustle of the trees, the splashing of waters or the song of birds, the whistling of the wind or the rumble of thunder, but I sense in them a testimony to Thy Unity and a proof of Thy Incomparableness; that Thou art the All-prevailing, the All-knowing, the All-wise, the All-just, the All-true, and that in Thee is neither overthrow nor ignorance nor folly nor injustice nor lying. O God, I acknowledge Thee in the proof of Thy handiwork and the evidence of Thy acts: grant me, O God, to seek Thy Satisfaction with my satisfaction, and the Delight of a Father in His child, remembering Thee in my love for Thee, with serene tranquillity and firm resolve.[17]

St Francis of Assisi would have joined this chorus in the praise of the Lord through the reflection of His Beauty and Wisdom in His creation.

The goal of the inward life in Islam is to reach the Divine as both the Transcendent and the Immanent. It is to gain a vision of God as the Reality beyond all determination and at the same time of the world as 'plunged in God'. It is to see God everywhere.[18] The inward dimension is the key for the understanding of metaphysics and traditional cosmology as well as for the penetration into the *essential* meaning of religion and of all religions, for at the heart of every authentic religion lies the one Truth which resides also at the heart of all things and most of all of man. There are of course differences of perspective and of form. In Christianity, it is the person of Christ who saves and who washes away the dross of separation and externalisation. In Islam, such a function is performed by the supreme expression of the Truth Itself, by the *Shahādah, Lā ilāha illa'Llāh*. To take refuge in it is to be saved from the debilitating effect of externalisation and 'objectivisation' and to be brought back to the Centre, through the inward dimension.[19]

It is not for all men to follow the interior life. As already mentioned, it is sufficient for a Muslim to live according to the *Sharī'ah* to enter Paradise after death and to follow the interior path after the end of his terrestrial journey. But for those who seek the Divine Centre while still walking on earth and who have already died and become resurrected in this life, the interior path opens before them at a point which is here and a time which is now.

> It is related that one night Shaykh Bāyazīd went outside the city and found everything wrapped in deep silence, free from the clamour of men. The moon was shedding her radiance upon the world and by her light made night as brilliant as the day. Stars innumerable shone like jewels in the heavens above, each pursuing its appointed task. For a long time the Shaykh made his way across the open country and found no movement therein, nor saw a single soul. Deeply moved by this he cried: 'O Lord, my heart is stirred within me by this Thy Court displayed in all its splendour and sublimity, yet none are found here to give Thee the adoring worship which is thy due. Why should this be, O Lord?' Then the hidden voice of God spoke to him: 'O thou who art bewildered in the Way, know that the King does not grant admission to every passer-by. So exalted is the Majesty of His Court that not every beggar can be admitted thereto. When the Splendour of My Glory sheds abroad its radiance from this My sanctuary, the heedless and those who are wrapped in the sleep of indolence are repelled thereby. Those who are worthy of admittance to this Court wait for long years, until one in a thousand of them wins entrance thereto.'[20]

No religion would be complete without providing the path for the 'one in a thousand'. Islam as an integral tradition and the last plenary message of Heaven to the present humanity has preserved to this day the possibility of following the interior life, a life which, although actualised fully only by the few, has cast its light and spread its perfume over all authentic manifestations of the Islamic tradition.

Notes

1 See F. Schuon, *Dimensions of Islam*, trans. P. Townsend, London, 1969, chapter 2.
2 See S. H. Nasr, *Ideals and Realities of Islam*, London, 1966, chapters 1, 3 and 4.
3 See F. Schuon, 'Imān, Islām, Insān', in his *L'Œil du cœur*, Paris, 1974, pp. 91–4, where the relation of this division to the tripartite division of the Islamic tradition into *Sharī'ah*, *Ṭarīqah* and *Ḥaqīqah* is also explained.
4 Concerning Shi'ism see 'Allāmah Ṭabāṭabā'ī, *Shī'ite Islam*, trans. by S. H. Nasr, New York and London, 1975.
5 On Muslim prayers from both Sunni and Shi'ite sources and dealing mostly with this 'intermediate' domain of religious life, between external religious acts and the 'prayer of the heart', see C. E. Padwick, *Muslim Devotions, A Study of Prayer-Manuals in Common Use*, London, 1961.
6 For a rather remarkable instance of this second category dealing with a prayer written by Ibn 'Aṭā'allāh al-Iskandarī in a famous Shi'ite prayer attributed to Imām Ḥusayn, the third Shi'ite Imam, see W. Chittick, 'A Shādhilī Presence in Shi'ite Islam?', *Sophia Perennis* (Journal of the Imperial Iranian Academy of Philosophy), vol. 1, no. 1, spring 1975, pp. 97–100.
7 Quoted in M. Smith, *The Sufi Path of Love, An Anthology of Sufism*, London, 1954, 82.
8 *Mishkāt al-maṣābīḥ*, trans. with explanatory notes by J. Robson, Lahore, 1972, p. 278.
9 The external movements of the prayers are said, by traditional Islamic authorities, to be reflections in the world of form, movement, time and space of the states experienced by the Holy Prophet during his nocturnal ascension.
10 Concerning the symbolism and inner meaning of the details of the movements, actions and words of the prayers as reflecting in the teachings of one of the greatest of the Sufi masters of the recent period, see M. Lings, *A Sufi Saint of the Twentieth Century*, London, 1971, pp. 176 ff.
As for the inner meaning of the prayers as seen by a Shi'ite theosopher and saint, see Ḥājjī Mullā Hādī Sabziwārī, *Asrār al-ḥikam*, Tehran, 1380/1960, pp. 456 ff.
11 Jāmī has said, 'Oh, happy man whose heart has been illuminated by invocation, in the shade of which the carnal soul has been vanquished, the thought of multiplicity chased away, the invoker transmuted into invocation and the invocation transmuted into the Invoked'. (Quoted in F. Schuon, *Understanding Islam*, p. 12).
12 *Mishkāt al-maṣābīḥ*, vol. II, p. 417, where many *ḥadīths* of this kind are recounted.
13 In modern times, few virtues have been as externalised, depleted of their spiritual significance and even made into a channel for demonic rather than celestial forces as charity, whose modern, secularised understanding in the West is the direct caricature and parody of the authentic Christian conception of this cardinal virtue. See F. Schuon, *Spiritual Perspectives and Human Facts*, trans. D. M. Matheson, London, 1953, pp. 171 ff.
14 Considering the spiritual principles of Islamic art see T. Burckhardt, *The Art of Islam*, trans. P. Hobson, London, 1976; and his *Sacred Art, East and West*, trans. Lord Northbourne, London, 1967, chapter IV; also S. H. Nasr, *Sacred Art in Persian Culture*, London, 1976.
15 Concerning the spiritual and interiorising effect of music in Sufism see J. Nourbakhsh, '*Samā'*', *Sophia Perennis*, vol. III, no. 1, spring 1977; and S. H. Nasr, 'Islam and Music', *Studies in Comparative Religion*, winter 1976, pp. 37–45.

16 Concerning the Islamic and traditional view of nature and its contrast with the modern view see Nasr, *Science and Civilization in Islam*; Nasr, *Man and Nature*, London, 1976; Nasr, *An Introduction to Islamic Cosmological Doctrines*; Nasr, *Islamic Science – An Illustrated Study*; also Th. Roszak, *Where the Wasteland Ends*, New York, 1973; and Roszak, *Unfinished Animal*, New York, 1975.

'Les vertus, qui par leur nature même témoignent de la Vérité, possèdent elles aussi une qualité intériorisante dans la mesure ou elles sont fondamentales; il en va de même des êtres et des choses qui transmettent des messages de l'éternelle Beauté; d'où la puissance d'intériorisation propre à la nature vierge, á l'harmonie des créatures, à l'art sacré, à la musique. La sensation esthétique – nous l'avons fait remarquer bien des fois – possède en soi une qualité ascendante: elle provoque dans l'âme contemplative, directement ou indirectement, un ressouvenir des divines essences.' (F. Schuon, 'La religion du cœur', *Sophia Perennis*, vol. III, no. 1, spring, 1977).

17 A. J. Arberry, *Sufism*, London, 1950, pp. 52–3.

18 See F. Schuon, 'Seeing God Everywhere', in his *Gnosis, Divine Wisdom*, pp. 106 ff.

19 See Nasr, 'Contemporary Western man, between the rim and the axis', in his *Islam and the Plight of Modern Man,* pp. 3 ff.

20 From 'Aṭṭār, quoted in M. Smith, *Readings from the Mystics of Islam*, London, 1950, pp. 26–7.

19

Contemplation and Nature in the Perspective of Sufism

Creation's book I studied from my youth,
And every page examined but in sooth
I never found therein aught save the 'Truth',
And attributes that appertain to 'Truth',
What mean Dimension, Body, Species,
In Mineral, Plant, Animal degree?
The 'Truth' is single, but His modes beget
All these imaginary entities.[1]
('Abd al-Raḥmān Jāmī)

I

Contemplatives of all ages from the prophets who are the prototypes of spirituality to the forest seers of the Upaniṣads and the early desert fathers, the medieval saints, and such contemporary sages as Śri Ramana Maharshi have turned to nature as a source of spiritual nourishment and retreat for the contemplative life. If in this essay the relation between contemplation and nature is limited to the Islamic tradition it is because of the limitation of the knowledge of the author rather than the lack of universality of the subject-matter, for, as the Sufis say, 'Truth like the Sun shines wherever no obstacle is put before it.'

Contemplation, from the Islamic point of view, is not a passive response nor an emotional or even mental activity. It involves, strictly speaking, the faculty of intellection symbolised by 'the eye of the heart' which 'sees' the spiritual world in a direct manner much like the physical eye which possesses the same power in the sensible world and in opposition to the faculty of reason which functions discursively and 'knows' indirectly. In the hierarchy of human faculties the senses occupy the lowest realm, the faculties of the soul the main one of which reason is the intermediate realm, and 'the eye of the heart' or the instrument of the intellect – as used in its original sense – the highest level.

Contemplation, then, is dependent upon the functioning of the faculty of intellection just as physical vision is dependent upon the possession of healthy eyes. The contemplative 'sees' the Truth and knows it through the realisation of identity. At the end when he has reached the state of 'union' through the effective realisation of the Truth or through gnosis (*ma'rifah*), his knowledge becomes perfect and, because knowing is essentially being, his being also partakes of the 'perfume' of the Divine knowledge thus acquired. The limited being and his finitude thus disappear like a drop of water in the infinite ocean of Being.

II

Not-being is the mirror of Being, that is, of Absolute Being. In it is reflected the glory of the Creative Truth. When not-being is placed opposite Being, in an instant the reflection appears in it. Not-Being is a mirror and the world the reflection and man like the reflection of an eye, the eye of the Hidden One. Although the place which is the centre of the heart is small, it is yet found to be a fitting dwelling-place for the Lord of the two worlds.[2] (Maḥmūd Shabistarī)

Of the many worlds of Reality, only the highest which is the world of the Divine Essence (*'ālam al-dhāt*) is absolutely Real. The other worlds are its multiple reflection in the mirror of non-being. This is the only image that can convey to a certain extent this ineffable aspect of the Truth, for the transition from Unity to multiplicity is an ultimate mystery which no human language or thought can hope adequately and fully to express. From a negative point of view, each lower world can be said to be the shadow of the one above it, each shadow being paler and farther away from the Absolute Reality as one descends from the world of the Essence through the intermediate realms to the world of earthly existence which is the lowest in this hierarchy. The world may thus be considered as the shadow of God.

If negatively this world is a shadow, positively it is a reflection and symbol of the worlds above it. In essence it has no reality outside of God – for there cannot be two completely independent orders of Reality. This essential identity, however, does not imply any form of pantheism despite what a cursory glance may imply to certain people. It may be said of the Sufi that 'he does not for one moment imagine that God is in the world; but he knows that the world is mysteriously plunged in God'.[3] The Universe is united and one with its Divine

Principle not materially but in essence. And, because it is thus united, every particle in the Universe reflects the Divine Beauty.

'Under the veil of each particle is concealed the soul-refreshing beauty of the Face of the Beloved. To that one whose spirit lives in contemplation of the Vision of God, the whole world is the book of God Most High'[4] (Shabistarī).

> Being's the essence of the Lord of all;
> All things exist in Him and He in all;
> This is the meaning of the Gnostic phrase;
> 'All things are comprehended in the all'.[5]

If from a certain point of view each world is a shadow of the one above it and a symbol of a higher realm of Reality, from another the Universe or macrocosm itself is a symbol of the microcosm or man. From the Divine Metacosm the two realms of microcosm and macrocosm are created in such a manner that they preserve an analogy with each other. As the Sufis say, 'The Universe is a great man, and man is a little Universe'. The Reality which lies in the centre of the heart of man also lies behind the veil of the appearances of nature. Consequently, every event, every particularity in nature, corresponds to an element within man, but since the soul of fallen man is like a dark forest his eyes cannot see the analogies with himself.

> Being, with all its latent qualities,
> Doth permeate all mundane entities,
> Which, when they can receive them, show them forth
> In the degrees of their capacities.[6]

Besides being a little Universe, man is also the central link in a great chain of being which extends from the lowest creature of the mineral kingdom to the archangels. Man alone, because of the free will accorded to him, can ascend to a realm even beyond that of the angels, to the Divine Presence itself, or descend below the level of the beasts of the field.

> I died as mineral and became a plant,
> I died as plant and rose to animal,
> I died as animal and I was a Man.
> Why should I fear? When was I less by dying?
> Yet once more I shall die as Man, to soar
> With angels blest; but even from angelhood
> I must pass on: all except God doth perish.
> When I have sacrificed my angel-soul,
> I shall become what no mind e'er conceived.

Oh, let me not exist! for Non-existence
Proclaims in organ tones: 'To Him we shall return'.[7]

Placed in a hierarchy below the order of angels and the world of subtle forms, in the world of generation and corruption which is the lowest of all levels of cosmic existence, man occupies a central position with respect to other creatures in the terrestrial environment. He is to other creatures as the centre of the circle is to the points on the circumference. Only man, by virtue of his central position, can acquire gnosis and sanctity, and is thereby given power over other creatures on earth. He is for them a channel of Divine Grace, a source of light in an otherwise dark room. But, also, only man can dominate nature and even destroy it. If this channel of grace is narrowed or diminished in any way, a corresponding darkness occurs in nature. And when man himself turns away from the higher realities to concentrate all his efforts within this world of shadows, then the light which was destined for nature is cut off, and the inner darkness of man's soul is projected unto nature. The modern growth of the cancer of urbanisation and the destruction of the natural environment are historical examples of this principle.

> Although each of the various kinds of existent things is a mirror, man is a mirror revealing the whole Universe; although each individual being in the existent world is a goblet, the knowing man is the goblet that reveals the stages [of being], the 'great electuary' [*ma'jūn-i akbar*], the goblet that reveals the world . . .[8] ('Azīz ibn Muḥammad Nasafī)

> Man is the link between God and nature. Every man is a copy of God in His perfection; none is without the power to become a perfect man. It is the Holy Spirit which witnesses to man's innate perfection, the spirit is man's real nature and within him is the secret shrine of the Divine Spirit. As God has descended into man, so man must ascend to God, and in the Perfect Man – the true saint – the Absolute Being, which has descended from its absoluteness return again unto itself.[9] ('Abd al-Karīm al-Jīlī)

The symbols which are found everywhere in nature, in such phenomena as rain, lightning and thunder, the rose and the lily, or the sun and the moon, correspond to the immediate appearance of things, an appearance that is known to man through the senses and not through a conceptual scheme dependent upon ratiocination. Symbols, just because they are related to the sensible realm, symbolise the highest realm, which is that of the Spirit. The Hermetic saying, 'That which is lowest symbolises that which is highest', expresses a basic law of the science of the symbolic interpretation of nature. The contemplative, by contemplating the phenomena of nature, is carried beyond the intermediate realm of reason to the realm of pure forms or 'Platonic ideas' (*'ālam al-jabarūt*). He studies nature not to analyse it according to some conceptual scheme but to come to know himself through the analogy existing between the microcosm and the macrocosm. And, by knowing himself, man comes to know God, for as the Prophet said, 'He who knoweth himself, knoweth his Lord'. Many of the ancient cosmological sciences were constructed precisely for this purpose and were therefore based on the analogy which exists between various realms of being. That is why in medieval times such contemplative groups as the Brethren of Purity in Islam and Taoists in China – and not primarily the rationalists – cultivated the sciences of nature.

It is natural then to see that sages and gnostics have again and again made use of immediate experience of the natural world to express the highest realities and to contemplate the spiritual world in the grand theophanies of nature. It is due to this law of inverse analogy also that poetry has remained throughout the ages the language of seers and prophets, expressing in symbols and images what the language of prose cannot easily convey. Prose has always been more suitable for the expression of ideas belonging to the intermediate realm of reason, while poetry or other forms of expression which lend themselves easily to symbolism, such as music and geometry, have always been the suitable vehicle for the contemplative.

> Kings lick the earth whereof the fair are made,
> For God hath mingled in the dusty earth
> A draught of Beauty from His choicest cup.
> 'Tis that, fond lover – not these lips of clay –
> Thou art kissing with a hundred ecstasies,
> Think, then, what must it be undefiled.[10]

As an example of traditional cosmological sciences one may cite alchemy, which is also based on the analogy between the microcosm and macrocosm. The forms of nature are ever changing in their cycles of generation and corruption. From the *materia prima* which is the ground and 'stuff' of all forms, the Divine Artist builds ever-new forms. But among these forms certain have nobility and beauty which reflect in a more direct manner the Beauty of the Artisan. Among stones the diamond is transparent to light and has a 'divine nature' in comparison with common stones which are opaque. And among metals gold has a nobility like that of the sun, a nobility which is reflected in the fact that it is resistant to corrosion and destruction, unlike the base metals which corrode easily.

The soul of most men is like base metal ever tempted by the desires of the world and corrupted easily under every evil influence. In the hands of the spiritual master, who functions as the vicegerent of the Divine Artist, the base soul of the disciple is melted into its *materia prima* from which a noble soul is formed, a soul which like gold shines with the spiritual virtues and is incorruptible when placed under the influence of the corrosive forces of evil. The traveller upon the path in his journey towards perfection and ultimately gnosis finds at each step forms in nature which symbolise his inner state as his inner state reflects the noble forms of nature.

The contemplative also finds nature a sanctuary which relative to the transient works of man represents the 'eternity' of God's handiwork. He becomes the channel of grace for nature, and nature becomes in turn for him a vast book of Divine Wisdom, an image of the Divine Word which in Christianity is Christ and in Islam the Quran. The rest of human society also shares in this exchange because the contemplative who has reached the goal of gnosis also becomes the means by which grace is dispensed to the society in which he lives. As Ghazzālī has said, 'The saints are the salt of society and what keeps it together'.

Man, by dissecting nature and raping her with animal ferocity to satisfy his never satiated passions, ultimately dissects and destroys himself. What seems to him 'the conquest of nature' becomes ultimately the conquest of his own higher nature by the infra-human elements within him. But he whose soul is thirsty for the Truth and who has been endowed by God with the power of contemplation seeks not to conquer nature but to come to know it intimately and to benefit spiritually from it. Such a person knows that nature participates in man's spiritual perfection and that it has its own metaphysics and spiritual method. He knows that, through the inner sympathy between man and nature, the prayer of the spiritual man is in the end united with the prayer of virgin nature. He sees in nature the operation of the same spiritual principle that inwardly governs him.

> 'Man prays and prayer fashions man. The saint has himself become prayer, the meeting place of earth and Heaven; and thus he contains the universe and the universe prays with him. He is everywhere where nature prays and he prays with and in her; in the peaks which touch the void and eternity, in a flower which scatters itself or in the abandoned song of a bird.'[11]

Notes

1 'Abd al-Raḥmān Jāmī, *Lawā'iḥ*, translated by E. H. Whinfield and M. M. Kazvini, London, 1928, p. 21.

2 M. Smith, *Reading from the Mystics of Islam*, London, 1950, p. 112.
3 F. Schuon, 'Aperçus sur la tradition des Indiens de l'Amérique du Nord', *Études Traditionnelles*, 1940, p. 164.
An observation made originally with respect to the North American Indians but which applies equally well to Sufism.
4 M. Smith, op. cit., p. 112.
5 Jāmī, op. cit., p. 39.
6 ibid., p. 40.
7 R. A. Nicholson, *Rumi, Poet and Mystic*, p. 103.
8 *Spirit and Nature*, *Eranos Yearbooks*, New York, 1954, vol. I, p. 189.
9 Smith, op. cit., p. 119.
10 Nicholson, op. cit., p. 45.
11 F. Schuon, *Spiritual Perspectives and Human Facts*, p. 213. Concerning the traditional versus the modern conception of nature, see Nasr, *Man and Nature, the Spiritual Crisis of Modern Man*, and Roszak, *Unfinished Animal.*

Postscript

The Islamic Response to Certain Contemporary Questions

Jesus Through the Eyes of Islam

Centuries of confrontation with the Christian West followed by a period of intense missionary activity, which still continues in certain regions of the Islamic world in new forms, have created among some contemporary Muslims an aversion not only to Christianity but, in the case of some of the modernised classes, even to the Islamic conception of Christ and Mary. In response to the aggressive attack made upon Islam by so many Christian sources during the past, certain modernised Muslims have tried to forget or push into the background the clear teachings of Islam concerning Christianity. There have been even more extreme reactions among the Muslims of the Indian subcontinent. As a result, they have created a Christology in certain quarters that is, to say the least, completely removed from the traditional Islamic teachings on the subject.

In this short exposition it is not with such recent reactions but with the traditional Islamic teachings concerning Jesus that we shall concern ourselves. It might appear unconvincing to certain Christians that Islam places such an emphasis upon the role of Jesus, but to understand the total perspective of Islam this emphasis is of significance. Moreover, in the secularised world of today it might be of spiritual comfort for Christians, besieged by a corrosive atmosphere which seeks to eat away the very sinews and bones of religion, to realise that millions of Muslims on earth bear witness to the Divine origin of Christianity and revere its founder, although naturally in a different perspective.

Islam does not accept the idea of incarnation or filial relationship. In its perspective, Jesus the son of Mary, 'Īsā ibn Maryam, was a major prophet and spiritual pole of the whole Abrahamic tradition, but not a God-man or the son of God. Nevertheless, his miraculous birth from a virgin mother, who is in fact referred to in the Quran as the woman chosen above all the other women of the world, is explicitly mentioned. So is the fact that he was 'the Spirit of God' (*rūḥallāh*). His special function as the bringer of a spiritual way rather than a religious law is also basic to Islamic teachings. The Quran, however, does not accept that he was crucified, but states that he was taken directly to heaven. This is the one irreducible 'fact' separating Christianity and Islam, a fact which is in reality placed there providentially to prevent a mingling of the two religions. All the other doctrines, such as the question of the nature of Christ or the Trinity, can be understood metaphysically in such a way as to harmonise the two perspectives. The question of the death of Jesus is, however, the 'fact' that resists any interpretation which would be common to the Christian and Islamic views of the event. It could be said that this event was greater than any single description of it. In any case the meaning of the crucifixion and the idea of redemption it signifies are perhaps the most difficult of all aspects of Christianity for an ordinary Muslim to grasp.

The Prophet of Islam held Christians in special esteem and emphasised the function of Christ within Islam by referring to Christ's second coming at the end of the world. Islamic eschatology, therefore, although not identical with the Christian, is related to the same central figure of Jesus. Through the eschatological role assigned to Jesus in Islam as well as the many references to him and the Virgin Mary in the Quran, Jesus plays a role in the daily religious consciousness of Muslims equal to that of Abraham and following, of course, the role of the Prophet. Moreover, in Islamic esotericism he plays a major function to which the many writings of Sufis such as Ibn 'Arabī, Rūmī and Ḥāfiẓ attest.

If the Quranic description of Jesus is closely analysed, it will reveal Jesus as possessing three aspects, pertaining to the past, the present and the future, and corresponding respectively to his function of preserving the Torah, celebrating and perpetuating the Eucharist and announcing the coming of the Prophet of Islam. The Muslims interpret the *perikletos* (meaning the Illustrious) as *parakletos* (the Praised), which corresponds to one of the names of the Prophet of Islam, Aḥmad (from the root *ḥmd* meaning praise). The Quran states: 'And when Jesus son of Mary said: O Children of Israel! Lo! I am the messenger of Allah unto you, confirming that which was (revealed) before me in the Torah, and bringing good tidings of a messenger who cometh after me, whose name is the Praised One (Aḥmad)' (LXI, 6). For Muslims it is inconceivable that such a major religious manifestation as Islam should have been passed in silence by Christ, and they see in his announcement of the reign of the Paraclete a reference to the coming of Islam. His function in the future is in fact, as stated in the above Quranic verse, to announce the coming of the Prophet of Islam and of course also to bring the present human cycle to its end.

In the traditional Islamic religious consciousness, Jesus joins with Moses and Abraham to represent the ternary aspect of the monotheistic tradition whose summation is to be found in the Prophet of Islam. In this perspective, Abraham represents faith, Moses law and Christ the spiritual way. The Prophet of Islam as the final Prophet, 'the seal of prophecy', is the synthesis of all these aspects. Also in the same way that the Prophet is the 'seal of prophecy' Christ is considered by most

Sufis as the 'seal of sanctity' in the Abrahamic tradition. There is in fact a special type of 'Christic' wisdom (*ḥikmah 'īsawiyyah*) within Islam, consisting of elements of inwardness, anteriority and a kind of Divine elixir or nectar which can be seen in certain forms of Sufism. Moreover, this wisdom as well as the spiritual personality of Jesus are closely related to the Virgin, and the Quran refers to the two as a single reality. It states, for instance, 'And We (Allah) made the Son of Mary and his mother to be a (miraculous) sign' (XXIVI, 50).

Despite differences which exist, and which in fact must exist if each religion is to preserve its own spiritual genius and authenticity, the Islamic conception of Jesus provides a firm basis for an understanding of Christianity by Muslims if they only refrain from reacting to the intimidations caused by modern attacks against Islam and return to a close study of their own traditional sources. But this conception can also aid Christians to grasp better what Islam really means to those who breathe within the universe it has brought into being. Perhaps the Islamic conception of Christ can serve as a basis for a better understanding of Islam on behalf of Christianity. It could enable Christians to realise that the sun of their spiritual world which they so love is also a shining star in the firmament of another world and plays an important role in the religious and spiritual economy of another human collectivity.

The Role of Women – The Islamic View

One of the greatest errors of the modern world is the attempt made everywhere to destroy all qualitative differences and to reduce all things to a least common denominator in the name of equality and democracy. It is one of the most conspicuous features of the tendency towards the total reign of quantity from which the modern world suffers. This error is to be seen especially in the question of the relation between the two sexes and the role of women in society. It is said that women should become equal to men. Such a statement could only be made by a woman who is no longer proud of being a woman and does not fully comprehend all the possibilities inherent in the female state. Feeling a sense of inferiority in what she is, she seeks to become another male, to become something which in fact she can never really become. For a woman to seek to emulate the male condition is for her to become at best a second-rate male, in the same way as if a man were to seek to emulate the female state.

In Islam the role of men and women is seen as complementary rather than competitive. Before God, man and woman stand as equals. They have to perform the same Islamic rites and, before Him, they must bear the same responsibility for their actions. Hence it may be said that in their relation with the metacosmic Reality they are equal. But on the cosmic level, which means the psychological, biological and social levels, their roles are complementary. In the same way that procreation implies a biological union of the two sexes, a union that embraces both of them and in which they participate in a harmonious rather than contending manner, a meaningful social structure must also be based on the harmonious co-operation of the two sexes. Islam believes that in the social order duties must be divided in such a way that men are able to perform what enables them to realise their potentialities as men, and likewise women must have a role in conformity with the genius and nature of their sex. A society in which the machine crushes the very possibility of the full growth of human nature, whether it be the male or the female, or one in which existing pressures are such that men become ever less masculine and virile and women ever less feminine and receptive, stands at the very antipodes of the Islamic social ideal. When the male and female types are blurred by the very chaos of a social order in which it remains wellnigh impossible for men to remain men and women women, the possibilities of spiritual development become very dim, for men and women can approach the Divine only by remaining faithful to the form in which the Creator has made them and according to their destiny. Now it must be remembered that men and women do not determine their own sex. Their sex, like their race and colour or place and date of birth, is determined by God and cannot be rebelled against if men or women want to realise the full possibilities of their own nature. A normal and healthy society, of which the traditional Islamic society is an excellent example, is one in which both men and women are given the possibilities to develop fully their natures and to contribute to that richness and diversity which characterise creation and reflect the Unity of the Divine Principle. Now more than ever, it is the duty of all who are concerned with 'man' in a serious way, 'man' in both the male and female forms, to rise to defend consciously the values of traditional societies, which are challenged from so many directions by the fallacies which parade in the modern world in the form of 'current ideas' and the 'spirit of the times' and which claim to speak for the well-being of mankind whereas in reality they are nothing but a poison which kills the spirit of both men and women and drags them to the infra-human level.

Why Do Muslims Fast?

Certain truths are by nature evident and need not be discussed in normal circumstances. But, in a day and age when the most evident truths are shrouded by the clouds of doubts and questioned, one is forced to discuss even the most obvious of them. One such truth is the necessity for an ascetic element in human life. Without an element of self-denial and asceticism no religion and therefore no human culture is possible. One must withdraw occasionally from the full life of the senses even in order to be able to enjoy the fruit of sensual perception. As the Taoist saying affirms, it is the empty space of the wheel which makes the wheel. It is only a certain degree of restraint from the material objects of the senses that makes even the life of the senses balanced, not to speak of making possible an opening in the human soul for the spiritual life.

One such practice of restraint is fasting, promulgated in Islam as obligatory for the month of Ramaḍān and recommended for other periods of the year. As the Holy Quran asserts, it is a practice which existed in older religions and in Islam it was only revived and institutionalised in the form of the *ṣawm* of Ramaḍān. Fasting during this month possesses, of course, many social and external benefits and features which have been discussed often and in fact even somewhat overemphasised in certain quarters, where the chief virtue of fasting is reduced to charity towards the poor. This element of charity is, of course, there but like all true charity it becomes spiritually significant only when it is directed towards God. And in fasting it is the obeying of the Divine Will which has as its fruit charity towards the poor and the needy and an actual participation in their hunger and thirst.

But the most difficult aspect of the fast is the edge of the sword of abstention directed toward the carnal soul, the *al-nafs al-ammārah* of the Holy Quran. In fasting, the rebellious tendencies of the carnal soul are gradually dampened and pacified through a systematic submission of these tendencies to the Divine Will, for at every moment of hunger the soul of the Muslim is reminded that it is in order to obey a Divine Command that the passions of the carnal soul go unheeded. That is also why the fast does not include only food but also abstention from every form of lust and carnal passion.

As a result of this systematic restraint, the human soul becomes aware that it is independent of its immediate natural environment and conscious that it is in this world but not of it. A person who fasts with complete faith becomes aware very rapidly that he is a pilgrim in this world and that he is created as a creature destined for a goal beyond this material existence. The world about him loses somewhat its materiality and gains an aspect of 'vacuity' and transparence which in the case of the contemplative Muslim leads directly to a contemplation of God in His creation.

The ephemeral and 'empty' nature of things is, moreover, compensated by the appearance of those very things as Divine gifts. Food and drink which are taken for granted throughout the year reveal themselves during the period of fasting more than ever as gifts of heaven (*ni'mah*) and gain a spiritual significance of a sacramental nature.

To fast is also to wear the armour of purity against the passions of the world. It is to incorporate even 'physically' in one's body the purity of death which is of course coupled with spiritual birth. In fasting, man is reminded that he has chosen the side of God over the world of passions. That is why the Holy Prophet loved fasting so much. It was a basic element of that 'Muḥammadan spiritual poverty' (*faqr*), about which he said, '*al-faqr fakhrī*' (spiritual poverty is my glory).

This death of the passions cleanses the human soul and empties it of the putrid water of its negative psychic residues. The individual and through him the Islamic community is renovated through this rite and reminded of its moral and spiritual obligations and goals. That is why the arrival of the blessed month is greeted with joy. For in it the doors of heaven are opened further for the faithful and the Divine Compassion descends upon those who seek it. To have completed the fast of Ramaḍān is to have undergone a rejuvenation and rebirth which prepares each Muslim to face another year with determination to live and act according to the Divine Will. The fast also bestows a spiritual perfume upon the human soul whose fragrance can be perceived long after the period of abstinence has come to an end. It provides for the soul a source of energy upon which it feeds throughout the year. The holy month has therefore been called 'the blessed', *mubārak*, one in which the grace or *barakah* of God flows upon the Islamic community and rejuvenates its deepest sources of life and action.

Why We Should Keep the Hijrah *Calendar*

A religion contains within itself providentially all that it needs for its later growth and development. Inasmuch as Islam was destined to become a world-wide religion and its rites and religious observances are based on the temporal rhythm of day and night, it could preserve equality and justice among its followers only by forbidding intercalation. To make the lunar Islamic year into a solar one by adding an extra month every three years or eleven days a year, as has been suggested by so many modernists during the past few years, would be to destroy the justice Islam envisaged by forbidding the act of intercalation. To show how the cause of justice among believers is served by the rotation of the lunar year through the solar seasons and year, it is sufficient to point to two of the basic rites of Islam, fasting and the pilgrimage.

Since Muslims live in many countries with different geographical latitudes and even in the southern hemisphere where the seasons are reversed, they experience different lengths of day and night. Only on the two days of vernal and autumnal equinoxes are the lengths of day and night the same. On every other day of the year a Muslim living in Central Asia experiences a different day length from one living in southern India, or one living in London a longer or shorter day than a person in Nigeria. If the season for fasting, let us say, were to be fixed in the solar year, throughout his life a Muslim in the northern latitudes would fast a shorter or longer day than one in the south. Likewise, if the *ḥajj* season were to be fixed in the winter for the northern hemisphere it would always be in the summer for the southern hemisphere, and vice versa. In both cases there would be an inequality of conditions for the believers. There is only one way in which the obligation of rites placed upon the shoulders of Muslims can be applied to all believers equally, and that is that the lunar year should rotate through the solar year as Islam has ordered. In this way compensation is made for the inequalities of day and night over different regions of the earth during a man's earthly life. The Muslim living in London who fasts nineteen hours during the summer will be able to break his fast in winter at about four o'clock in the afternoon. During a lifetime his summer hardships are compensated by easier fasting conditions during the winter and balance out to become at the end like conditions imposed on one living, let us say, in Persia, Afghanistan or Pakistan.

As for the few living in very northern regions, such as Sweden, where in certain seasons the sun never sets completely, their problem would not be solved by fixing the fasting season at a particular time anyway. Moreover, if the season were to be fixed, others living in other climates would be in differing, and, in the case of people in the southern hemisphere, opposite conditions. In such extreme cases as the very northern or southern regions a *fatwā* is needed to decide upon the number of hours one should fast and in fact the times of prayer. It is illogical and absurd to sacrifice the order and equilibrium of the religious life of the vast majority of Muslims for a few exceptional cases which do not amount to more than a few thousand believers at most.

As for making the Islamic hijrah calendar more important in life, it is not at all necessary to make it into a solar year in order to add to its importance. Throughout history, Muslims have also had a solar calendar which has, however, remained subservient to the Islamic lunar one. What has lessened the importance of the Islamic calendar for many people today is not its lunar character but the weakness that Muslims show in so many other domains of life before things Western. Why is it that there are so many books published in the Muslim world today with the Christian solar calendar whereas all books throughout Islamic history have used the Islamic hijrah dates? If many Muslims use Western months and Sunday holidays and even celebrate Western feasts, it is only because so many people in the Muslim world have become completely enamoured with Western ideas and customs. Khayyām, who participated in devising the Jalālī calendar, the most perfect solar calendar ever devised and used, always employed hijrah dates in his writings.

It would be a tragedy for the Muslims to change their lunar year by fixing it within the solar year. It would cause inequalities in the religious duties of Muslims and cause more heterogeneity and division within the *ummah* than homogeneity and unity, not to speak of the grievous sin of breaking the *sunnah* of the Prophet. It is high time for modern Muslims to seek to understand and apply Islam rather than seek to change the Divinely given tenets of Islam only to placate the fashions of the times. If we penetrate the meaning of Islamic tenets, we realise that they are all placed there for a purpose and have a profound meaning. It is for us to understand this purpose and to apply and defend these tenets, not to try to change them through the excuse of rediscovering a 'pure Islam' which is usually no more than our own individualistic whim and fancy moulded by various deviations of modernism. The modern history of Christianity should be a good lesson for all Muslims on the effect of religious innovation and a defensive attitude *vis-à-vis* various forms of modern thought. Only that religion survives which remains faithful to both the spirit *and* the form ordained for it by God.

Index